BRUCE LEE
A WARRIOR'S JOURNEY

JOHN R. LITTLE

Contemporary Books

Chicago New York San Francisco Lisbon London Madrid Mexico City
Milan New Delhi San Juan Seoul Singapore Sydney Toronto

Library of Congress Cataloging-in-Publication Data

Little, John R.
     Bruce Lee: a warrior's journey / John R. Little.
         p.   cm.
     Includes index.
     ISBN 0-8092-9722-1
       1. Lee, Bruce, 1940–1973.   2. Game of death (Motion picture : 1978)
   3. Bruce Lee, a warrior's journey.   I. Title.

     PN1997.B7682L58   2001
     791.43'72—dc21   00-45157

Contemporary Books
A Division of The McGraw·Hill Companies

All Bruce Lee/*Game of Death* writings, script notes, choreography writings, and photographs
copyright © Linda Lee Cadwell. Used with permission.
All photographs taken in Korea copyright © John Little.
Materials from Lee's interview with Pierre Berton copyright © 1994 Little-Wolff Creative
Group. Used with permission.

1 2 3 4 5 6 7 8 9 0 VL/VL 0 9 8 7 6 5 4 3 2 1

ISBN 0-8092-9722-1

This book was set in Village
Printed and bound by Vicks Lithograph

Cover design by Todd Petersen
Cover photographs copyright © Media Asia and Linda Lee Cadwell
Interior design by Amy Yu Ng

CONTENTS

CERTIFICATION OF VITAL RECORD

STATE OF CALIFORNIA
DEPARTMENT OF HEALTH SERVICES

STATE OF CALIFORNIA } ss.
City &
County of San Francisco

L-000

STATE OF CALIFORNIA
DEPARTMENT OF PUBLIC HEALTH
VITAL STATISTICS
AFFIDAVITS FOR CORRECTION OF A RECORD

Local Registered No. 8363
City or
Town of San Francisco

Ho Oi Yee
(Name of Affiant)

20F2

18 Trenton St., 40-111834

California, being first duly sworn, deposes and says that he/she is the blood mother
(If related, specify degree—if friend or otherwise, so state)

of Bruce Lee (Lee Jun Fon) who was born in the City of San Francisco
(blooded)

County of San Francisco on the 27th day of November, 1940

as stated in a certificate of birth*/death filed by Mary E. Glover
(Name of Physician or Midwife for Birth—Undertaker for Death)

with the Local Registrar for the City of San Francisco County of San Francisco California

on the 5th day of December, 1940

That the following facts set forth in said certificate are not correctly stated therein, to wit:

Item #3 (B) - usual residence of mother

That affiant upon his/her own knowledge states the true facts to be, and the changes necessary to make the
record correct are, as follows: Item #3 (B): California - one year two months

(Affiant) Ho Oi Yee

(Address) 18 Trenton St., San Francisco, Cal.

Subscribed and sworn to before me this 11th day of February, 1941

Notary Public in and for the County of San Francisco, State of California

STATE OF CALIFORNIA } ss.
City &
County of San Francisco

Emma Ung of 1111 Powell St., San Francisco,
(Name of Affiant) (Address)

California, being first duly sworn, deposes and says that he/she has knowledge of the facts hereinbefore alleged and that
the said facts as stated therein are true.

(Affiant) Emma Ung

(Address) 1111 Powell St., San Francisco, Cal.

Subscribed and sworn to before me this 11th day of February, 1941

Notary Public in and for the County of San Francisco, State of California

*For correction of a marriage certificate, in rare instances where necessary, the words "were married," "marriage," and "minister," "priest," "judge" or "justice," etc., may be inserted specially by way of substitution throughout this blank.

This is to certify that this document is a true copy of the official record filed with the
Office of Vital Records and Statistics

S. Kimberly Belshé, Director and State Registrar of Vital Records and Statistics

by: Michael Davis

MICHAEL DAVIS, CHIEF
OFFICE OF VITAL RECORDS AND STATISTICS

050074

DATE ISSUED
MAY 1 5 1995

This copy not valid unless prepared on engraved border displaying seal and signature of Registrar.

ANY ALTERATION OR ERASURE VOIDS THIS CERTIFICATE

Affidavit for correction of Bruce Lee's birth certificate from the city of San Francisco. Although Lee was born in the United States, his parents lived in Hong Kong. This document shows his mother's change of address to California.

CHRONOLOGY OF BRUCE LEE'S LIFE

November 27, 1940. San Francisco. Bruce "Jun Fan" Lee is born in the hour of the dragon (between 6:00 A.M. and 8:00 A.M.) and the year of the dragon.

February 1941. San Francisco. Appears in his first film. He is three months old.

1941. Lee moves to Hong Kong with his parents.

1946. Hong Kong. Begins to film the first of what will total eighteen Cantonese-language films before he reaches the age of eighteen.

1952. Hong Kong. Enters La Salle College, a Catholic boys school.

1953. Hong Kong. Begins to study gung fu under the venerated grandmaster Yip Man of the wing chun system.

1958. Hong Kong. Wins the "Crown Colony Cha-Cha Championship."

March 29, 1958. Hong Kong. Enters Saint Francis Xavier high school.

April 29, 1959. Hong Kong. Departs Hong Kong for voyage back to America.

May 17, 1959. **San Francisco.** Arrives in America.

September 3, 1959. Seattle. Settles in Seattle, Washington. Enters Edison Technical School.

December 2, 1960. Seattle. Graduates from Edison.

May 27, 1961. Seattle. Enters the University of Washington.

March–August 1963. Hong Kong. Returns to visit his family for the first time in four years.

May 1964. Leaves the University of Washington.

July 19, 1964. Oakland. Leaves Seattle to establish a Gung Fu Institute in Oakland, California.

August 2, 1964. Long Beach. Performs at the International Karate Tournament in Long Beach, California.

August 3, 1964. Oakland. Starts gung fu instruction in Oakland.

August 17, 1964. Seattle. Marries Linda Emery.

February 1, 1965. Oakland. Son, Brandon Bruce Lee, is born on Chinese New Year's Eve day in the year of the dragon.

February 8, 1965. Hong Kong. Father, Lee Hoi Chuen, passes away.

March 1966. Los Angeles. Lee family moves to Los Angeles.

June 6, 1966. Los Angeles. Shooting of "The Green Hornet" TV series begins.

February 5, 1967. Los Angeles. Officially opens the Los Angeles chapter of the Jun Fan Gung Fu Institute.

July 1967. Los Angeles. The first appearance of the words "jeet kune do" in his journal.

May 6, 1967. Washington, D.C. Performs at National Karate Championships.

June 24, 1967. New York. Appears at All-American Open Karate Championship at Madison Square Garden.

July 14, 1967. Los Angeles. Hired to appear in one episode of the "Ironside" TV series.

July 30, 1967. **Long Beach.** Performs at the Long Beach International Karate Tournament.

June 23, 1968. **Washington, D.C.** Attends the National Karate Championships.

July 5, 1968. **Los Angeles.** Hired as technical director for the movie *The Wrecking Crew.*

August 1, 1968. **Los Angeles.** Hired to play a bad guy in MGM's *Little Sister* (later renamed *Marlowe*).

October 1, 1968. **Los Angeles.** Moves to Bel Air.

November 12, 1968. **Los Angeles.** Films an episode of the television series "Blondie" for Universal.

April 19, 1969. **Santa Monica.** Daughter, Shannon Emery Lee, is born.

1970. **Hong Kong.** Returns to Hong Kong with his son, Brandon, to visit his family.

1970–1971. **Los Angeles.** Works with actor James Coburn and screenwriter Stirling Silliphant on a screenplay about the philosophy of martial art entitled *The Silent Flute.*

June 27, 1971. **Los Angeles.** Films the premier episode of the television series "Longstreet" for Paramount.

1971. **Los Angeles.** Begins to collaborate with Warner Bros. on developing a TV series called "The Warrior" (later renamed "Kung Fu").

July 1971. **Thailand.** Films *The Big Boss* (called *Fists of Fury* in North America) for Golden Harvest Studios, which breaks all previous box-office records in Hong Kong.

December 7, 1971. **Hong Kong.** Receives official word that he will not star in "The Warrior" TV series and that the part has been given to American Caucasian David Carradine.

1972. **Hong Kong.** Films second movie for Golden Harvest, *Fist of Fury* (called *The Chinese Connection* in North America), which breaks all records set by his last film, *The Big Boss.* Also forms his own production company, Concord, and makes his directorial debut in his next film, *The Way of the Dragon* (called *Return of the Dragon* in North America), which, again, shatters all previous box-office records in Hong Kong.

October–November 1972. Hong Kong. Begins preliminary filming of fight sequences for his next film, *The Game of Death*.

February 1973. Hong Kong. Interrupts filming of *The Game of Death* to begin filming a feature film for Warner Bros. entitled *Enter the Dragon*.

July 20, 1973. Hong Kong. Passes away in Hong Kong, his death the result of a cerebral edema caused by hypersensitivity to a prescription medication.

July 31, 1973. Seattle. Laid to rest in Lakeview Cemetery. His pallbearers are friends and students Steve McQueen, James Coburn, Dan Inosanto, Peter Chin, and Taky Kimura, and his younger brother, Robert Lee.

ABOUT BRUCE LEE

Bruce Lee was born in San Francisco in 1940. He returned to Hong Kong with his parents at the age of three months. While growing up in Hong Kong, Lee made a total of eighteen films. At the age of eighteen, he boarded a ship that returned him to America. After staying briefly in San Francisco, Lee finally settled in Seattle, where he went on to study philosophy at the University of Washington. Lee published his first book in 1963, entitled *Chinese Gung Fu: The Philosophical Art of Self-Defense*. After researching the human sciences of kinesiology and physiology, Lee began to create his own method of self-defense—predicated for the first time in the history of combat on unconditional freedom of expression for the individual practitioner.

As a direct result of his personal applications of his research, Bruce Lee quickly emerged as the leading martial artist of his generation, eventually opening three schools in Seattle, Oakland, and Los Angeles. In 1964, he married American Linda Emery, then a student in one of his Seattle gung fu classes. Together they formed a perfect example of yin-yang, with each one complementing the distinctive qualities of the other. Their union also brought forth two children, Brandon Bruce Lee (born February 1, 1965) and Shannon Emery Lee (born April 19, 1969). Lee was a devoted family man, who much preferred staying home with his wife and children to attending parties and premieres and indulging in the celebrity trappings that accrue to a successful career in film.

After an electrifying demonstration at a Long Beach karate tournament in 1964, Lee was offered the role of Kato in "The Green Hornet" television series. The syndication of the show gave Lee a substantial following, and after continuing to ply his trade both as an actor and as a teacher in America, he accepted an offer to star in two movies in Hong Kong—*The Big Boss* and *Fist of Fury*. The films were huge box-office successes in Southeast Asia

The financial success of the two films gave Lee the creative latitude to direct his next film, *The Way of the Dragon*, which he also scripted, coproduced, and starred in. At the same time, he began to formulate an idea for a film that would more fully express his martial philosophy. He entitled it *The Game of Death*. However, before he could complete any more than one-third of the picture, he was signed to star in *Enter the Dragon*, his last film, and the first coproduction between American and Hong Kong film studios. The film proved to be an interna-

tional hit, famous as much for its pearls of wisdom ("It is like a finger pointing a way to the moon—don't concentrate on the finger or you will miss all that heavenly glory.") as it was for its spectacular martial art action sequences. He did not live to complete *The Game of Death*.

During his lifetime, Bruce Lee cultivated a personal philosophy, a synthesis of Eastern and Western insights into the human condition, which helped him to overcome many adversities and to achieve unparalleled greatness in his career. Lee died at age thirty-two on July 20, 1973, the result of hypersensitivity to a pain medication he had taken to alleviate a headache. Despite his passing, Lee's thought continues to inspire and influence thousands of individuals from all walks of life, while Lee's contributions to the action-film genre opened the door for all of the action films and their stars that have followed.

INTRODUCTION

Kareem Abdul-Jabbar (left) and Bruce Lee square off in a publicity shot from the most eagerly anticipated martial arts film of all time, *The Game of Death*.

In the five years that followed Bruce Lee's passing, the biggest buzz in the martial arts and action-film world was Bruce Lee's *Game of Death*. Was his death a publicity stunt—to be revealed when the film finally finished shooting? If his death wasn't a publicity stunt, would the film ever be released? What was it about? How much footage of Bruce actually existed that had never been seen?

In 1978, Golden Harvest Films (Hong Kong) and Columbia Pictures put together a movie called *Game of Death* incorporating eleven minutes and eight seconds of footage that Bruce Lee had shot for the film prior to his death. The film ignored Bruce Lee's original plotline, it was poorly made, and the footage of Bruce Lee appeared only during the last fifteen minutes—the result was hardly satisfying. In fact, it was in many ways an insult to the memory of a visionary artist such as Bruce Lee.

Nevertheless, the film proved to be a substantial success at the box office, as so many of us went to the theaters on repeated visits in order to see our hero's final performance. Despite the success of the film and the bittersweet belief that this was the last of the Bruce Lee footage to be seen, a rumor began to circulate—and continued to do so for more than twenty-five years—that there was more footage of Bruce Lee that had been edited out of the 1978 release.

Moreover, people who knew Lee and worked with him in the film were saying that the story line of the finished version of *Game of Death* bore no resemblance to the film that Bruce had intended to make.

This rumor remained unconfirmed until 1994 when I discovered Bruce Lee's original shooting script and choreography notes for *The Game of Death* perfectly intact in a filing cabinet containing Bruce Lee's artifacts and personal papers that had been placed in a storage locker in Boise, Idaho, by the Lee estate. I happened upon them by accident while working with Linda Lee Cadwell in researching materials that were written in Bruce's hand for what would become The Bruce Lee Library Series, now published by the Charles E. Tuttle Publishing Company, Boston.

Stumbling upon those script notes and choreography writings—the majority of which are included in this book—filled me with hope that the footage that they indicated had been shot in 1972 was still in existence and that, if it could be located, these materials would point the way to their correct reassembly. With Linda's blessing, I established contact shortly thereafter with Golden Harvest Studios and even flew to Hong Kong in 1994 to meet with the studio's senior executives about the project. A search was initiated for the footage that Lee's handwritten materials indicated had been shot—but that had never been seen publicly.

To make a long story short, after a six-year search the footage was located. It's amazing that the script and choreography notes themselves were still in existence after the passage of more than a quarter of a century, but as if by Bruce Lee's own hand, doors began to open where there had been no doors before. Linda Lee Cadwell provided the materials, an investor came on the scene, and Warner Bros.—the company that had coproduced Lee's last and biggest film, *Enter the Dragon*—came on board to distribute the completed film.

Also assisting in the production of the film were the publishers of this book, NTC/Contemporary Publishing Group. Having published two of my previous books on Bruce Lee, and believing deeply in the subject matter, editor Betsy Lancefield and publisher John Nolan got behind the project early on, and their advance monies went toward the production budget of the film. Everyone involved in the production cared about Bruce Lee and his legacy. It was a pleasure to reedit Bruce Lee's original footage for *The Game of Death* according to his own exact specifications, replacing all of the scenes that were unceremoniously excised from the Golden Harvest release in 1978. Having always been a fan of Bruce Lee's, I found this project to truly be a dream come true—in fact, just seeing the footage for myself was a dream come true!

As you will see for yourself, the choreography notes that Bruce left behind are both meticulous and precise—thank God!

His written directions made it possible for me to lend Bruce my hands, allowing him to put the film together properly. His notes were much like the directions to assembling a complicated model; without them, it would have been impossible to know exactly which takes of which scenes Bruce wanted included and the sequence that he wanted them edited into.

Not to mislead you; the final product, *Bruce Lee: A Warrior's Journey*, featuring all of the *The Game of Death* footage, is not a complete film. With Bruce's passing, there is just no getting around this unfortunate fact. But through viewing the film and reading this book, it is at least now possible for you to share his vision, to see the drama and the pacing, to experience the motif as he had intended. With just the footage that Bruce shot, it is completely different from—and far superior to—the film that we all saw back in 1978 (and perhaps more recently on video and DVD).

There is one scene still missing that has evidently been lost to the ravages of time: the fight scene between Dan Inosanto and Chieh Yuan, in which Chieh Yuan attacks Dan with a huge log and Dan dispatches him with his escrima (stick fighting) techniques. This scene was choreographed by

Bruce Lee as the first fight sequence he filmed in the movie; where it is now is anybody's guess.

Having conceded this, I'm delighted to say that every scene involving Bruce Lee has been preserved; from the moment he enters by sprinting up the stairs to face Dan Inosanto, to the moment he walks down the final flight of stairs in a state of near collapse after having disposed of Kareem Abdul-Jabbar—it's all here, and all Bruce Lee.

Likewise with this book; extensive quotations from Bruce Lee are to be found within each chapter, so that wherever possible, you will be able to hear directly from Bruce Lee himself. The first part of this book follows the format of the film. The narrative overview incorporates quotations from Bruce Lee and those who knew him best: his wife of nine years, Linda Lee Cadwell; his closest friend and highest-ranked student, Taky Kimura; and Kareem Abdul-Jabbar, who was not only one of Lee's private students, spending many hours training with Lee after Lee had formally closed his martial art schools, but also a close friend.

The second part of the book allows us to look more in-depth into key areas and influences in Bruce Lee's life and development, ranging from his writings on Bud-dhism to his commitment to the scientific method in formulating his incredible martial art. While the first part of the book provides a solid overview of Lee's "journey" and struggles to make *The Game of Death*, the second part provides a more scholarly approach to his discoveries and insights.

My hope with the film and now with this companion book is to educate the audience about the significance of this project, to shed some light so that they might better appreciate the work that Bruce Lee put into it and what his message in this film was, instilling (hopefully) a deep-seated appreciation in the audience for the footage they have waited so long to see—and for the message he had worked so hard to communicate throughout his life.

In reading about Lee's quest to make this film, it should give us pause to recognize that it was occupying his final thoughts on the last day of his life. It was an important film to Lee, and it must be considered with the proper degree of respect and reverence as representing the last on-camera communiqué from Bruce Lee to his public. Lee not only wrote the story line, which is presented here for the first time, thus ending many decades of speculation, but also choreographed all the action and was the cinematographer, the set designer, the lighting man, the director, the producer, and the star.

It has been my most fervent wish for well over two decades to locate this footage and reedit the film as Bruce Lee intended. Ever since I was twelve years old, I had pondered what Bruce's vision had been for this film. Now, with the assistance of Linda Lee Cadwell, this wish has finally been realized.

To my knowledge, there has never before been an attempt to essentially recut a film in such a manner as to allow a deceased individual to have a say in how his legacy is presented. Rather than simply soliciting other people's opinions, I am in a position to go to the source, Bruce Lee himself, and am thus able to—after some twenty-eight years—finally present Bruce's original version of the film. The feeling that attends being part of such a project borders on the spiritual and cannot be adequately framed by words.

In many respects, despite its ominous title, this is a film about life—not death. It is about the "hero's journey" that each of us must take alone to confront those who would bar us from pursuing what we are destined to become. You will see in this a film of pain, effort, and redemption—and the cinematic showcase of Bruce Lee's mar-

tial philosophy of personal liberation: jeet kune do.

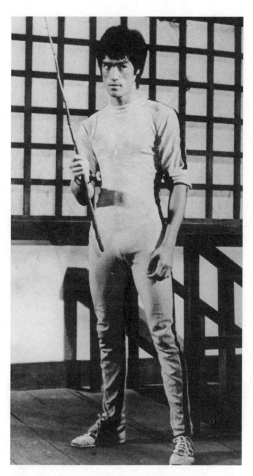

Bruce Lee: A Warrior's Journey marks the first-ever presentation of Bruce Lee's final film in the exact manner that he wanted it to be shown.

PART I

A WARRIOR'S JOURNEY

CHAPTER 1
BACKGROUND

Definitely in the beginning I had no intention whatsoever that what I was practicing—and what I'm still practicing now—would lead to this. But martial art has a very, very deep meaning as far as my life is concerned because as an actor, as a martial artist, as a human being—all these I have learned from martial art. **—Bruce Lee**

Hong Kong in the fall of 1972 was then much as it is now: a bustling island of modern industry and commerce playing against a backdrop of culture and tradition that has remained largely unchanged for more than one thousand years.

The biggest news from within the city in September of that year was the rapid growth of its motion picture industry. Formerly an enterprise of no consequence to anyone but local theater owners, the Hong Kong movie industry was now attracting the attention of the biggest film studios in the world.

The reason for the sudden surge in interest was the meteoric rise to fame within the city of a thirty-one-year-old man named Bruce Lee. Lee's dynamic on-screen presence coupled with an audience empathy that cut across all cultural boundaries resulted in his films' shattering of box-office records, records that had stood unassailed for more than half a decade.

Producers the world over had come to see in Lee the key that would unlock the door to the future of the industry. They began to flood the young artist with offers that even six months previously would have

Lineups formed early for Bruce Lee's second film, *Fist of Fury*. It would go on to break box-office records throughout Southeast Asia.

film market. However, the very notion of "formulas" and "methods" held no appeal whatsoever for Bruce Lee.

Instead, Lee began work on a movie entitled *The Game of Death*, which he termed a "multilevel film," in which his personal philosophy of martial art would be presented for the first time. He spent from early September to late October of 1972 filming three sequences—the finale, it turned out—of the movie.

been impossible for him to have imagined. After years of battling against cultural and professional bigotry and economic and emotional hardship, as well as the exhausting effort required to sustain the integrity of his art, Lee's perseverance had finally been rewarded: he was now the most sought-after motion picture actor in the world.

With such power now at his disposal, Lee could easily have chosen to rest on his laurels and play it safe by making the kind of "formula" pictures that were then being offered him daily. No one—certainly no one in Hong Kong—would have begrudged him this option. In fact, many would have encouraged it. The customary Chinese wariness of foreigners had, for the moment, been put aside as they watched Lee, single-handedly, bring fresh commerce, ideas, dignity—and an international future—to the Chinese

Bruce Lee was always front-page news for Hong Kong newspapers in the early 1970s.

Bruce Lee (right) worked long and hard in crafting his fight sequences for *The Game of Death*, working on everything from choreography to camera angles.

In one sequence involving his handling a nunchaku, Lee performed no less than ten takes until he felt he had it down perfectly, even though the on-camera time of the sequence was less than four seconds.

Lee performed the work and assumed the responsibility of no fewer than eight people in the creation of this film: he was the director, the producer, the choreographer, and the author of the screenplay, in addition to having a hand in the set design, the cinematography, and the lighting. And, of course, he was to be the leading actor.

Martial artists who had been hired as cast members and were not accustomed to the camera had to be taught how to "sell" a strike or a reaction for optimal dramatic effect. Again, this fell to Lee to look after. Take after take of precision martial-art choreography was performed. In some instances Lee spent up to four days filming what would turn out to be only a five-minute fight sequence.

He was most demanding of himself, of course. A case in point is one shot involving his handling a nunchaku—a double-segment wooden rod that is connected by a length of chain or cord. The nunchaku was originally used as a rice flail but was converted into a weapon during the Japanese occupation when all traditional weapons were confiscated. He shot this scene no fewer than ten times to capture one small

Fred Weintraub (left) visits Bruce Lee on the set of *The Game of Death* in October of 1972 to deliver news that Warner Bros. was ready to offer Lee a starring role in a feature film (*Enter the Dragon*).

Bruce Lee's agreement to make *Enter the Dragon* marked the first time that Chinese and American film studios would work together on a feature film. Lee's wife, Linda (second from left) was on the set when the news arrived.

twirling sequence with the weapon that would appear on screen for a mere three and a half seconds.

The Game of Death was not simply another "Chinese boxing movie," which were plen-

tiful in the Hong Kong of the early 1970s. It was to have been the most important film of his budding career. Though fate had other plans, in the end, his labor paid off in exactly the way he had intended.

Production on *The Game of Death* was suspended in October of 1972 when word reached the set that Warner Bros. was now keenly interested in coproducing Lee's next film, which was then tentatively titled *Blood and Steel*.

Lee's widow, Linda Lee Cadwell, recalls:

There had been talk during this period of time about a possible Warner Bros. film, a coproduction. There were, in fact, discussions that had been going on for quite some time—months, and probably more than a year—with Ted Ashley, who was the CEO of Warner Bros. and was a private student of Bruce's. So, they were friends as well as teacher and student. Bruce had been trying to motivate Ted to produce the biggest worldwide martial arts film ever.

Lee had viewed the potential collaboration with Warner Bros. as the first step in raising the standard and profile of Chinese films, with the ultimate goal of broadening global understanding of Chinese culture and, thus, allowing Chinese films, actors, directors, and producers to eventually be accepted into the international film market. Prior to beginning his career in martial art films in Hong Kong in the early 1970s, Lee had gone to see the current crop of martial art films. After sitting through the top-grossing film released by then new production company Golden Harvest Films, he turned and asked company president Raymond Chow, "Is that the best you can do?" Chow recalls, "I was ashamed to admit that it was. But Bruce told me with full confidence, 'I can do better.'"

In a 1971 interview with Pierre Berton, Lee spoke of the quality of Chinese films.

Pierre Berton: Did you look at many Mandarin movies before you started playing in your first one?

Bruce Lee: Yes.

Pierre Berton: What did you think of them?

Bruce Lee: Quality-wise, I would have to admit that it is not up to the standard. However, it is growing and going toward that standard that I would term "quality."

The Warner Bros. proposal was the fulfillment of a lifelong dream of Lee's, a film that would, in his words, allow "nation to speak to nation," marking the first time in the history of East-West relations that a Chinese film studio and an American film studio would collaborate on a feature project.

By the end of 1972, Lee and Chow were business partners, Lee's two-picture contract with Golden Harvest Films having expired. Chow had quickly proffered an invitation to his young star to start a production company, with Lee as 50 percent partner, rather than risk losing him and his earning potential to a rival studio.

By Hollywood standards, Chow's company was a primitive production facility. The soundstages, built initially to house a modest textile mill, contained an odd placement of pillars and were perched precariously on a hilltop that, some feared, might have collapsed at any time, given the ferocity of the typhoons that have been known to hit Hong Kong.

Nevertheless, the smaller facility was able to secure Bruce Lee's services and

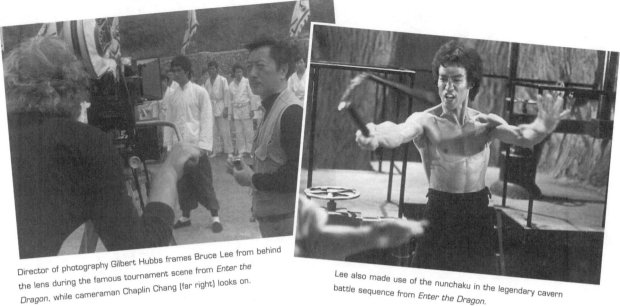

Director of photography Gilbert Hubbs frames Bruce Lee from behind the lens during the famous tournament scene from *Enter the Dragon*, while cameraman Chaplin Chang (far right) looks on.

Lee also made use of the nunchaku in the legendary cavern battle sequence from *Enter the Dragon*.

loyalty by being the only studio at the time willing to offer the one thing that was most important to him: not simply a paycheck but complete creative control over his own projects—the lifeblood of all true art.

In November of 1972, Chow was patting himself on the back for his prescience as he and his new partner found themselves on a plane en route to Los Angeles to complete negotiations with Warner Bros. for what would prove to be Lee's last and biggest film. Although the screenplay underwent at least two more title changes, it was ultimately named *Enter the Dragon* and went on

to become the greatest martial arts picture in history, the classic of its genre.

January to early April of 1973 Lee gave over to the filming of *Enter the Dragon*. As with *The Way of the Dragon* and the elements of *The Game of Death* before, Lee oversaw every aspect of *Enter the Dragon*'s production and postproduction. By the time his schedule finally allowed him to return to work on *The Game of Death*, it was mid-July—the last week of his life.

July 20—his final day on earth—he spent discussing script ideas for the film. On this fateful day, Lee, with characteristic opti-

The quality of Bruce Lee's movies set standards that have never been surpassed.

Linda Lee Cadwell recalls the immense pride that the Chinese people had in what Bruce Lee had accomplished:

Bruce's films inspired pride in his Chinese countrymen. Not only were some of the historical outrages that had been perpetrated against the Chinese brought to light, but also the Chinese were shown to be heroes. I think that this led to great pride in the Chinese breast. It also served to show the rest of the world some of the atrocities that had been committed in history against the Chinese nation and to show the value and worth of Chinese people as citizens of the world. I think in that way Bruce helped to bridge any gap that existed between China and the rest of the world.

mism, opened his journal and looked ahead to September 20, 1973. He wrote there of his intention to resume filming *The Game of Death*. These were the last words he would ever write.

Word of Lee's passing hit the residents of Hong Kong like a tidal wave, unleashing a torrent of emotions. Lee had represented many different things to many different people within the Chinese community, both in Hong Kong and abroad. There had been so much more the young man had to accomplish, so much more he had to achieve for the Chinese people, so much more he had to live for. And then—nothing.

As Lee's spirit passed quietly into the night that rainy July evening, along with it passed his vision of educating the public about the ultimate truth and deeper meaning of martial art. Another casualty of his passing was the movement toward realism

Bruce Lee (second from left) on the set of *The Big Boss*. To Lee's right is Lo Wei, the director of the film.

Bruce Lee performs a dramatic flying side-kick from the final battle in the 1971 box-office blockbuster *The Big Boss*.

in Eastern cinema that he had pioneered. Almost immediately, martial art films reverted to being unbelievable and hokey.

In an eerie prognostication, an audio dictation that Lee had recorded in the privacy of his home only weeks prior to his death contains his comments on the distinction between his films and those made by less dedicated production companies and foreshadows the trend in martial art films immediately following his passing:

Ever since *The Big Boss* there seems to be a wave, a hot wave in fact, of finding "another Bruce Lee" among all types of people, particularly martial artists. Ranging from karate men, hapkido men, judo men, etcetera, etcetera.

Forgetting about whether or not they possess the ability to act, just so long as they can halfway decent kick or punch and know a few tricks or gimmicks, the producers will make them a "star."

Now, let's stop about here. Is it that simple to become a star? Well, I can assure you it's not that simple. Also, I can tell you that as more [of] Bruce Lee's films are shown, the audience will soon realize—not only in acting ability but in physical skill as well—they will see the difference.

Of course, "It is only moviemaking," people will say, but certainly the audiences are not so insensitive as to not be able to see and judge for themselves.

The film titled *Game of Death*, released by Golden Harvest and Columbia Pictures in 1978, proved to be a commercial success, but it was a disappointment to Bruce Lee's legions of fans.

Within three years, the genre that Lee had rendered so popular was also dead. Lacking Lee's artistry and vision, the Hong Kong film industry returned to producing "traditional" and heavily stylized "kung-fu" movies that were long on fighting and violence and short on meaning and message. The American action-film industry followed suit with a long series of appallingly bad films—*Hot Potato, Gymkata,* and *Breaker! Breaker!* among them.

Five years after his passing, excerpts from the film on which Lee had worked so feverishly during the final months and hours of his life were edited into a movie featuring the title of *Game of Death,* but it bore no resemblance to Lee's original multilevel vision.

Without Lee's choreography notes, script outline, and motif, the producers had been uncertain how to complete the film. Moreover, they had quickly discovered that Lee had been such a perfectionist that, of the 100 minutes he had shot, two-thirds turned out to be outtakes and retakes—shots that Lee had discarded as sequences that were beneath his standard of quality.

Rather than contact the Lee estate or people who understood what Lee had intended to accomplish with the movie, the producers opted to create a whole new story line and to film new fight sequences. They billed it as a "Bruce Lee film," but of the 100 minutes of footage they had in their possession, only eleven minutes and eight seconds made it into the final product.

The movie *Game of Death* was uneven from start to finish. Using stand-ins, and even cardboard cutouts, to replace Bruce Lee, in addition to actually incorporating footage from Lee's public funeral in Hong Kong, the end result was viewed by many as being nothing more than an exploitative and grotesque joke played on the great artist's legacy.

Lee's closest friend and highest-ranked student, Taky Kimura, says that when he saw the film in the theater, he was very disappointed:

I just went in with an empty mind and tried to enjoy it. When I saw that some of the characters weren't Bruce—I understand that two or three guys play his role in different parts of the movie—and that kind of thing, it really just took the wind out of my sails . . . because, having known Bruce as well as I did, and knowing that it wasn't really to the purpose or the goal of what Bruce wanted to do with that movie, having to see all of those distractions in there, it just didn't bring out that excitement that Bruce's real films, like *Return of the Dragon*, did for me.

The use of the three stand-ins to impersonate Bruce Lee (none of whom looked particularly like him) underscored just how big a hole the producers were attempting to fill. The pacing was peculiar as well: just as the audience becomes used to seeing these impersonators, the producers drop in some clips of the real Bruce Lee from the original footage. Even the last fifteen minutes of the film—the portion containing the only real and consistent footage of Bruce Lee in the movie—is so heavily edited that it is very disjointed and hard to follow. Nevertheless, the film did well at the box office, but it was a disappointment to those who had come to look upon a "Bruce Lee film" as something special.

By the 1980s, small grabs of excised footage from *The Game of Death* turned up in a documentary entitled *Bruce Lee: The Legend*, produced by Golden Harvest Films. It was only one of several documentaries made about Lee's life, but its contents provided Lee's fans with the glimmer of possibility that additional footage that Bruce Lee had originally shot for inclusion in *The Game of Death* was still in existence.

However, by the early 1990s, with nothing further having surfaced, even Lee's most zealous fans began to believe that the original footage that Lee shot was gone and that it would never be possible to see the film as Lee shot it in its entirety, nor to ever learn what his original story line for the film was.

Fast-forward to April 2000. I am in a remote Buddhist village in South Korea, kneeling on a prayer mat before a 100-foot-high bronze Buddha and lighting a candle to the memory of a man I have never met. It should be the most foreign and certainly the most incongruous enterprise in which I, a former writer for a bodybuilding publication, could possibly be involved, and yet, having pored over this man's private writings, journal entries, and essays dating back to his earliest days—papers that no one else, except perhaps his wife and children, had

The Buddha of Popju-sa.

Director John Little (front row, third from right) traveled to Popju-sa in South Korea in order to have Bruce Lee's original twelve-page story line for *The Game of Death* enacted before the cameras for *Bruce Lee: A Warrior's Journey.*

Veteran South Korean cinematographer Hoo-gon Lee (left) discusses a shot for the Popju-sa sequence for *Bruce Lee: A Warrior's Journey* with director John Little.

ever seen—I have come to feel that I know this man and his mind, better in some instances than I know my own.

And that is why I now find myself more than six thousand miles away from my home and family in America; I'm simply doing my part to help Bruce Lee realize a dream he had first envisioned twenty-eight years ago and had attempted to fulfill before destiny intervened. It is my intention, not to complete his film—that would be impossible without his physical presence—but to deliver his message: to make it clear what

the film was to have been about and what his story line had been, and to provide some background on the journey of labor he endured to reach this vision. The hope is that if people can see the footage as Lee intended it to be shown, with some understanding of what he was trying to say and why it was important to him, they will come to better know Bruce Lee the human being and to more clearly understand his thought, which was decades ahead of its time. At the very least, it would be immediately obvious why Bruce Lee was something unique and not simply some "martial arts guy."

Bruce Lee has always been his own best ambassador. Despite having written and edited more than sixteen books on the man and now having completed two films, I would never consider myself to be a spokesperson for Bruce Lee. He, being the individualist that he was, continues—despite corporeal absence—to speak for himself. My only task has been to bring forth the authentic materials that flowed directly from the mouth (via audio recordings and video interviews) or pen of Lee, thereby allowing him a platform to speak for himself.

For many decades, Lee has been poorly represented by people who claimed to be speaking for him or to have been his protégé. Such claims, when viewed in the spirit of how Lee looked at his life and art, would be laughable—were not the damage done to his legacy so brutal. Lee had no interest in turning out a protégé; he had no interest in creating "another Bruce Lee." His interest was to instill in his students a desire to become their own protégés, to develop into themselves. That is why it is imperative that the film I'm overseeing is authentic, and why I've pored over and included as much original material from Bruce Lee as possi-

Bruce Lee (left) delivers a right lead punch to the face of his adversary, played by hapkido grandmaster Ji Han Jae, in the battle on the fourth floor of the pagoda in *The Game of Death*.

ble; the motif of the film is Lee's own motto of "Using no way as way; having no limitation as limitation."

To aid authenticity, I sought out support players who were actually on the set when the cameras were rolling, not only to provide their recollections but also to loop their own dialogue—as Bruce Lee had originally had them speak it in the fall of 1972. All but one obliged. Making this film authentic is the number one priority. That is why I've spent hundreds of hours going through war cry excerpts to find the ones that perfectly match both the emotion and mouth positions that Lee displays in the footage he

Two pages from Bruce Lee's handwritten choreography notes for his battle with real-life student Dan Inosanto in "the hall of the tiger" sequence. The notes were believed lost for more than twenty-eight years.

shot. That is why a copy of his notes and shooting script are by my side throughout the shooting, editing, and final sound mix.

Every artist seeks to be understood, and Lee had been robbed of that when the previous film was released in 1978. His message must be rendered with this film in the manner he intended. And that is why I now find myself genuflecting before a giant Buddha statue and lighting a candle to the memory and the journey of Bruce Lee, the great phi-

losopher, martial artist, and filmmaker who died in 1973, before he could complete the film on which I am now working.

My involvement in this story actually began in the fall of 1994, during research conducted for a multivolume book series on which I was working with Linda Lee Cadwell, Bruce Lee's widow. The book series, which comprises Lee's surviving writings, had required me to travel to Boise, Idaho, to meet with Linda. During that visit, Linda took me to an old storage locker and left me alone to go through Lee's papers. To me, having been a zealous fan since the age of twelve, this was the equivalent of being a kid in Aladdin's cave: everywhere I looked, I saw historical documents and artifacts that had been instrumental in shaping Lee's life, art, and career. Lee's career and art had had a profound impact on my own life, and I now felt as though I were among holy relics containing illuminating facts to better explain to me my own fascination with the man and his teachings.

It was while sifting through a large filing cabinet that I first happened upon Lee's original script and choreography writings for *The Game of Death*. Just seeing the title of this ill-fated project momentarily took my breath away. I began to flip through the pages, pages that Lee himself had been the last to hold, and it struck me that this project had occupied the very last hours of his life.

And what a project it was! As I continued to peruse his choreography writings, sketches, and story line, the fact that this man had been wronged by whoever was responsible for the film bearing the title *Game of Death* screamed out at me with every turn of every page. Here was substance, message,

A page of Lee's choreography writings for his fight sequence with Korean hapkido grandmaster Ji Han Jae.

and truth—a truth that he had labored so long to discover and to relate—and all of it had been cast aside in favor of creating a "fight film."

The script notes and, more particularly, the choreography writings, revealed what many of us had long suspected: that Lee had, indeed, shot considerably more footage for the film than had been seen to date. Stumbling upon these documents filled me with hope that the footage that they indicated had been shot in 1972 was still in existence and that, if it could be located, these materials would point the way to their correct reassembly.

The next week, I returned home with more than sixty pounds of photocopied material from the storage locker. The project wouldn't leave me; Lee had been wronged. His message and, by extension, his legacy had been corrupted by the passing off of a film bearing his name and title but none of his message. Moreover, even the footage used had been severely edited. As an accomplished filmmaker, Lee had a wonderful sense of pacing, of drama and story—all were gone from the 1978 film.

As the weight of this fact grew heavier and heavier in my mind, I contacted Linda and told her that I thought it would be worthwhile to try to locate the missing footage. "Surely if Golden Harvest were interested in doing anything with it, they would have done it by now," I explained. "They've had it for twenty-three years." Linda concurred and was supportive of my quest to at least locate the footage. What I would do with it once I had located it was still a big question mark. After all, I had never produced or directed a feature film before.

With Linda's blessing and a letter of introduction, I established contact shortly thereafter with Golden Harvest Studios and flew to Hong Kong in March of 1994 to meet with the studio's senior executives. I explained my interest in "doing right" by Bruce Lee by making use of Lee's own script notes to restore the footage to the way that he had intended.

They were not particularly enthusiastic about assisting me in my quest to locate the footage. In the years subsequent to Lee's passing, Golden Harvest had sold its interest in Lee's films—to whom, they would not reveal. I returned from Hong Kong empty-handed and profoundly disappointed at having traveled so far only to return less optimistic than when I had left.

My mission had, I later learned, at least served to stimulate peripheral interest in locating the footage. I continued to probe and ask questions, following leads—most of which proved vacuous—for the next six years.

Then, in the summer of 1999, word crossed the Pacific from one of my contacts that more than ninety-five minutes of excised and outtake footage had been discovered in the vaults of Golden Harvest studios. The man who physically pulled the footage from its storage shelf was Bey Logan, an employee of Media Asia—the company that, I later learned, had obtained the licensing rights to the footage from Star Television, which had acquired it from Golden Harvest.

It was miraculous that this footage and the script notes should have been preserved at all, given the passage of so much time. But, as if by Bruce Lee's own guidance, both his script and his footage were finally reunited in December of 1999 after having been separated for more than twenty-seven years.

That is why I found myself kneeling before the Buddha on this day. In front of a thick wax candle, I placed a pamphlet from the Bruce Lee Educational Foundation that had a cover shot of Bruce Lee, lit the wick, and bowed three times—as I had been taught by Lee's widow—in conformity with the Chinese custom: honoring heaven, earth, and man in between. And then it struck me: "You did it, Bruce," I whispered. "Your dream has finally been realized."

This was, indeed, the fulfillment of Lee's dream. And, as with all dreams that are worth pursuing, it had not been easy to bring to fruition. It entailed not just the reassembly of the footage that he had shot for the film but also the enacting of his original story line, taking images and scenarios that had existed until now only in his head and on twelve sheets of paper, and bringing

them to life with actors and a film crew—and in the location he had envisioned.

I wondered just when the dream of making such a meaningful statement on film had first occurred to Bruce Lee, when he had first set out on his journey to discover a truth of martial art that would prove so difficult to reach that no martial artist before him had dared risk the journey. What was this message that caused him to endure racism, poverty, and censure in order to

On the set of *Bruce Lee: A Warrior's Journey*, where South Korean actor Hak-kyu Kim (who played Hai Tien), John Little (producer/director), and Bill Katz (coproducer) united to bring Bruce Lee's story line to life.

bring it to the public's attention through the medium of film?

It was not a journey to something external, such as a championship title or a trophy or even public acknowledgment. It was a journey inward to the center of the human soul, to better understand the nature of the energy that informs and molds one's life. How, I wondered, had Lee begun that journey that was now completing itself here in a small Buddhist village high in the hills of South Korea?

CHAPTER 2
THE JOURNEY

LEE: I don't believe in system, Mr. Longstreet. Nor in method. And without system, without method, what's to teach?

LONGSTREET: But you had to learn. You weren't born knowing how to take apart three men in a matter of seconds.

LEE: True, but I discovered the cause of MY ignorance.
                    —1971 season premier episode of "Longstreet"

February 1965. Los Angeles. Twenty-four-year-old Bruce Lee sits before a camera crew to audition for a television series that will never be made.

The director of the screen test sits off camera, feeding Lee directions such as, "Now look directly into the camera, Bruce—directly at it. Now give me a three-quarter this way. And hold it. And give me a profile that way—all the way. Good. Hold it. Now come back for a profile on the other side and hold that. Give me a three-quarter on that side. And then give me a right-into-the-camera again."

A twenty-two-year-old Bruce Lee practices gung fu in the Hong Kong countryside.

Bruce Lee assumes the famous bai-jong (ready position stance) of wing chun gung fu in a Seattle parking lot in 1963. Lee would later come to view both this stance and wing chun as too restrictive.

Lee obliges with great patience. He is no stranger to the camera, of course, having made no fewer than eighteen Chinese-language films in Hong Kong prior to returning to America—the land of his birth—at the age of eighteen.

In nineteen months, he will be known to American audiences as Kato from "The Green Hornet" TV series. In five years, he will have discovered a truth that will forever alter the course of martial art history. And in eight years, he will be the most famous motion picture actor in the world.

But at this point, he is unknown, and neither he nor the American crew conducting his screen test has any inkling of the momentous destiny that fate has in store for him.

The screen test proceeds:

Question: And you worked in motion pictures in Hong Kong?

Bruce Lee: Yes, since I was around six years old.

Question: And when did you leave Hong Kong?

Bruce Lee: 1959. When I was eighteen.

Question: I see. Now look over to me, Bruce, as we talk. I understand you just had a baby boy?

Bruce Lee: (smiles) Yeah.

Question: And you've lost a little sleep over it, have you?

Bruce Lee: (laughs) Oh, three nights.

Question: And tell the crew what time they shoot the pictures in Hong Kong.

Bruce Lee: Well, it's mostly in the morning because it's kind of noisy in Hong Kong, you know? Around three million people there, and so every time when they have a picture it's mostly, say, around 12:00 A.M. to 5:00 A.M. in the morning.

Question: I see. (sarcastically) You love that, do you?

Bruce Lee: (smiles)

Question: And you went to college in the United States?

Bruce Lee: Yes.

Question: And what did you study?

Bruce Lee: Ah, philosophy.

Bruce Lee's interest in philosophy—defined by the Western ethos as the "love of wisdom"—was a passion that remained with him throughout his life. He had been teaching Americans about Chinese philosophy and culture for six years, lecturing in the Pacific Northwest on the subtleties of Chinese thought. But his great passion was gung fu—an ancient Chinese fighting art unknown in the America of 1965.

Lee's scrapbook from this period reveals brief descriptions of many of the arts and traditions of the venerated masters of gung fu. The only martial arts known to America at this time were judo and jujitsu, two Japanese arts that were taught to American servicemen during the Korean War.

Lee regarded himself as an ambassador for Chinese gung fu, teaching all who would listen about the ways of the Chinese masters, so he welcomed the opportunity to share with his interrogators on this day some of the origins and methods of the art:

Question: Now, you told me earlier today that karate and jujitsu are not the most powerful or the best forms of Oriental fighting. What is the most powerful or the best form?

Bruce Lee: (smiles) Well, it's bad to say "the best," but in my opinion, I think gung fu is pretty good.

Question: And would you tell us a little bit about gung fu?

Bruce Lee: Well, gung fu was originated in China. It is the ancestor of karate and jujitsu. It's more of a complete system, and it's more fluid. By that I mean it's more flowing; there's continuity in movement, instead of one movement, two movement, and then stop. . . . The best example of gung fu would be a glass of water. Why? Because water is the softest substance in the world, yet it can penetrate the hardest rock or anything—granite, you name it.

Bruce Lee's first and only formal martial arts instructor, the legendary Yip Man—one of the greatest wing chun practioners of all time.

most talented and articulate exponents. His teacher in this art was an elderly Hong Kong Chinese master by the name of Yip Man—a man Lee held in particularly high regard, writing in his scrapbook:

Professor Yip Man
(Leader of the Wing Chun School)

The last master of the wing chun school is Professor Yip, born in Fut San in Southern China. Professor Yip started a study of the various schools of gung fu at the age of eight, until he met Professor Chan Wa Shun and immediately devoted his full energies to his art, the wing chun school. Now he is the present leader of that school. Professor Yip is truly a gung-fu great, and is respected by other instructors of various schools. He is famous for his "sticking hands," in which he attaches his hands to the opponent and subdues him with his eyes shut! Even at the age of sixty he was still active, and none of his students could touch him.

Water is also insubstantial. By that I mean you cannot grasp hold of it; you cannot punch it and hurt it. So, every gung fu man is trying to do that: to be soft like water and flexible and adapt to the opponent.

Question: I see. What's the difference between a gung fu punch and a karate punch?

Bruce Lee: Well, a karate punch is like an iron bar—whack! A gung fu punch is like an iron chain with an iron ball attached to the end, and it goes Whang! And it hurts inside (laughs).

Lee had studied a system of Chinese gung fu for the past nine years called wing chun and was considered one of the art's

Although his views would eventually diverge sharply from the teachings of the wing chun system of gung fu, Bruce Lee always had the utmost respect for his teacher in this art, Yip Man (left).

Question: Show me now the difference between jujitsu, which is long and involved, and gung fu, which is very quick, if you have an opponent.

Bruce Lee: All right. For instance, you will read it in a book, in a magazine and everything, that when somebody grabs you (grabs his own collar), you will "first do this, and then this, and then, and then, and then, and then"—thousands of steps

Despite his proficiency in this style of gung fu, Lee was studying philosophy, which caused him to search for the ultimate truth of martial art, and he began to question why most martial artists—Chinese and otherwise—seemed more concerned with preserving tradition than with looking more deeply into the matter.

Acting on his inquisitiveness, Lee began to research and develop his own method of gung fu, which he described as "nonclassical" in nature and which he called the "Jun Fan method," Jun Fan being Lee's Chinese-language name. His method takes as its core the principles of economy of motion, simplicity, and directness.

Again, during his screen test this day, Lee welcomed the opportunity to share his insights with the camera crew:

Bruce Lee (left) demonstrates the trapping and striking technique of wing chun with James Yimm Lee, Bruce's friend and assistant instructor in the "Jun Fan method" of gung fu.

Bruce Lee and his wife of nine years, Linda Lee. No one knew Bruce Lee better.

before you do a single thing. Of course (smiles), these kinds of magazines would teach you to be "feared by your enemies and admired by your friends" and everything, see? But in gung fu, it always involves a very fast motion. Like, for instance, a guy grabbing your hand: It's not the idea to do so many steps; (he stomps the ground sharply with his right foot) stamp him right on the instep—he'll let go. This is what we mean by simplicity. *Same thing in striking and in everything: it has to be based on a very minimum motion so that everything would be directly expressed (gestures to strike)—Wham!—in one motion, and he's gone. Doing it gracefully. Not going (karate yell) "Aaaagh!," yelling and jumping all over him, but to do "Hoight!"—(a sudden motion, and he enacts watching his opponent fall to the ground; Lee then straightens himself up, adjusts his cuffs, and looks down at his imaginary opponent) "Excuse me."*

Despite his eloquence and willingness to promote martial art, both the American and Chinese martial art communities resented his iconoclasm. For such a young man to stand up against thousands of years of tradition and venerated authority was considered a direct threat to the status quo and its entrenched power base.

The Chinese community vehemently opposed Lee's having committed what they perceived as the gravest of transgressions: teaching the Chinese art of gung fu to non-Chinese students—specifically, African Americans, Hispanics, and Caucasians. And despite claiming to be "the land of the free," America, Lee learned, was willing to extend its liberties only so far. Many Americans were upset by the fact that Lee chose to marry outside of his race—a Caucasian girl, named Linda Emery. Linda recalls:

When I first met Bruce in Seattle in 1963, I was very fortunate in the fact that I went to a high school and a junior high school in the central city district of Seattle, Garfield High School, that was very much mixed— racially, ethnically, economically. It drew from all sections of the city. I had many, many girlfriends and guy friends who were of different races: Japanese, Chinese, other Orientals, blacks; it was very well mixed. So, I had been accustomed in my growing-up years to just looking straight across at people, not considering them first as whatever race they were. And I think this paved the way actually for Bruce's and my relationship getting off on a very good start. I didn't think of him as any different because he was Chinese. I just looked at him as the man that he was.

It wasn't always so for everyone else, and his first introduction to my family was difficult. My family of course was looking out for my best interest and thought that we would suffer the consequences of an interracial marriage by societal standards at that time. I know they were looking out for our best interests, but heedless as we were at that young age, we decided to get married, and I must say that during our marriage, on a personal level, I never felt that we suffered racism or racist thought against us, because most everyone who met Bruce was instantly attracted to him. He was very appealing, you know. He was a showman when he wanted to be. He was

extremely courteous and well spoken, and so, no one ever looked down on him or made any racial slurs. However, there were some incidents where it might be interpreted that there was a racist feeling in how he was treated, especially professionally.

Linda and Bruce, the proud parents of Brandon Bruce Lee. The Chinese characters on the scrolls on the wall read: "Using no way as way; having no limitation as limitation."

The professional slights were still to come, but when they did, it is both surprising and a testament to Lee's character that there is no evidence that he held a grudge or ever felt sorry for himself. Rather than gnash his teeth at his misfortune, Lee held out optimism that one day America would make the effort to see beyond the shape of his eyes to the content of his character.

Too proud to bend his knee before the false altars of ignorance and compromise, Bruce Lee continued to live his life by his own terms: he would love his wife—irrespective of bigoted opinions—and would continue to teach his interpretation of gung fu to whomever was open to the experi-

Bruce Lee (right) teaching gung fu to his student Doug Palmer in Seattle in 1963. Lee had to fight for the right to teach his art to non-Chinese students.

ence, regardless of their ethnic makeup. The perhaps predictable result was that it wasn't long before trouble showed up on his doorstep. Taky Kimura recalls:

Prior to Bruce's coming to this country, gung fu was alive in almost all of the Chinese communities, but there was nothing taught to outsiders. Then Bruce came along, and with that basis of trying to create equality among all people regardless of race, he chose to let anybody into his school regardless of what color or race they were. As long as he knew that what was in their heart was good and positive, he took them in. When he was teaching in Oakland, trouble started in San Francisco, where the Chinese community was much more like being in China, and they took exception to it, and he had to fight his way out of it.

Linda Lee Cadwell picks up the story, noting that something positive grew out of the confrontation:

ruce was so highly skilled that he did not run into racism on a daily basis because he made believers out of people right away. However, there were expressions that you might say had to do with race, particularly from the Chinese community of martial artists.

For instance, when we lived in the San Francisco Bay Area, Bruce had opened a martial arts school, a gung-fu school, with James Lee in Oakland. He received a challenge from the San Francisco Chinese martial arts community, which read that if Bruce were to be defeated in this challenge, he would have to cease teaching Caucasian or non-Chinese students because traditionally the Chinese martial arts were taught only to Chinese. This idea stemmed from a historical viewpoint ranging back to the Boxer Rebellion in China, where the Chinese felt that if they were to teach the bigger, stronger Caucasians their martial arts, they would never have a chance against them. That idea was still prevalent in the Chinese martial arts community in San Francisco.

This challenge went forward, and the Chinese martial artist came over from San Francisco to Bruce's studio in Oakland, and a very formal challenge took place. I was present; in fact, I was eight months pregnant with our son, Brandon. James Lee was also there. [James Lee was an assistant instructor in Bruce Lee's art who ran the Oakland school.]

The fight with this Chinese martial artist lasted about three minutes. It consisted of a lot of running. The Chinese martial artist took off and started running around the room, and Bruce was pursuing him. Bruce finally got a hold of him and took him down to the floor and made him give up.

Then, after the challenge ended with the Chinese martial artist being soundly defeated, and they all went away, Bruce—now having won the right to teach anyone he wanted to—used this incident to turn inward and to analyze what had happened. It became a turning point in his martial arts education, you might say, because he was very disappointed in himself that he had allowed this fight to go on for three minutes. And he was disappointed that there had been all this running and that he had been very winded at the end of the three minutes.

And so, he realized that, number one, there had to be better techniques to catch a hold of someone who's running away, and number two, he needed to be in better physical condition so that he wouldn't be winded after three minutes of aerobic exercise. So, I would say that this was a real turning point where he really began to dissect his martial art and to incorporate new ideas that would work for him. It was also the catalyst for him to begin his program of physical fitness that led to his becoming in great physical condition.

Kimura adds:

When Bruce was in the Seattle area, he was basically teaching us a modified wing chun approach to gung fu. In his estimation, the most important part of this art was that it was void of a lot of classical-ness; it was straight to the point, without any flares. During those years, he often told us, "It's not going to be a fifteen-round prize fight." He said, "You're just going to get it done with, over in just a matter of seconds—at the longest, minutes." He taught us that it was just a quick block or whatever, then you just use a straight-blast punching system.

And he had been proof of this. He was once forced to fight a young Japanese martial artist who had taken exception to what Bruce was teaching us in Seattle. When it finally came to a point where they had to have a fight, he beat this young man in eleven seconds! So, at that point of his life, I think because he was gifted with such coordination and such speed and he had a terrific sense of rhythm, he felt that that was really the answer to fighting.

But when that fellow came to fight him from San Francisco—and this other fellow was much bigger than Bruce— this guy actually turned on his heels and ran. According to what Bruce told me, it took him three minutes to put him down, and that was sort of the awakening period for Bruce; he found

that technique isn't the whole picture. That's when he began to think about nutrition, and he started running and doing other things that made him the complete man that he was soon to be.

Bruce Lee (right) works out with his student and best friend, Taky Kimura, in Seattle in the early 1960s. Kimura would become Lee's highest-ranked student and the only one, according to Lee, whose judgment he trusted to train instructors in Lee's art.

Despite all of his trials and tribulations both personally and professionally, and despite the birth of the Civil Rights movement and the strides made by its leading activists, in the Hollywood of the mid-1960s,

Bruce Lee learned that an Asian male was still looked upon as little more than a prop for a scene.

Nevertheless, his screen test did not go unrewarded. Although the television series for which he was auditioning, "Number One Son," was canceled before it began, a new breed of television action hero was starting to emerge. Lee reflected on this transition during a television interview conducted in 1971 by Canadian journalist Pierre Berton:

Pierre Berton: Is it true that the first job you had was being cast as Charlie Chan's Number One Son?

Bruce Lee: Yeah, "Number One Son."

Pierre Berton: They never made the series?

Bruce Lee: No, they were going to make a new Chinese James Bond type of a thing: you know, "The old man Chan is dead; Charlie is dead, and his son is carrying on."

Pierre Berton: Oh, I see. But they didn't do that.

Bruce Lee: No, "Batman" came along, you see. And then everything started to be going into that type of a thing.

Pierre Berton: Like "The Green Hornet."

Bruce Lee: Yeah.

Television producer William Dozier, fresh from his success with the "Batman" TV series and eager to repeat his success with another superhero series, opted for a remake of the old radio serial "The Green Hornet"—about a newspaper publisher who dons a mask to fight crime as the Green Hornet. Lee was cast as Kato, the Green Hornet's trusty sidekick. Lee later recalled:

I did "The Green Hornet" television series back in 1965, and as I looked around, I saw a lot of human beings, but when I looked at myself, I was the only robot there. I was trying to accumulate external "security," external "technique"—the way to move my arm—but I never stopped to ask, "What would Bruce Lee have done if such a thing had happened to me?"

While Lee might have been displeased with his acting in "The Green Hornet," he

Bruce Lee was not just a student of martial art but also a devout student of philosophy.

was nevertheless delighted by the opportunity that the series afforded him to introduce the Chinese art of gung fu to mainstream America. This, he believed, would encourage the cultures to become more familiar with each other, and with the increase in familiarity, he hoped, would come an increase in understanding, tolerance, and compassion. Kimura recalls:

Bruce was telling me quite often that he was frustrated that the Chinese were depicted in the American movies as a kind of a heathen-type person with his arms in his sleeves and pigtails, and about the only thing you heard from them was "Chop-chop!" He said, "I'm going to try through the medium of the movies to create some equality among people, you know? Not based on race or color or anything like that."

Bruce Lee enjoyed the opportunity his role as Kato on "The Green Hornet" TV series gave him to introduce the Chinese art of gung fu to America in the mid-1960s.

Despite Lee's popularity, when "The Green Hornet" series was canceled after one season, Hollywood closed its doors to the young martial artist as quickly as it had opened them. According to Linda, there were some tough times ahead for the young family:

When he played the role of Kato in "The Green Hornet," that was fine because Kato was supposed to be an Oriental man. He sparked a lot of interest through that role and at that point in his life had decided that he was going to make the film business his career rather than teaching martial arts on a mass basis. So, he tried to pursue the idea of getting roles in film and TV. After "The Green Hornet," however, he had a great deal of trouble securing really leading roles. He had a number of roles in small pictures. He did a lot of choreography for fight scenes in pictures. But as far as really promoting his career as a leading man, he had a lot of difficulty in America at that time.

Bruce Lee gives a lecture on martial art to students in the Los Angeles branch of his Jun Fan Gung Fu Institute in February 1967.

reality, consisting of rehearsed "self-defense" routines that were performed by rote in predictable and patterned rhythms. Lee noted that real combat was not predictable, but spontaneous, not something that could be anticipated with infallible certainty. Instead, "combat, as it is," is made up of irregular, or "broken," rhythm that a martial artist could not anticipate—only respond to.

Even the "World Championship" karate tournaments of the era were noncontact affairs, settled not on knockouts but on an

With a wife and young child to support, Lee returned to teaching gung fu full-time. By February of 1967, he had three schools operating in Seattle, Oakland, and Los Angeles, each of which taught his own interpretation of gung fu, the "Jun Fan method," which was based on the results of Lee's investigations into the "ultimate reality" of gung fu.

With more free time to devote to investigating the ultimate reality of martial art, Lee saw far more clearly the problems inherent in the manner that most martial arts were then being practiced in America. Most, he observed, lacked a solid grounding in

Bruce Lee (second from left) considered only character—not race—in determining whom he would accept as students of his art.

accumulation of points awarded for blows that never touched an opponent. A victory was determined by a team of judges, who concluded which combatant would "probably have" hurt the other combatant more— *had contact been allowed.* Kimura recalls:

In those days, the tournament rules were that karate was noncontact; if you hit somebody, you lost a point or the match. And of course, the other thing that controlled the outcome of matches in those days was that if you hit somebody, that meant you "didn't exercise coordination." The referees were pretty much within those systems and structures, so it was pretty much a concluded dimension. And Bruce used to say, "Well, if I hit you, that means you didn't block me—that's why I hit you." He felt in those days, if you went into a tournament like that, obviously you would be limiting yourself to the principles of what the other systems were. Therefore, it just didn't match up with his thinking, which was why he didn't go into it.

Lee had no use for such styles of pseudofighting, which he labeled "organized despair" and "dryland swimming." Lee's criticism of the arts could be attributed, in part, to his background in Hong Kong, which consisted not of noncontact karate tournaments but of full-contact street fights and challenge matches fought on Hong Kong rooftops.

When not fighting against exponents of different styles of gung fu, Lee fought frequently against opponents who were armed with knives and chains. In such "real-world" encounters, so-called referees and judges are not necessary.

Rather than participating in noncontact karate tournaments, which he considered little more than glorified games of "tag," Lee devoted himself to continuing to refine his own system of gung fu. His journey now led him in the direction of a more scientific approach to unarmed combat. He came, in time, to be enamored with the techniques and principles of European fencing and Western boxing, in which efficiency, not tradition, is the touchstone. NBA superstar Kareem Abdul-Jabbar, who came to know Lee and train under Lee's tutelage during this period, recalls Lee's fascination with Western boxing, and with one boxer in particular:

Bruce understood the advantage of hand techniques over kicks, especially coming from the wing chun background, where they do very little in terms of kicks; everything is focused on the hands and on the placement of the hands. He understood the whole idea of getting inside and slugging, and he knew how to do it. The fighter that he admired the most—and who can blame him?—was Sugar Ray Robinson. We saw Muhammad Ali as just a larger version of Sugar Ray Robinson. But he really felt that Sugar Ray Robinson had really had it *all* down in terms of movement and ambidexterity and effective hand techniques using either hand. The only thing Bruce added to that was the fact that in his martial art, we kicked, and you had to be able to use your legs. That was an important aspect of it.

Bruce Lee (right) introduced the notion of full-contact training to the American martial art world in the late 1960s.

Along with the principles of boxing and fencing, Lee was also looking into a discipline based not on tradition but rather on empiricism—the science of Newtonian physics. He quickly realized that the principles and laws have a direct bearing on and application to all human beings, regardless of cultural or martial backgrounds, and that if one came to understand these "laws of motion," one could better amplify one's use and manipulation of force in human combat.

Lee pored through textbooks on physics and kinesiology, researching how moving objects become more powerful (damaging) and the factors influencing speed (inertia, momentum) and power production (the law of reaction). As these were scientific principles that were universally true, it didn't take long for Lee to conclude that many of the

The defining principle of Lee's art of jeet kune do was that of interception. Here, Lee (left) intercepts student Ted Wong's left cross with a right hook kick.

classical martial art techniques that he saw his colleagues practicing and teaching—as well as many gung-fu techniques that he had been taught and practiced during his youth—actually possessed little scientific validity and therefore were, by definition, inefficient.

This insight caused the chasm between Lee and the traditionalists to widen, as the traditionalists, like latter-day dwellers in Plato's famous cave, didn't want to know about the young man's *new* insights and discoveries because their "systems," which had been created and passed down by the

ancients, were predicated on a given technique's being delivered in a particular fashion only. Kimura explains:

Bruce had witnessed a great many martial arts before he came into this country at eighteen. He was very aware of many of them over there in Hong Kong, and I think that as time went on, he recognized more than ever that there was too much classical mechanicalism in a lot of these styles. You know, you have to look at it from another aspect: we as human beings are awed by something that simply isn't normal. Something that has a different little twist to it catches our eye, and we often get stuck on those kinds of things. We're always looking for something that has that different thing to it that makes it exciting, but when you really examine and assimilate all of that, that's fine in one way, but it leads you away from the direction of simplicity, the natural course of life that makes up a human being or life in general.

Kareen Abdul-Jabbar holds Bruce Lee's son, Brandon, in his arms prior to a jeet kune do workout in Lee's backyard. Abdul-Jabbar would later take part in one of the most famous fight sequences of Lee's movie career when the two squared off in *The Game of Death*.

Kareem Abdul-Jabbar concurs:

Bruce didn't think that styles were really that important. He thought that quickness and agility and knowing what you're doing and knowing things that work for you was the best way to approach the whole idea of individual combat. And those ideas of his: when they were first exposed, people did not embrace them at all. It's really amazing the about-face that's taken place, with all of the "no-holds-barred" fighting that is so prominent now. People understand that the real test of any art is:

How's it going to help you when your chips are down and nobody is enforcing any rules? Bruce understood that.

The fact that people were so caught up in "their style," as opposed to any other style, he saw as a disadvantage that limited people's effectiveness and limited their outlook. It was a type of "us-versus-them" mentality. If it's not the "Chinese style" versus the "Japanese style," then it's the California practitioners of one style versus people from Chicago in the same school. They're at odds, and it's an illusion.

Lee's research caused him to understand that the only litmus test of a combative technique's worth was whether or not it could be landed effectively on an opponent with maximum impact. Anything that was ornamental was discarded from his style; he retained only those techniques that he had determined to be practical in real self-defense situations.

Lee became the first martial artist in North America, if not the world, to have his students don boxing gloves, headgear, and body protectors—and spar all-out. Nothing is rehearsed. No punches are pulled. Full-contact, reality-based martial art became the order of the day. In 1967, Lee introduced the concept of full-contact sparring at the International Karate Tournament in Long Beach, California.

Defense was not emphasized in his new, reality-based sparring method because this would have been the equivalent of allowing one's opponent to set the tone and tempo in a real fight. Instead, the focus of Lee's new approach to combat was centered squarely on attack—or, more precisely, on intercepting his opponent's attack with an attack of his own.

By midsummer of 1967, Lee had determined that the defining principle of this new approach to martial art was in fact the principle of interception. As the Cantonese term for unarmed combat is typically indicated by a character representing a fist, Lee christened his new approach "jeet kune do"—"the way of the intercepting fist." In the television series "Longstreet," Lee cowrote an episode entitled "The Way of the Intercepting Fist" and therein explained the principle underlying his new art:

Duke: What is this thing you do?

Bruce Lee: In Cantonese, jeet kune do—the way of the intercepting fist."

Duke: "Intercepting fist," huh?

Bruce Lee: Or foot. Come on, touch me any way you can. (Duke steps toward Lee and is intercepted by a side-kick to the shin.) You see? To reach me, you must move to me. Your attack offers me an opportunity to intercept you. This time, I used my longest weapon, my side kick, against the nearest target, your kneecap. This can be compared to your left jab in boxing. Except it's much more damaging.

By now, word was out concerning Lee's art, and he began to attract the attention of America's top martial artists, as well as a large number of prestigious southern California actors and athletes. James Coburn and

Bruce Lee (left) during his demonstration at the 1967 International Karate Tournament in Long Beach, California.

Steve McQueen were added to his growing roster of students in jeet kune do who were eager to learn how to explore themselves more thoroughly in order to handle themselves more efficiently in a combative situation. Abdul-Jabbar recalls:

He said if I were going to use, let's say, a judo throw, it would be impractical stuff: imagine me trying to get my hips underneath him to throw him for a hip throw! He'd joke, "You're going to try and do that while I'm beating you down?" He'd be hitting me with something else while I was trying to get into position for the throw—and he was absolutely right.

Bruce Lee (left) demonstrates the finer points of the art of trapping an opponent's hand while simultaneously delivering a strike during a workout at his Chinatown school in Los Angeles, California.

Bruce Lee's Los Angeles school, located in the heart of Chinatown, without any advertising pulled in—not newcomers to the martial arts—but seasoned black belts, all of whom now looked upon Lee's art as revolutionary and upon his talent as otherworldly.

In a dictation made in 1973, Bruce Lee cited a newspaper article that referred to the "world champion" karate practitioners who were now coming to him for instruction:

In the Sport Week section of the *Washington Star*, printed in Washington, D.C., on August 16, 1970, it was written:

"Three of Bruce Lee's pupils, Joe Lewis, Chuck Norris, and Mike Stone, have between them won every major karate tournament in the United States. Joe Lewis was Grand National Champion three successive years.

"Bruce Lee handles and instructs these guys almost as a parent would a young child, which can be somewhat disconcerting to watch. It's like walking into a saloon in the Old West and seeing the fastest gun in the territory standing there with notches all over his gun. Then in walks a pleasant little fellow who says, 'How many times do I have to tell you? You're doing it all wrong!' And the other guy listens. Intently . . .

"Chuck Norris, the American karate champion who recently did a movie with Bruce called *The Way of the Dragon*, readily admitted to millions of people watching TV in a recent interview in Hong Kong that Bruce was his 'teacher' and considers him 'fantastic.' I must also add here that, at the same time, two other champions in karate, the heavyweight champion, Joe Lewis, and the light heavyweight champion, Mike Stone, have, along with Chuck, been taking lessons from Bruce. Now, all three of these men are from different styles and all are well established. Yet, they come to learn under Bruce."

With the top martial artists in America now coming to his home for private instruc-

American martial arts legends (from left to right), Ed Parker, Joe Lewis, Bruce Lee, and Mike Stone pose with actor Dean Martin (middle) during a break in filming *The Wrecking Crew*, on which Lee served as the stunt coordinator. Both Lewis and Stone studied privately with Bruce Lee for a short time during the late 1960s.

tion, Lee was the toast of the martial arts world. However, by the end of 1969, he had grown concerned that his students were looking at jeet kune do as containing a secret "way"—special techniques that alone were responsible for success and ability in unarmed combat.

To Lee, such a thought was nonsensical; there was no such thing as a magic system, the only "secret" to martial art success being a willingness to train hard enough to cultivate one's innate ability to the highest possible level. Under no circumstances did Lee look on his art as being merely a warehouse of "secret" techniques.

Bruce Lee (right) delivers a simultaneous trap and kick to student Dan Inosanto during a photo session in Palos Verdes, California. Inosanto was also Lee's assistant instructor at the Los Angeles branch of the Jun Fan Gung Fu Institute.

Taking matters into his own hands, Lee then did something that was unheard of in martial art circles: in January of 1970—at the height of his popularity and reputation in the martial art world—he closed all three of his Jun Fan Gung Fu schools, in effect, setting his students free from his own influence. In a 1972 telephone conversation recorded by one of his students, Daniel Lee,

Bruce Lee explained that "I've disbanded all the schools of jeet kune do because it is very easy for a member to come in and mistake the agenda as 'the truth' and the schedule as 'the way.' You know what I mean?" He further elaborated on this point during an interview with reporter Alex Ben Block:

Many people will come to an instructor and say, "Hey man, like what is the truth? Hand it over to me!" So, one instructor would say, "I'll give you my Japanese way of doing it." And another guy would say, "I'll give you the Chinese way of doing it." To me that's all baloney. If you go to a Japanese style, then you are expressing the Japanese style; you are not expressing yourself. Nationalities don't mean anything. We must approach it with our own self. Art is the expression of our self.

Lee then trained only a handful of students privately. Since his art was about personal growth, he felt that he must come to know each student thoroughly in order to assist him in developing the skills and confidence required to free himself of the chains of limitation, whether physical or psychological. Kareem Abdul-Jabbar, one of these select students, recalls:

When Bruce closed the schools, he felt he was unburdening himself of having to prove through his students that his system had merit. He didn't want to get into that. He wanted them to evolve and teach. But it was not a thing where "You have to teach what I taught." You have to teach what you *learned*. And that's going to be more than what he taught, hopefully, for the students who understood what he was doing.

When he taught me, he always emphasized that people were going to attack my legs and were going to use the fact that I'm so long against me. I had to know what to do to deal with that approach. It was fortunate for me that I learned what I learned in the sequence that I did.

Lee is his own best example of the potency of his beliefs. He had detected his own weaknesses and limitations, and by the application of intellect and hard work, he overcame them, raising his physical ability to a level that bordered on the phenomenal. He routinely performed one-finger push-ups on one hand and executed elevated V-sits for extended periods, he cannonaded opponents several feet back from a punch he delivered from only one inch away, and his side kicks had so much power that, in the words of one recipient, they "felt like being hit by a car."

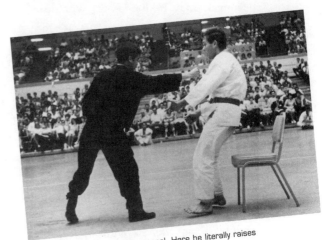

Bruce Lee's power was phenomenal. Here he literally raises a man off the ground with his famous "one-inch punch" during a demonstration at a Southern California karate tournament.

It was during a bout of weight training that Bruce Lee suffered the back injury that almost ended his career.

He continued to train hard, pushing to discover the outer limits of expression for the human body. He found out—with disastrous consequences—on August 13, 1970. Linda recalls:

———————————— ❦ ————————————

Bruce injured his back in 1970. It didn't seem severe at the time because it was just a weight-training accident. He was doing an exercise called a "good morning," in which he put a barbell on his shoulders and bent over from the waist and straightened up. But unfortunately he did this without warming up—which he would warn against, and he usually practiced that: warming up and warming down. But on

this day, he did not warm up; he just picked up this barbell and bent over, and he felt a twinge in his lower back.

The injury became exacerbated over the next few days, and it was a constant source of pain. So, he went to a doctor, and he had an MRI and the various tests and some cortisone injections to relieve the pain. The results of the tests were that Bruce had injured his fourth sacral nerve. They really did not expect that he would ever be doing martial arts again—no kicking, any of that kind of thing. He was advised that he needed to have bed rest for an interminable amount of time until it healed. That was the only way it was going to heal.

Well, for Bruce to be lying down in bed twenty-four hours a day for approximately six months was an impossible thought; you could not contain him like that. But he did, because he knew that if there was to be any future, even to walk normally, he would need to give this time to heal. So, he spent a great deal of time resting: flat on his back for quite a time, quite a long time. And then also just sitting, sitting in a chair.

———————————————————

Bruce Lee's greatest progress as a martial artist came from constant practice. Here, he practices his finger jab on an apparatus that he had designed specifically to practice this technique. He would routinely perform up to two thousand strikes per day.

The damage caused by the injury proved to be far more than physical; unable to function fully, he could no longer teach private lessons to clients who often required him to be available at a moment's notice, nor could he fly to film sets on overseas locations. What little film work that might have been offered him was now withdrawn: Hollywood had little interest in Asian actors to begin with—and no interest at all in injured ones.

It is often in times most bleak that truths most real are manifest. In Lee's case, his physical nadir proved to be his intellectual and spiritual zenith. With no money and no prospects, and lacking the ability to effectively teach his beloved martial art, Lee spent hour upon hour in the company of the world's wisest men via the printed page, seeking wisdom and insights that he hadn't had time to ponder when possessed of superior health. Linda recalls:

Bruce was not one just to waste time. So, he spent this amount of time doing a lot of research in his vast library, which included books on the martial arts, all combative arts, all hand-to-hand arts—whether they be Western, Eastern, modern, or ancient—and all types of philosophy and psychology, especially in the motivational field. Now that he was injured and his future was in jeopardy, he felt that he needed to self-motivate all the time, which he did. He would write down these motivational phrases and look at them every day and repeat them, to get his engines going and moving forward.

Philosopher, warrior, legend—Bruce Lee.

Abdul-Jabbar, who converted to the spiritual tradition of Islam during the time that he knew and studied under Bruce Lee, recalls:

The writings of the Buddha, Alan Watts, Bertrand Russell, Hermann Hesse, Plato, Carl Rogers, David Hume, René Descartes, Lao-tzu, Confucius, Frederick Perls, Daisetz Suzuki, and Jiddu Krishnamurti became his constant companions. He filtered their insights through his own razor-keen intellect and profound compassion. Kareem

Bruce had read so much about everything that he could talk to you about anybody's thoughts. We really both enjoyed Hermann Hesse; we discussed Hermann Hesse a lot. And he was aware of different Islamic writings. Although he wasn't [Muslim], and he didn't get or draw a lot from [the

Islamic writings], he was aware of where I was coming from. He really enjoyed the Sufi teachers because they spoke about getting to "the heart of things" and "the essence" of it, which is a big thing, because in Islam you have formal worship and then what you really, sincerely believe, what sincerely comes from your heart. And those two things are two different strains of where the focus is in Islam. Bruce also read some of the Persian poets, Rumi and Omar Khayyám. He liked Omar Khayyám.

We had so much in common. I, too, am a bibliophile. I feel I should have everything so I can go and have an instant reference.

And to anything spiritual or philosophical, Bruce could go right to his library and talk about where they were coming from and what they understood. Bruce saw that as how it was supposed to be done. We live our lives in a way that we physically enact things that we have to learn with our hearts. The two are supposed to work hand in hand.

One section from Lee's incredible home library. By 1973, he had amassed more than three thousand books dealing with martial art, philosophy, psychology, literature, and art.

Of all of the authors Lee read, he was particularly taken by the thought of Jiddu Krishnamurti, who states that truth cannot be organized without invalidating it. In 1974, in a rare television interview titled "What Is Communication with Others?" with Professor Allan W. Anderson, Krishnamurti commented on this perspective with an incident from his personal history:

In 1928, I happened to be the head of a tremendous organization, a religious organization, and I saw around me various religious organizations, sects, Catholic, Protestant, all trying to find truth. So, I said, "No organization can lead man to truth." So, I dissolved it, the property, an enormous business. I can never go back to it. When you see something as poison, you won't take it again. It isn't that you say, "By Jove, I've made a mistake; I should go back and . . ." It is, sir, like seeing danger. When you see danger, you never go near it again. . . . Now, that means you have to be a light to yourself, not take the light of a professor, or an analyst, or a psychologist, or the light of Jesus, or the light of the Buddha. You have to be a light to yourself in a world that is becoming utterly dark. That means *you* have to be responsible.

Lee saw a direct analogy between what Krishnamurti had been saying about religious organizations and martial art organizations. He saw articulated in the writings of Krishnamurti truths that he himself had experienced. Linda recollects:

Often when reading Krishnamurti's works, Bruce would underline certain passages or write a note in the margin where he related what he already had thought about, say something in martial arts, to what Krishnamurti said in his text. Bruce already had many of these ideas that were being expressed in Krishnamurti's writings, and so, he almost felt a kinship. Bruce was very interested in Krishnamurti's philosophy, particularly toward the end of his life, when he read his books avidly. I believe that part of the concept that he enjoyed so much within that philosophy was that of self-reliance, that if you're looking for truth, you must look *inward* rather than outward and that freedom is something you find within yourself. You free yourself from restraints, from societally imposed restrictions.

Lee immediately saw an application of these insights to martial art and began to write about it with passion and intensity. His writings fill seven large volumes. Linda relates:

The best thing that came out of the back injury was that he turned that stumbling block into a stepping-stone by using that time with a purpose, meaning that, that is the time that he compiled the seven volumes of his writings about martial art. We are blessed to have these writings now and to know what Bruce was doing in the martial arts, what he was thinking about. And these lessons that he penned during those six months of recovery can go on to benefit all of us, and future generations.

Slowly, Lee began to battle back. Although the back injury turned out to be a permanent problem, within six months he had proved both the naysayers and the medical community wrong. Not only was he able to kick again, but he became a better martial artist than he ever had been before. The injury left him stronger, not weaker. It was a vision of perseverance and will that remains with Taky Kimura to this day:

He didn't let that bother him. He just kept moving on; he kept succeeding and going around it and doing these other things. That's something that has kept me alive all of these years. I've run through a lot of tragedy, but Bruce was a guy that helped me to put things in perspective. You have to be awed. Even in my late days, I tried to shape my life in a more positive way because of Bruce's attitude. He didn't know what defeat was; he just didn't accept it. Everything was going to be conquered one way or the other.

Lee's harrowing experience and new insight underscored for him the validity of his belief that there is no help but self-help—including help in the form of instruction in the art of unarmed combat. Even his own

Bruce Lee was able to overcome his back injury through intellect and hard work. He would become a better martial artist after his recovery.

beloved creation, jeet kune do—by far the most scientific of all martial arts—was not exempt from his solvent analysis. In a handwritten essay titled "Toward Personal Liberation" from 1971, the first of two drafts, Lee writes:

The founder of a style might be exposed to some partial truth, but as time passed by, especially after the founder passed away, this partial truth became a law, or worse still, a prejudiced faith against the "different" styles. In order to pass along this knowledge from generation to generation, the various responses had to be organized and classified, and presented in logical order. Creeds are invented, reinforcing ceremonies are set to glorify, separative philosophies established, and organizations erected. So a definite form results, and all those who come to learn will only be bound by that form.

So, what might have started off as some sort of personal fluidity of its founder is now solidified knowledge, a sort of preserved cure-all for mass conditioning. In so doing, the faithful followers have made this knowledge not only a holy shrine but a tomb in which the founder's wisdom is buried. Because of the nature of organization and preservation, the means would become so elaborate that tremendous attention must be devoted to them, and gradually the end is forgotten.

If we honestly look at reality as it is, and not as we would like [it] to be, I am sure we cannot help but notice that a style tends to bring about partiality, adjustments, interpretation, justification, condemnation, denials, etc. In short, the solution being offered is the very cause of the problem, placing obstacles and limitations in the light that will illumine our shadows [and impede our] way to understanding. If we really and totally see organically, then we find that the end is also in the means, the answer is in the question, each being the cause as well as the result of the other.

At any rate, the followers of a style often accept its "organized segment" as the total reality of combat. Of course, as a direct reaction to "the other truth," another founder or maybe a dissatisfied disciple would "organize" an oppositional approach, and pretty soon, it, too, would become a large organization with its laws and fixed fragmentary patterns. These styles arise from the division of a unitary total; not only [do they] tend to be separated in thoughts from each other, and consequently in opposition to each other—thus keeping people apart—but each style also claims to posses "truth" to the exclusion of all the others. So, the individual is total and universal, while a particular style is partialized, blinded by that chosen segment, and therefore is never the total—the style has long become more important than its practitioners. . . .

Remember that the whole is evidenced in all parts, but an isolated part, efficient or not, does not constitute the whole. In the field of law, there are criminal lawyers, business lawyers, etc.; unfortunately, no such thing occurs in "all-in/total fighting." Favorite segments do not fare too well in "all-in/total fighting." So, one can say "a little learning is a dangerous thing" applies appropriately to those who are conditioned to a particular approach to combat.

When I first arrived in the United States, I was teaching my own version of the wing chun style—I had my "Chinese" system then. However, since then, I no longer am interested in systems or organization. Organized institutes tend to produce patternized prisoners of a systematized concept, and the instructors are often fixed in a routine. Of course, what is worse is that by [forcing] members to fit a lifeless preformation, their natural growth is blocked.

At the time he wrote these words, Lee had recognized that he had been heading in the wrong direction; he had been striving to create the ultimate "way" or "style" of martial art to teach to his students. He had first thought that he had it with the "Chinese way" of martial art and, then, in his newly created "way of the intercepting fist." But he had now come to see that the ultimate truth of martial art was to be found not in the "ways" and "styles" of others, but within the soul of each human being. According to Linda:

Bruce was insightful. He often wrote down his thoughts about his personal evolution, and we are fortunate to have a record of that because it's something we can learn from every day. In the early years, when Bruce first came to the United States, he had every intention of teaching martial arts and of creating a chain of gung fu schools and teaching it on a mass basis. You could say he thought of himself as a "gung fu man" at that time. In fact, he described himself that way.

And then as he progressed in his martial art and as his own way of martial art, which he called jeet kune do, developed, he would refer to himself as a "jeet kune do man," but with a different viewpoint on the martial arts.

By this time, he was no longer going to reproduce his way of martial art on a mass basis. And as he continued in the later years, in his filmmaking days, and was aware of the process he was undergoing in his own development, I think he began to regard himself more as, simply, a "human being," rather than a *this* man or a *that* man or a Chinese man, or just a martial artist or a filmmaker—more as a human being. He would often say that the highest compliment he could ever receive was just to be regarded as a "quality human being." I think that this is an evolution that we can all learn from in our own lives, this moving toward simplicity, as Bruce used to say.

He used to call it the "Three Stages of Cultivation," where you start off not knowing anything, totally ignorant. You move to the stage of knowing so much that you're always analyzing every part of yourself or every movement that you make. In other words, it's a "taking-apart" process until you arrive at that process that Bruce was undergoing, where everything returns once again to the simplicity stage. That's when Bruce was regarding himself as simply a human being. But it didn't come from nowhere; it came from this process of inner evolution.

To Lee's way of thinking, the problem with any type of "way" or "style" in martial art was its very sectarianism, its denial of our commonality as human beings and limiting the potential of human movement to one small area of emphasis. Lee commented on this insight during the 1971 interview with Pierre Berton cited earlier:

I do not believe in styles anymore. I do not believe that there is such a thing as, like, "the Chinese way of fighting" or the "Japanese way of fighting," or any way of fighting, unless some human beings have three arms and four legs—then there will be a different form of fighting. Basically we only have two hands and two feet. So, styles tend to separate men, because they have their own doctrines, and then the doctrine becomes the gospel truth—that you cannot change. But if you do not have style, if you just say, "Here I am as a human being. How can I express myself totally and completely?," now, that way, you won't have style, because style is a crystallization; this is a process of continuing growth.

Bruce Lee was forever committing to paper his thoughts on martial art, filmmaking, and life.

Linda Lee Cadwell picks up on her husband's point:

Then it's just two people who are being aware of their own movements, who are observing the other person's movements and able to fit in with that person's movement, so that there's no set pattern—no, "Well, when he does this then I do this." It's just a total freedom really to react to what the other person does. In fact, Bruce inscribed it perfectly on the back of a medallion, where he wrote the words that have become his motto; it says, "Using no way as way; having no limitation as limitation."

Over the years, this phrase has been somewhat misinterpreted, and people think of "using no way as way" to mean "anything I do is OK—and anything I do is 'my way.'" I don't think Bruce really intended it to mean this. He just meant not to be boxed in by a certain way. To give an example: If you have a strength—let's say that in fighting, your left hook is your biggest strength—when you're fighting an opponent you're always looking for an opportunity to use that left hook. Well, if your opponent knows that about you, he's never going to give you that opportunity. But you are stuck in that way of using the left hook, and so, you are going to go down to defeat. From a martial arts standpoint, I believe that's what he meant as "having no way," using "no way" as your way. You need to be able to adapt to what the other person is doing.

Of course, that is only a mini example of how one would conduct his or her life through the JKD way of thinking, so that you never get into a situation where there is only one response. You adapt to what the situation calls for. I think Bruce had that down pretty well.

Lee recognized the fact that as soon as a style or "way of fighting" was established, it had effectively become a closed system or dogma, thereby shutting off all future possibilities of learning and growth. In a telephone interview granted in 1972 to journalist Alex Ben Block, Lee expounds on this point:

Alex Ben Block: This philosophy that you have, doesn't it go against much of what is taught in martial arts by normal instructors?

Bruce Lee: Well, yes, because most of them are so doggone stubborn, you know? I mean, their approach is something like, "Well, two hundred years ago, it was taught like this," but to maintain that type of attitude today means you've had it! I mean, you would still be back there; you will never grow, because learning is a discovering thing. It's a constant discovery thing. Whereas, if we follow the old method, it is simply a continuous repetition of what was being handed down several hundred years ago.

Lee had put it even more succinctly during the telephone conversation referenced earlier with his student Daniel Lee, when he said:

Bruce Lee (standing) gives a demonstration of his new approach to martial art, jeet kune do, during an appearance on Hong Kong television in 1971.

Despite the fact that each member of a style is a unique human being, they were made over time to dress the same, move the same, react the same—to believe the same doctrines and to teach the next generation of students to be the same robots that they had become. To Bruce Lee, this was simply a formula for becoming someone else's product, not yourself. In a radio interview on Radio-Television Hong Kong, Lee said:

Where there is a way, therein lies the limitation. And when it limits, it traps, and when it traps, it's lifeless, and if it is lifeless, it rots.

The original founder of the style started out with a hypothesis. But now [that hypothesis] has become the gospel truth, and people who go into it become the product of it. It doesn't matter who you are, how you are structured, how you are built, how you are made—it doesn't matter. You just go in there and be that product. And that, to me, is not right.

Lee refused to make his art a robot factory and his students into automatons by teaching them a "one-size-fits-all" or "cookie-cutter" system that would deny them the opportunity of total self-actualization. He had designed a miniature tombstone that he placed on the desktop in his office that read: "In Memory of a Once Fluid Man, Crammed and Distorted by the Classical Mess." Lee spoke on this topic during his interview with Alex Ben Block, August 1972:

Alex Ben Block: You once were quoted as saying: "Man, the living creature, the creating individual, is always more important than any established style." Do you mean by this that one must change one's style all the time . . . ?

Bruce Lee: No, I mean this: We are always in a learning process, whereas a "style" is a concluded, established, solidified something. You cannot do that, because you learn every day as you grow older.

Free of the chains of styles, Lee's mind was now free to look at martial art from an unconditioned and fresh perspective, with the result that he now saw another—even more profound—vision. Lee saw in martial art no longer simply an efficient means to dominate an opponent, but a means of spiritual realization and a means by which to liberate the individual from the grip of ego, fear, and insecurity.

What most people see as weapons of destruction—the kicks, the punches, the grappling—Lee saw as tools to liberate the spirit. The whole thrust of Lee's teaching now reflected this power of martial art as liberating agent. Whereas in earlier writings, Lee had focused primarily, if not exclusively, on martial technique and combative principles, his later writings express fundamental truths that gracefully transcend the confines of physical technique. In the handwritten essay "Toward Personal Liberation," Lee wrote:

As he matures, the martial artist will realize that his kick is really not so much a tool to conquer his opponent, but a tool to explode through his ego, his anger, his consciousness. . . .

In fact, all the tools are ultimately means for penetrating the depth of his being, so that he will achieve this imperturbability of his inner center of gravity. . . . All the training is to round him up to be a complete man and not some sort of superman.

In a radio interview with Hong Kong–based journalist Ted Thomas, Lee commented that to him the most important aspect of martial art is that it's a means to self-knowledge:

That is to me the most important thing, and that is: How can I—in the process of learning how to use my body—come to understand myself?

For him, this became the ultimate purpose of martial art: to take the individual from the shore of ignorance to the shore of enlightenment, thereby liberating the human soul from the manacles of the ego. The "I" is a product of the past—past memories,

past conditioning—and the past does not exist in the present. There is only now—the moment. To always be in the "now," to live

Bruce Lee sporting a gold medallion upon which he wrote his personal motto: "Using no way as way; having no limitation as limitation."

every second afresh, with each nerve fully exposed to life's experiences, is to know the eternal, the unsullied, the pure. As Lee told Daniel Lee in 1972:

---------------- 🌀 ----------------

It's becoming more and more simple to me as a human being. More and more I search myself, and the more questions are listed, the more I see clearly. What it is is that what man has to get over is the consciousness—the consciousness of himself. . . . Really what it is is that it utilizes the body to come to some sort of realization in regard to whatever your pursuit might be; in my case, the pursuit of becoming, moment to moment—whatever that thing is—and constantly questioning myself: What is this, Bruce? Is it true or is it not true? Do you really mean it or not mean it? Once when I've found that out, that's it.

Lee called this process "the art of dying." By that, he meant dying to the illusion of ego, dying to the petty worrying and the possessive, false image of self that we have made into an oppressive idol of the ego. In an episode of the television show "Longstreet" Lee said:

---------------- 🌀 ----------------

Like everyone else, you want to learn the way to win—but never to accept the way to lose. To accept defeat, to learn to die, is to be liberated from it. So, when tomorrow comes, you must free your ambitious mind and learn the art of dying. May it be well with you.

It is this illusion of ego that is the martial artist's worst enemy, as it seeks to preserve itself at all costs and so becomes rapacious, worrisome, and fearful of losing anything that feeds and reinforces its existence.

In combat, emptying the mind of all thoughts of survival allows the martial artist to be free of the fear of death and personal injury and thus to react naturally. To Bruce Lee, the true martial artist had no sense of self, and thus, his weapons moved subconsciously—as if by their own accord—to strike at the precise moment necessary. Lee had even attempted to communicate this point during a martial arts teaching scene that he had written into the premier episode of "Longstreet":

Lee: Now how did it feel to you?

Longstreet: Like "I" didn't kick; "it" kicked.

Lee: Very good. Now once more.

Longstreet: Wait a minute, I have to think . . .

Lee: If you have to think, you still do not understand!

Less than two years later, Lee attempted to teach this same lesson in a scene from his last film, *Enter the Dragon*—a scene that was later cut from the original version:

Monk: What were you feeling just now?

Lee: There is no opponent.

Monk: Yes? And why is that?

Lee: Because the word I does not exist.

Monk: Continue . . .

Lee: A martial artist does not become tense, but ready. Not thinking, yet not dreaming. Ready for whatever may come. When the opponent expands, I contract, and when he contracts, I expand. And

when there is an opportunity, "I" do not hit—it hits all by itself.

In his critically acclaimed appearance in the episode of "Longstreet" entitled "The Way of the Intercepting Fist" and cowritten by Lee and his real-life student, Academy Award–winning screenwriter Stirling Silliphant, Lee first spoke the words that have since been taken by many to encapsulate his personal philosophy:

Longstreet: There's so much to try and remember.

Lee: If you try to remember, you will lose. Empty your mind. Be formless, shapeless, like water. Now, you put water into a cup, it becomes the cup. You put it into a teapot, it becomes the teapot. Now, water can flow, or creep, or drip—or crash. Be water, my friend.

The summit of Lee's journey to discover the ultimate truth of martial art led him full circle back to himself. His greatest battle turned out to be a battle to ascend in his own consciousness, to journey to the center of his soul to discover the nature of the energy that informed his life, and to express that energy as completely and honestly as possible. In his 1971 interview with Pierre Berton, Lee said:

To me—to me—ultimately, martial art means honestly expressing yourself. Now, it is very difficult to do.

I mean, it is easy for me to put on a show and be cocky and be flooded with a cocky feeling and then feel pretty cool and all that. Or I can make all kinds of phony things and be blinded by it. Or I can show you some really fancy movement. But to express oneself honestly—not lying to oneself—and to express myself: that, my friend, is very hard to do.

CHAPTER 3
THE STRUGGLE

Bruce Lee: I have already made up my mind that something about the Oriental—I mean, the true Oriental—should be shown.

Pierre Berton: Hollywood sure as heck hasn't.

Bruce Lee: You better believe it, man. It's always the pigtails and running around "chop-chop" with the eyes slanted and all that. I think that's very, very out of date.

—Interview with Pierre Berton, December 1971

Despite the profundity of the young artist's vision, Hollywood still had no interest in using him in productions—and even less interest in producing a film about the ultimate truth of martial art, which was a discipline considered far too esoteric and exotic to have any commercial appeal. Linda Lee Cadwell recollects:

After "The Green Hornet" folded, Bruce decided that he wanted to make filmmaking and television his career as a way, a medium, to show the beauty of his martial art. . . . He attempted to get roles in movies and TV but found it very difficult. Bruce never intended to be a bit-part actor, you know. He always set his sights higher, and he considered himself leading-man material. Although he did a number of small parts and he did choreography on a lot of films, he had difficulty finding major roles.

The Lee family (left to right), Linda, Shannon, Bruce, and Brandon, arrive in Hong Kong in 1971 to embark on a film career that would make history.

idea of a Chinese leading man. The show was later renamed "Kung Fu," and the lead role was given to Caucasian actor David Carradine. The show went on to substantial success and critical acclaim throughout the world. Linda recalls:

When he proposed the idea of the "Kung Fu" TV series and wrote up the idea as a treatment and submitted it, it was very well liked, and he had numerous discussions with the producers. Even after all that, when it came down to casting the role of the lead man in "Kung Fu," Bruce was not picked, and a Caucasian man was picked. The word came down that Bruce had not been picked because a Chinese man would not be a bankable commodity. He would not be able to pull an audience.

To counteract the paucity of opportunity, Lee wrote a screenplay entitled *The Silent Flute*, which detailed the personal quest of self-discovery of a young martial artist. It was promptly torpedoed by Hollywood. Not thwarted, Lee turned his attention to television and began to develop the concept of a series featuring both philosophy and martial art, which he entitled "The Warrior." The network loved the idea—but not the

In an interview granted to Canadian broadcaster Pierre Berton the day after receiving the news that he had been passed over for the part, Lee—though disappointed at the cultural bigotry to which he was being subjected—was nevertheless characteristically upbeat:

Pierre Berton: Let me ask you, however, about the problems that you face as a Chinese hero in an American series. Have people come up in the industry and said, "Well, we don't know how the audience is going to take a non-American"?

Bruce Lee: Well, such questions have been raised. In fact, it is being discussed, and that is why "The Warrior" is probably not going to be on. Because, unfortunately, such thing does exist in this world, you see. Like, I don't know, in a certain part of the country, right? Where they think that, business-wise, it's a risk—and I don't blame them. I don't blame them. I mean, in the same way, in Hong Kong, if a foreigner came and wanted to become a star, if I were the man with the money, I probably would have my own worry of whether or not the acceptance would be there. But that's all right, because if you honestly express yourself, it doesn't matter. You're going to do it!

Lee recognized that Hollywood wanted Asians to play only grossly inaccurate stereotypes. With a wife and now two small children to support, Lee's dignity and philosophical principles came at a huge price. With money rapidly running out, he now realized that the dream was over, he was wasting his time with Hollywood. He told Alex Ben Block in an interview:

H ere I am—a Chinese. I mean, not prejudiced or anything but realistically thinking, How many times in film is a Chinese required? And when it is required, it is always branded as the typical "Tung-de-de-lung-lung-dung-dung-dung." That type. So, I said, "The hell with it."

Once again, Lee found himself up against his old foe: ignorance—and, once again, he stood alone. Linda recalls:

S o, with that rejection in mind, I guess you could say that was an overt expression of racism in the film industry in the early '70s. And at that time, we went to Hong Kong. Bruce had decided that if he couldn't make it in the American film industry through the front door, he would go to Hong Kong and come back in through the side door, which is precisely what he was doing.

Rather than wring his hands in despair, in 1971, armed with nothing but his indefatigable belief in truth lying deeper than surface prejudices, Bruce Lee headed back to Hong Kong. His goal: to create a series of films that would, step by step, educate his audience and prepare them for his message of the ultimate truth of martial art and of its implications for individual freedom, self-knowledge, and universal brotherhood.

The films Lee had in mind included plenty of action to keep things interesting, but there would also be something deeper—for those with eyes to see it.

Lee told the Hong Kong press in an interview shortly before his death:

I believe that I have a role here in Southeast Asia. The audience needs to be educated, and the one to educate them has to be somebody who is responsible. We are dealing with the masses, and we have to create something that will get through to them. We have to educate them step by step. We can't do it overnight. That's what I am doing right now. Whether I succeed or not remains to be seen. But I don't just *feel* committed; I *am* committed.

Lee recognized that the majority of mainstream America did not comprehend what martial art was, let alone its deeper meaning. They were not ready for his message—yet. Conversely, he also realized that on the other side of the Pacific, while the majority of his Southeast Asian audience was familiar with martial art, their very familiarity was also a wall of misconception that would blind them to his message of personal liberation. They, too, were not

Bruce Lee's first film, *The Big Boss*, electrified moviegoers throughout the world with Lee's unique brand of action.

ready for his message—yet. Here is an excerpt from the 1971 interview with Pierre Berton:

Pierre Berton: You're fairly hip: are you too hip for your Oriental audience?

Bruce Lee: Man—how! I have been criticized for that!

Pierre Berton: You have?

Bruce Lee: Oh, definitely, definitely. Let me say this: When I do the Chinese film, I will do my best not to be as American as I have been . . . for the last

twelve years in the States. But when I go back to the States, it seems to be the other way around. You know what I mean?

Pierre Berton: You're too exotic, eh?

Bruce Lee: Yeah, man. They want me to do too many things that are simply for the sake of being exotic.

He was offered very little money to star in his first film—but then, money had never been his sole objective. The true wealth, to Lee's mind, lay in the huge opportunity a starring role in a feature film afforded. The first film Lee made during this period was entitled *The Big Boss*. Filmed in the small Thai village of Pak Chong and made on a shoe-string, it became the highest-grossing film in Southeast Asian history.

Lee followed up that unprecedented success with a second film,' *Fist of Fury*, which promptly proceeded to smash the record set by *The Big Boss*.

At the time, Chinese action films were largely swordplay films—or, as Lee so aptly described them—simply "one long—armed—hassle." He told Pierre Berton:

Bruce Lee's second film for Golden Harvest, *Fist of Fury*, firmly established him as the biggest star in Southeast Asian history.

I would hope that the picture I am in would explain why the violence was done—whether right or wrong, or what-not. Unfortunately, pictures—most of them here [in Hong Kong]—are done mainly just for the sake of violence.

Lee insisted that the fight sequences in his films be realistic and artistic, revealing not what swords are capable of but rather what the human body, in toto, was capable of in terms of hand-to-hand combat. The result was that Lee's new style of martial art choreography was perceived by the Chinese viewing audience as both vital and real.

According to Linda:

When Bruce first went to Hong Kong and made *The Big Boss* and *Fist of Fury*, which were scripts written by others and directed by another, there were quite a few pretty violent fight scenes in those films. And he would say that he "didn't invent the

Lee delivers a reverse hook kick to Bob Baker during a photo shoot for *Fist of Fury*. Baker, apart from playing Lee's adversary in the film, was a real-life student of Lee's art of jeet kune do.

Bruce Lee effectively demonstrated not only his incredible martial art skills but also his phenomenal strength during the fight scenes for *The Big Boss*.

gore in Mandarin films" but that the violence in his films was always with "just cause." So, there were not these protracted fight scenes where a guy gets kicked in the face five hundred times and can still get up and go at it. They were more efficient, the way that Bruce's martial art was, and more dramatic.

His first two films, the second one in particular, strongly stressed Chinese pride and dignity and how a Chinese man and a Chinese art were by no means inferior to other cultures. These films served to not only reassert the dignity of Chinese people in their own eyes but also substantially elevate their culture in the eyes of the rest of the world.

Lee, who had spent his formative years in Hong Kong, was keenly aware that over the centuries, Chinese people had been repressed, particularly in Hong Kong, and made to feel much like second-class citizens in their own country. Realizing that he could communicate with his Chinese audience about racial equality in any meaningful manner only after first leveling the

Lee delivers a high hook kick to the jaw of Chuck Norris during their climactic battle in the Roman Colosseum in his third film, *The Way of the Dragon*.

based on the proven success in Southeast Asia of his first two films, which strongly promoted Chinese patriotism and nationalism. There was a ready and paying audience for this message, and his product had now become so successful that other domestic studios actively bid for his services.

However, Lee had his quest and was about to take the second step toward its fulfillment. This step was to infuse a lesson of compassion for one's fellow man—especially when that fellow man is of a different race or culture.

This second step Lee inserted into the final moments of his third film, *The Way of the Dragon*, which he wrote, directed, and produced. In the climactic moments of the film, Lee allows his adversary (played by his onetime student Chuck Norris) to die a heroic and noble death. Lee's character, rather than seizing the moment to underscore the superiority of Chinese martial art, pauses to make a symbolic gesture of respect to a fellow human being. It was yet another example of Lee's communicating to his audience a piece of his personal philosophy regarding the brotherhood—rather than the differences—among all races. Lee addresses this distinction in the 1971 interview with Pierre Berton.

cultural playing field, he opted to make two films that would reveal to his countrymen that they were the equal of any other culture and had much to be proud of. The films effectively accomplished the first step of Lee's quest: to deliver a message that would right the balance of racial equality and thus pave the way for his bigger message to follow.

Had Lee wished simply to make money, he could have continued to make movies

Pierre Berton: Do you think of yourself as Chinese, or do you ever think of yourself as American?

Bruce Lee: You know how I like to think of myself? As a human being. Because, I don't want this to sounds like "As Confucius say," but under the stars, under the heavens, there is but one family. It just so happens that people are different.

Bruce's view of filmmaking was very closely related to his view of martial art. That is, he didn't want to be segmented in such a way that he could do only Chinese movies or do only Chinese martial arts. He didn't view himself as only a Chinese man; he viewed himself as a citizen of the world who had a mission that really had nothing to do with what his nationality was. He wanted to bring his views of martial art and of life and of the culture that he had experienced in his short lifetime to audiences all over the world.

The first movies that he made were indeed intended for a Chinese audience. You can tell by the Chinese historical themes that are represented and by the type of humor that appeals to a Chinese audience, such as the jokes, especially when it's in the Chinese language. But this Bruce looked at as a stepping-stone to his greater vision of what he wanted to do.

The Way of the Dragon was another box-office smash, decimating the records set by his previous two films. His audience was

Bruce Lee (left) works out with Kareem Abdul-Jabbar on the set of *The Game of Death,* the first cinematic presentation of Lee's martial philosophy of jeet kune do.

not only enjoying his brand of action but also, to his delight, proving receptive to his philosophical message. Linda remembers:

After the first two movies, Bruce progressed into making *The Way of the Dragon*, which was his own creation, then *The Game of Death*, of course, and then *Enter the Dragon* came along. I think you can see that there is a progression in those films, where the fighting has even more justification, and that there's more material built around the fighting to explain the reason for it, first of all, and to also find expression for the philosophy underlying the martial arts. This was what Bruce was really aiming at. Bruce knew very well that a film is a commercial property; it needs to have appeal as well as message. I think he was trying to combine those.

Lee was now in a position to take the third step in his series of "edutainment" films—*The Game of Death*.

CHAPTER 4
PREPARATION

The Game of Death was Bruce Lee's "martial arts baby," according to his wife, Linda.

Bruce Lee's remarkable success brought with it more creative freedom for the young artist, with the result that he was able to move his "classroom" from modest American storefronts to motion picture screens around the world.

Having touched on elements of his martial philosophy in *The Way of the Dragon*, Lee now wanted to present a more comprehensive picture of what jeet kune do was all about. As Linda recalls:

This was his "martial arts baby," you might say, in that he had an idea of how he wanted to show his martial art to the viewing public; these are the various steps in finding your own way in martial art. The different styles and what styles mean and, more important, what they don't mean: that was Bruce's big message, the style of no style. *The Game of Death* was going to be the platform for these expressions.

Bruce had done a great deal of writing about the martial arts in the years before the making of *The Game of Death*, before he went back to Hong Kong. Many of his writings appeared in magazines such as *Black Belt*, where he wrote a definitive expression of what his way of martial art, jeet kune do, meant. I believe that this background of research and a building of a philosophy of jeet kune do is what Bruce intended to relate through *The Game of Death*— how all knowledge, as Bruce often said, is self-knowledge.

Bruce used martial art as a vehicle to learn about himself and to be able to express himself. So, everything he had learned to that point about himself he wanted to express in *The Game of Death* to show people what it meant to live life as a martial artist. In other words, all of his life was interpreted through the vehicle that he chose for self-expression, which he called jeet kune do.

Lee brought in real martial artists, including Dan Inosanto (right), to appear in *The Game of Death* to help him relate his belief regarding the problem of styles in martial art.

Bruce Lee threw himself into all aspects of filmmaking for *The Game of Death*, including selecting the backdrop for the film. According to Lee's original story line, it was Popju-sa, once a thriving Buddhist temple in the heart of South Korea's Sagni-san national park, that would provide the backdrop for the action.

Popju-sa is the largest temple in the Korean provinces and one of the most important. It is located three hours south of Seoul and can be reached only by a long, level entranceway that runs through a colonnade of tall trees.

Popju-sa has long been known not only for its beautiful surrounding scenery but also for its history and ancient cultural artifacts. Preserved within the Buddhist compound are three National Treasures and more than a dozen other historical properties. Ten hermitages in the hills beyond the village are also under its jurisdiction.

The village itself was founded in 553 and was rebuilt in 776, in time growing to include an incredible sixty buildings with seventy hermitages. Like most other temples in the country, it was destroyed in 1592 by the invading Japanese army, but it was subsequently rebuilt in 1624. Several of the buildings within the compound—perfectly

Bruce Lee's sketch of the village of Popju-sa in South Korea, based on photographs he had taken to assist him in crafting his story line for the flim.

The village of Popju-sa as it looks today.

preserved—date from this time. Extensive renovations were undertaken in the mid-1960s. Records from the temple reveal that Popju-sa once was home to some three

One of Bruce Lee's photos of the giant Buddha from Popju-sa. In 1988 the cement Buddha was replaced by one made of 150 tons of bronze.

of bronze and is claimed to be the largest such standing figure in all of Asia. In 1988, this statue replaced one of cement that had graced the temple for more than twenty years.

In a museum located within the base of the Buddha, one finds magnificent stained-glass windows with images representing heavenly spirits from Buddhist mythology, while beneath the windows resides a gold statue of Mirugposal, who, it is said, remains in the world of heaven dreaming of an ideal world to come.

Back outside and within the temple's main hall, which is a giant double-roofed structure toward the back of the village, sits the third-largest temple hall in the country. Within, three huge Buddha figures, made of wood and painted a brilliant gold, sit contemplatively on an altar. The main hall was originally built in 553 but also required restoration after the Japanese invasion.

Lee had several photographs taken of Popju-sa, from which he worked in designing the backdrop and story line for *The Game of Death* in 1972. Most prominently featured was P'alsang-jon (rechristened "Temple of the Leopard" for cinematic purposes), the five-story wooden pagoda that Lee had chosen as the setting for the climactic final battles of the film.

thousand monks. At one point during the twelfth century, more than thirty thousand monks gathered here.

The village's most striking object is its huge Buddha statue. Standing 100 feet high, it is visible even before you enter the village. It was cast in one mold with 150 tons

P'alsang-jon is the only large wooden pagoda remaining in Korea and is also one of the few wooden structures to survive from the early 1600s. It was rebuilt in 1624. Its design is breathtaking, and—unlike Bruce Lee's set—the pagoda is actually a facade of sorts. Rather than having five floors, it is one floor with a gigantic pole that runs up through the center of its ceiling to support its top roof. Four other posts surrounding this central pole and a complex post-and-beam and cantilever support system hold up the lower roofs.

A decorative metal finial perches atop the apex of the pagoda, and metal wind chimes with dragons carved into them hang from the corners of all the roofs. The chimes themselves are fish figures, crafted to reveal open eyes, symbolizing an ever-conscious, always-watchful approach to life, which, in the Buddhist tradition, is indicative of having attained satori, or enlightenment. Within the pagoda are a thousand miniature Buddhas sitting on an altar surrounding the building's central pillar. Behind these, two to a side, are murals showing scenes from the Buddha's life.

In Bruce Lee's story, this serene village was transformed into a martial arts training compound, with each floor of the pagoda protected by a skilled fighter. Lee was well

P'alsang-jon, this five-story wooden pagoda, served as the backdrop for the battles in *The Game of Death*.

aware of the symbolism of the Buddha figure in Popju-sa: it was dedicated not only to the unification of Korea but also to peace throughout the world, a cause to which he had hoped to contribute as well, through his work in martial art and film.

He immediately began designing the sets and conceiving of a scenario whereby such a locale could be justifiably employed. He also began contacting potential costars as the characters and story line fell into place. Linda Lee Cadwell recalls:

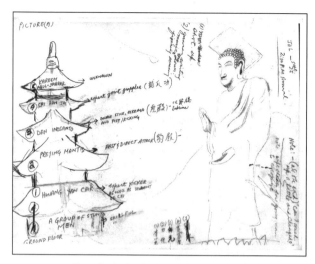

Bruce Lee's sketch of the pagoda and Buddah figure from Popju-sa, indicating the floors of the pagoda and the guardians of each floor.

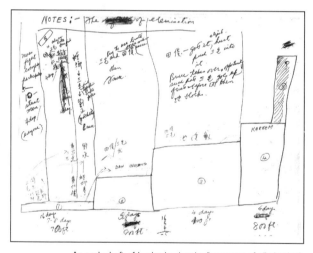

An early draft of Lee's showing the "sequence of elimination" that Lee and his colleagues would experience as they battled their way to the top of the pagoda and the number of days he estimated would be required to film each fight sequence.

Bruce had finished *The Way of the Dragon* and was now between projects. Bruce had always wanted to make movies about the martial arts that would raise the image of martial arts, particularly in the West, and the level of filmmaking in the East. With that in mind, he was always making notes about what types of films would be able to further that goal. He was always writing ideas down.

At the same time, we were going to be visited in Hong Kong by Kareem Abdul-Jabbar, who was a longtime friend of Bruce's. He had been a student of Bruce's in Los Angeles before we moved to Hong Kong, and Bruce and he had often talked about filming some sequences: how interesting they would be because Kareem, of course, is 7′2″ and Bruce was 5′8″. Bruce thought how interesting that would be from a martial arts aspect. So, they had talked about that, and they'd talked about Kareem's coming to visit Hong Kong because he had wanted to do that.

With Kareem's visit impending, Bruce decided this would be the ripe time to carry out a fight scene on film with him, and thus the idea started from there. Bruce took some of the ideas he had been gathering about the levels of martial arts combat in the pagoda, and Kareem came out. I believe that the first scenes that they shot were the fight scenes between Bruce and Kareem.

Bruce Lee poses with Hong Kong actress Nora Miao, who was Lee's original choice to play the role of his sister in the film. Miao is holding Lee's nunchaku, which he used in his fight with Dan Inosanto on the third floor of the pagoda.

Lee wanted solid actors, athletes, and martial artists for the cast. He always sought out what he called "competent deliverers" to appear in his films, and the message that he was envisioning delivering to his audience with *The Game of Death* was to be the most important one of his career.

THE PROTAGONISTS AND ACCOMPLICES

NORA MIAO

Nora Miao, an actress who had appeared with Bruce in all three of his previous movies, was Lee's choice to play the role of his sister. Photos exist of Nora, Linda, and Bruce in Lee's office in Golden Harvest Studios, in which both the nunchaku used by

Dan Inosanto and the one used by Bruce in their epic battle in the film are clearly visible. In fact, in one, Nora is holding the nunchaku that Bruce used, which would date the photo to September 1972, the time when he was finalizing his story line. Nora would play the role of Lee's sister, who, along with a "younger brother" who had not yet been cast, would be kidnapped by a malicious boss in order to get Lee's character to take part in the raid on the pagoda.

JAMES TIEN

Of what were to be five "accomplices," Lee wanted one to be slightly devious and antagonistic toward his character. This would

Bruce Lee (left) and James Tien square off in a publicity photo for *The Game of Death*.

remainder of his career. *The Game of Death* was to mark the first time that Tien would play the role of antagonist on screen.

CHIEH YUAN

Another accomplice was to be a simple-minded yet strong martial artist. These character attributes would allow for a different type of dynamic among the accomplices as they fought their way up each level of the pagoda. Lee initially considered future Hong Kong and U.S. action actor

create some interesting interplay between the two men, not letting the audience know for certain whether Lee's partners were actually "with" him or "against" him. For the role of the antagonistic accomplice, Lee chose James Tien, an actor who had appeared with Lee in two of his previous three films for Golden Harvest. Tien had been a popular actor in Hong Kong cinema, with many films to his credit, by the time he appeared in Bruce's first film for Golden Harvest, *The Big Boss*. After Lee's arrival at Golden Harvest in 1971, however, Tien was relegated to supporting-role status for the

Hong Kong stuntman Chieh Yuan was selected to appear as one of Lee's allies in *The Game of Death*, although Lee's first choice was Hong Kong action actor Samo Hung.

Samo Hung for the role but ultimately settled on Hong Kong stuntman Chieh Yuan. It would be the first time that these two had worked together.

THE OPPONENTS

Selecting the martial art opponents whom Lee and his accomplices would face inside the pagoda was a comparatively easy matter. Lee wanted professional martial artists for the role of his adversaries, since he believed that they could best assist him in bringing the scintillating martial art action to life in a manner that was totally believable.

In the pagoda, Lee and his accomplices would have to battle upward past five levels, each guarded by a martial artist of a particular style.

WONG IN SIK

According to Lee's notes, the first level was to be guarded by Wong In Sik, who was to portray a master of a kicking style. The "style" was not specified at the time of Lee's passing, although Wong was in real life a student of Ji Han Jae, a martial artist Lee had chosen to be the guardian of the fourth level of the temple. Wong had appeared as

Hapkido master Wong In Sik (far right) was supposed to be the guardian of the first floor of the pagoda in *The Game of Death*. Wong had also appeared in Lee's previous film, *The Way of the Dragon*.

one of Lee's adversaries in The Way of the Dragon.

TAKY KIMURA

Lee chose his most senior student, Taky Kimura, to play the guardian of the second floor. According to Kimura, Lee wanted him to utilize praying mantis gung fu, as well as some elements of wing chun gung fu—the first martial art that Lee had studied formally. Both arts emphasize in-close fighting, use of the hands predominantly, with kicks limited to below the waist, and virtually no grappling maneuvers. Kimura recalls:

Taky Kimura (left) was a man whose loyalty and friendship were very important to Bruce Lee throughout his life. Lee wanted him to play the role of the guardian of the second floor of the pagoda in *The Game of Death*.

Bruce was very kind to me. I think that he felt that there was a strong friendship and maybe that he owed me something; it was his way of paying me back. I think it was October of 1972 that he called me and said he wanted me to be in that movie. And I said, "Look, Bruce, I've got two left feet. You know it, and I know it. There's probably a thousand people in Hong Kong that could do better than I can. Just let me sit here and enjoy the fruits of your success. You know me: I don't need to be in that." He said, "No, I want you in it; I'm the technical director and the coproducer, so don't worry about it." I was reluctant for fear that he would kick my butt if I said no, so I said, "OK."

Lee sent Kimura a ticket to fly to Hong Kong to film his sequence, but two things precluded this from happening. First, Kimura had some pressing business from which he could not extricate himself, and second, Lee had signed to begin filming *Enter the Dragon* for Warner Bros. in January of 1973, only three months away. Again, Kimura recalls:

But this [filming] was to happen in October, and I was engaged in an import-export business with Japan at the time, and October was the month that I had to really get out to the various wholesalers to sell my product. So, I called back and got a hold of Linda, and I said, "Linda, I just can't make it."

"Well," she said, "don't worry about it. Bruce has been called to go to Warner Bros. in California to talk about a new movie project they're working on together, and if it goes through, we're going to postpone *The Game of Death* until after it's over with." Of course, that's what happened. But prior to that, he had already sent me an airline ticket and told me to bring my blue gung fu uniform.

Weeks or maybe a month or so before he died, after *Enter the Dragon* was all done and over with, he called me and said, "We are going to finish *The Game of Death* now." He said, "Send that old ticket back, and I'll get you a new one. I want you back in there again." And very reluctantly, I agreed. I was really worried because Bruce was a perfectionist, and I just didn't think I had it in me to measure up to what he wanted me to do. But unfortunately, he passed away just prior to that, and so that was history.

Bruce Lee (right) had known Dan Inosanto for many years and knew that he could count on him to deliver an exciting weapons performance in his role as guardian of the third level of the pagoda.

DAN INOSANTO

Lee had selected Dan Inosanto to be the guardian of the third floor, as he not only had been an assistant instructor in jeet kune do when Lee's Los Angeles Chinatown school was open but also was an advanced practitioner of kenpo karate and the Filipino stick-fighting art of escrima. Lee opted to have Inosanto employ methods from both arts in the film. Escrima would be employed to add an exciting visual element to the film to break up the unarmed combative sequences.

Bruce Lee, in the famous "on-guard" position of jeet kune do, prepares to intercept an attack launched by hapkido grandmaster Ji Han Jae (right) during their fight sequence on the fourth floor of the pagoda in *The Game of Death*.

KAREEM ABDUL-JABBAR

Casting the role of the calm, cool assassin who would employ the "formless form" of Lee's own martial art of jeet kune do was proving to be more problematic—that is, until he heard that one of his last and most diligent private students, Kareem Abdul-Jabbar, would be coming to Hong Kong for a brief vacation. According to Abdul-Jabbar:

Kareem Abdul-Jabbar was to represent the "formless" art of jeet kune do at the highest level of the pagoda.

JI HAN JAE

Grappling or joint locking would also serve to break up the "stand-up" fight sequences that Lee had intended to film as "prior" battles. For this, Lee settled on Korean hapkido grandmaster Ji Han Jae, who, at the time, was respected as a seventh-degree black belt in the art. Ji would be the man to stand guard over the fourth floor of the pagoda.

Lee and Abdul-Jabbar demonstrate how two individuals, both free of the restrictions of styles, engage in unarmed combat.

Lee brings Abdul-Jabbar to the ground, thus taking away his height advantage during their legendary battle in *The Game of Death*.

Bruce and I had talked about doing a film, and he liked having to work against the problems I presented with my reach and my agility and my ability to move. He felt that would be an interesting fight in the context of a film, and that was what he wanted to show: how someone his size would have to go about dealing with someone my size in a fight to the death.

Abdul-Jabbar fit the bill perfectly: he was an athlete of superior conditioning and coordination, a student of jeet kune do who had spent considerable time in private instruction with Lee, working out in Lee's backyard. Abdul-Jabbar would present the perfect combative riddle to solve for the last and most significant battle in the film—a battle of two individuals, both free of the restrictions of styles and both in the peak of athletic, mental, and spiritual condition.

With his cast now in place, Lee spent the next three months of his life, from August to October of 1972, putting his martial vision on celluloid. Extensive rehearsal and choreography takes were completed before the cameras until Lee felt that he and his costars had it down—not merely sufficiently, but *perfectly*.

Lee wanted his fight sequences not only to be exciting and artistic to watch but also to tell a story, revealing a message of the human spirit through the "language" of movement.

It was a message that was to become Bruce Lee's greatest teaching.

CHAPTER 5
THE STORY

It seems to be the thing now to go for sex and blood just merely for the sake of sex and merely for the sake of blood. . . . But I definitely do not believe in putting something in there just for the heck of it, because it is an exploitation. . . . My first question was, First of all, why do I start fighting?

—Bruce Lee

With his motto of "using no way as way; having no limitation as limitation" firmly in mind, Lee set out to craft a story that would justify his illustration of it cinematically. Lee never believed in exploiting violence in his films, but to illustrate this vital principle effectively, there could be no avoiding the fact that combat was the vehicle necessary to deliver the message to the audience. A juxtaposition of freedom of athletic expression and rigid martial arts styles would be necessary, and that meant "action."

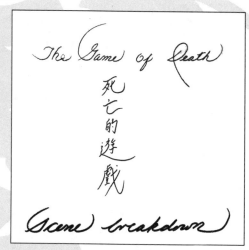

Bruce Lee's handwritten title page and scene breakdown heading for his story line for *The Game of Death*.

Bruce Lee took great pains to justify the violence or "action" in his films—and always in the films over which he had control. He was looking not simply to titillate his audience with the gratuitous use of sex and blood but rather to entertain and educate.

In every Bruce Lee film, Lee's character never seeks out violence for its own sake; he is always sorely provoked until he is thrust into a situation in which he has no alternative but to fight. It is at this point that his body becomes an instrument of communication, delivering a counterstrike on behalf of all individuals who have suffered from injustice, violence, and oppression. It makes his ultimate volcanic eruption of rage at the injustice all the more striking.

After long and careful thought, the story line for *The Game of Death* had come to him. Lee's character would be coerced into taking part in an attack on a five-story pagoda in the South Korean Buddhist village of Popju-sa.

The story would begin on an airplane en route from Hong Kong to Korea. A retired martial arts champion named Hai Tien (Bruce), his sister (Nora Miao), and their young brother are taking a tour of Southeast Asia. On the plane at Hong Kong's Kai Tak Airport, the young boy says that he wants a window seat. A passenger in an aisle seat across from Hai Tien recognizes him as a fighter who suddenly quit in the ring for no apparent reason. The passenger, whose name is Yu Ming, is a "martial art nut" who was at the fight. He asks Hai Tien why he quit. This causes the fighter to flash back to being wild and primitive in his fighting ability. The camera then cuts back to Hai Tien's "blank look," which dissolves to nonchalance. He is indifferent to the passenger's allegations that he "threw" the fight. Hai Tien's brother reproaches the passenger for his ignorance.

The plane has a one-hour stopover in Korea. At the Korean airport, the young boy sets out to get a cold drink, and the trio proceed to check out the shops and sights at the airport, when Hai Tien is paged over the public address system. He picks up the phone and is informed that his sister and brother have been abducted. He is given a stark command from the voice on the phone (James Tien) to walk outside, where a car will be waiting for him. He is to get into the car without causing a scene.

Hai Tien leaves the airport and finds an expensive car waiting for him. There are three individuals waiting for him by the car; a chauffeur and two thugs, all of whom are

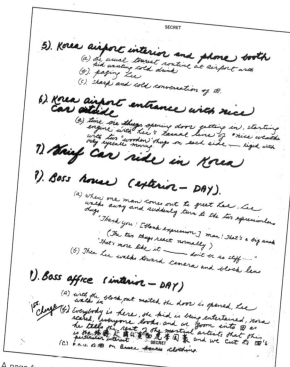

A page from Lee's handwritten story line.

in the boss's employ. Hai Tien is told to get in the backseat, as the two thugs sit on either side of him. They are stiff and rigid. Hai Tien mocks their seriousness by commenting, "Nice weather." There is no reaction from the thugs.

After a brief ride through Korea, they arrive at a large house. While leaving the car, Hai Tien turns and tells the thugs to look at the "big snake" at their feet. They jump back in fear, which causes Hai Tien to

comment, "That's more like it—don't be so stiff."

Once inside the house, Hai Tien is escorted to a meeting room. Upon his entrance, everyone turns to acknowledge his arrival. Hai Tien's sister is in the room and is obviously terrified. Hai Tien notices that his brother is also present—and safe, for the moment—but blissfully unaware of the danger he is in. Not wanting to alarm the boy, Hai Tien refers to the boss who has abducted them as "Uncle Wong." Wong now enters, accompanied by James Tien, who refers to Hai Tien as "Lee Gok Ho—known to foreigners as 'the Yellow-Faced Tiger.'"

The boss wants to introduce Hai Tien to his team of martial artists, but Hai Tien interrupts the introductions by stating that he would like a cup of tea. We cut to see the reaction of James Tien and others, and of their displeasure with Hai Tien. Hai Tien sends the young boy away to play. Concerned for their safety, he tells his sister, "Do not let the kid know [what's going on]. Stay inside and don't run around!"

Hai Tien returns to the main room, and the introductions are resumed. The boss reviews each person in attendance and what his specialty is. One individual is there because he is being paid $2,000, which he needs for his mother's operation. Another is an American who is participating simply because he is "practical" (and being paid). Another individual, somewhat simple-minded, is being paid only $700, but he is strong and loves to show his strength. A comment is made that another member, originally to have been played by veteran comedic actor Lee Kun, is on the team because he came "cheap because he is an alcoholic and a cheap, petty thief." According to statements that Lee Kun later made to the Hong Kong press, Lee had told him that his role was to be that of a master locksmith, who would pick the lock to the temple to allow the martial artists inside. The character would not join the other members of the team, instead staying down below as lookout.

Hai Tien is then introduced to James Tien's character. It is mentioned that he has cost the boss the most so far because he is "extremely efficient and is the current Asian champion." Tien looks to Hai Tien and says, "Like you were." He then says, "By the way, I do not like retired and undefeated champions." As Hai Tien turns to walk away, Tien refuses to let go of his hand. Tien continues his attempt at intimidation: "On top of that, for a retired champion, you sure

have a bad memory. I've just spoken to you at the airport not too long ago. How can you have forgotten my voice?" Hai Tien, not intimidated in the least, pauses briefly before responding: "You know something? You sound tougher than you look."

The boss attempts to placate Hai Tien by offering him money to take part in the mission (presumably to recover a Korean treasure of some kind) but is coolly turned down. The boss reminds Hai Tien that he will have to agree because the lives of his sister and brother hang in the balance.

Later that evening, in the same room, a movie projector is brought out, and a film is shown to the team. It is a blurred image of the "Temple of the Leopard." The boss then shows footage depicting the martial artists that guard each floor of the pagoda and what their specialties are, and what each attacker's duty will be. Hai Tien and James Tien's character will be in charge of the operation. It is clearly indicated who will fight with whom. The schematic of the tower is explained, along with the fact that guns are not allowed in the village. The boss also points out that a prior group of attackers had attempted to make it to the top but that only one man survived—and was unsuccessful in getting past the "Tower of the Unknown." The man's last words before being committed to a local insane asylum were: "Unbelievable agility and power!"

It turns out that Hai Tien had been the one who taught this "survivor" how to kick so effectively, which is the reason he was able to last as long as he did. The boss announces that the next day's meeting will start at 11:00 A.M. and tells everyone to rest up. He issues a "deadly warning" for those who know too much and emphasizes that he is committed to his goal.

Hai Tien then asks the boss for permission to use his car to visit his student in the asylum. The boss replies, "Of course you can use my car, but I can tell you it's a waste of time." Hai Tien answers, "Thank you for letting *just* me go." The boss says, "Ha! Ha! That is why I like you. You know you have to come back!"

The next morning, Hai Tien steps out of the boss's house to discover the chauffeur and James Tien's character waiting for him. They suddenly stop talking when they see him. Tien complains to the boss about Hai Tien's using the car. Then he says to Hai Tien, "I sure don't like the way you dress as a martial artist." Hai Tien responds, "How

does a martial artist normally dress?" Tien hesitates, allowing Hai Tien to finish his point: "It is not how he dresses—that's his own personal taste, anyway—but what really counts is what is behind those clothes of the martial artist, isn't it? By the way, have you looked at how you dress lately?" Tien does a slow burn.

Hai Tien then visits the sanatorium. He walks down the hallway until he comes to the padded cell that holds his former student.

When Hai Tien returns to the boss's house, he is obviously late for the 11:00 meeting. The boss, with James Tien standing next to him, is not pleased. Tien comments, "You have a bad habit of being late." Hai Tien ignores him and instead addresses the boss: "You want your job done, don't you?" The boss assures Hai Tien that the boy and girl are fine and know nothing about "our project."

Hai Tien says, "You have no choice anyway. You need me, and by the way, don't you or anyone in this house lay even one finger on either one of them!" Tien laughs at this, but the boss is more compassionate: "I can assure you that my guards personally will take good care of them. And I might even be generous enough to let you see them anytime you want—but don't even try or think that you can leave this house. My generosity, you see, has a limit."

The meeting resumes, and the boss explains that the purpose of the meeting is to set the date of attack. He tells his warriors to take "tomorrow morning easy and conserve your energy for today." The mission will begin the next day.

Later, Hai Tien steps out into the garden to train. Everybody is training; James Tien is bossing them around. Hai Tien's sister and brother are also present. Hai Tien pulls his sister aside. She has tears in her eyes and is deeply concerned about what will happen. He looks at his little brother and says, "I want you to remember me."

The boy is too innocent to understand the revelation within Hai Tien's message and replies simply, "Why? I see you every day." Hai Tien then exits. That evening (the night before the attack will be launched), another meeting is held. Hai Tien walks out for some air. It is at this point that the "game of death" is mentioned by the American.

Early the next morning, a small bus arrives at the front of the boss's house. Everyone taking part in the attack is wait-

Bruce Lee's scene breakdown for the ending of the film.

ing for Hai Tien. He finally arrives and non-chalantly says, "Good morning, fellas!"

The bus leaves for the temple, and preparations are made for the break-in.

The bus arrives at the temple. It is here that the big fight is to take place. The village of Popju-sa is to be turned into a martial arts training compound, with each floor of the pagoda protected by a skilled fighter.

Bruce Lee's character, along with the other four individuals, are to fight their way up to the top of the pagoda and retrieve the boss's treasure while the locksmith, according to Lee Kun's statement to the Hong Kong press, is to remain below as a lookout. On the first floor, one of the team members is to be killed. The second floor, the floor of the praying mantis, will see what was now the trio overcome the praying mantis master and proceed to the next level. But the third floor—this floor we know much more about. This battle—and the action on the remaining floors as well—Bruce Lee captures on film.

At the end of the film, an arrest is made. Hai Tien is reunited with his sister and brother and returned to the airport to leave for Hong Kong.

The story line perfectly justified the action that would be required, while the choreography in the fight sequences themselves would tell a story within a story of personal liberation in the art of combat.

CHAPTER 6
THE MESSAGE

Ted Thomas: There are a number of styles of fighting. . . . You must have been asked hundreds of times before—which do you think is the most effective?

Bruce Lee: There is no such thing as an effective segment of a totality. By that I mean that I personally do not believe in the word style. Why? Because . . . unless we have another group of beings on earth that are structurally different from us, there can be no different style of fighting. . . . We have two hands and two legs. The important thing is: How can we use them to the maximum.

—Interview with Ted Thomas

The Game of Death was to be a film with a substantial piece of thought at its core, and that thought was freedom, the freedom required to adapt to changing circumstances. Many of Lee's personal beliefs and teachings resonate throughout the footage that he shot for the film.

In the battle of the third floor, for example, Lee's character makes use of a green bamboo whip. The whip represents flexibility and pliability, two attributes that Lee felt a martial artist must possess if he is to

Bruce Lee sketches a figure of an old Taoist priest during a break in filming.

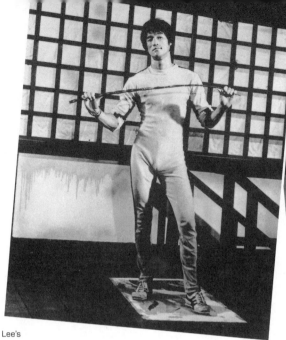

Bruce Lee wanted to convey that "man, the creating individual, is always more important than any established style."

Lee's character in *The Game of Death* would be taking on not just the various exponents of particular styles but also the very notion of styles itself.

be successful in combat. If you enter a combative situation with a rigid, fixed approach, you will lack the flexibility necessary to adapt to the ebb and flow of combat. Since combat, like life, is not predictable, Lee held that one must possess a choiceless, pliable awareness in order to "change with change."

The fact, then, that Lee's character in *The Game of Death* would be taking on advocates of different styles on each level of the temple was significant in a larger context than might be initially evident. Lee was taking on not just the various exponents of particular styles but the very notion of "styles" itself. According to Kareem Abdul-Jabbar:

Bruce understood style to be something that made people latch onto an outward appearance, as opposed to the *substance* of what you're supposed to be trying to do. So, people who got into a showy style that was not an effective fighting style he saw as being misguided and off on a tangent, as opposed to learning what they needed to know to be able to defend themselves. A lot of the *art* aspect of martial arts he saw as being totally superfluous and for show, and not related to the essence of what you're trying to do.

More symbolism was to follow. Lee has his character dressed in a one-piece, yellow and black tracksuit, to symbolize no affiliation with any known martial art school or style. He is an individual who has transcended all styles, using "no way as way" and "having no limitation as limitation," and is thus able to express himself totally and without restriction. According to Linda Lee Cadwell, the wearing of the yellow tracksuit in *The Game of Death* also marked a cinematic turning point for Lee:

The yellow tracksuit that Lee wears in *The Game of Death* symbolizes that his character had no affiliation with any known martial art school or style.

Bruce in his movies before *The Game of Death* had always worn a Chinese gung-fu outfit. But this was because of the setting of the films: they were set in prior times, in traditional times, and so that fit with the overall themes of the pictures. But people who understand Bruce's philosophy of martial art, the way he had taught from when he first came to the United States, the way he conducted his classes, his private lessons, the articles he wrote for magazines about what he felt about the martial arts—people who understand that would know that

Bruce would be called an iconoclast or rebel in the martial arts, someone who thought in a nontraditional way. So, I think the wearing of the yellow tracksuit was an expression of how he felt about the martial arts: that you need not be dressed in a traditional uniform in order to be an effective fighter. That yellow tracksuit is something that is comfortable. It's flexible; you can move without restriction. I think that is why he chose it.

By way of contrast, Lee's opponents in the film are each dressed in the particular fashion of their traditional martial art styles, indicating that their own unique individuality has been lost to the styles they serve and that they have become prisoners of their fixed styles, unable to adapt to the vicissitudes of combat.

Lee had hopes that this film would mark the birth of a "modern" era for martial art, presenting the possibility of personal liberation for martial artists the world over. His character in *The Game of Death* was to be the first cinematic example of martial totality, a man who is free to use any and all means available in a combative situation. According to Linda Lee Cadwell:

I think it's evident in *The Game of Death* how Bruce planned to fight a person of a different style, a very precise style, on each floor of the pagoda—and show how he could fit in with anybody else's style, having no style of his own—until he reached the top level, where Kareem also is a martial artist who, in the film, does not have any particular style.

Jeet kune do versus jeet kune do: Bruce Lee battles his biggest challenge, another free-form individual—Kareem Abdul-Jabbar.

As Lee progresses up each level of the pagoda, initially with four other martial arts stylists, the opponents they face become more challenging with each succeeding level. They find that each level of the pagoda has an art that is less traditional than the one before it. A shedding, or emptying, process is taking place: Karate, which was to be the ground level of the pagoda, is a very traditional Japanese art. Praying mantis gung fu, a very traditional Chinese art,

Jeet kune do versus escrima: Bruce Lee (right) executes a lead leg shin-kick to lower his opponent's guard during his battle with Dan Inosanto.

This "unknown" style was the essence of jeet kune do, the "formless" art of combat pioneered by Bruce Lee. A martial artist who has no form is unpredictable, pliable, and thus totally capable of successfully adapting to whatever his opponent throws at him. Furthermore, a martial artist who has no "style" or "method" has no "playbook" that his opponent can read in advance in order to anticipate the nature of his combative approach.

guards the second. The third level is escrima, a Filipino martial art, which is not as rigid as the first two but still has as one of its defining attributes a particular approach to stick fighting, which is what distinguishes it from all other "stick arts." Level four is hapkido, a comparatively recent art that is considered "eclectic" in approach. Hapkido originated in Korea and makes use of joint locks, strikes, and kicks and, despite having less chronological history than any of the other arts represented in the pagoda, still makes use of a particular "way," or approach to combat.

The highest level of the pagoda is presided over by an "unknown" style, which symbolizes the highest level of martial art.

"If you can move with your tools from any angle, then the clumsier, the more restricted the object is in front of you, the easier it is for you to potshot it." —Bruce Lee on jeet kune do.

It is only when Lee encounters Kareem Abdul-Jabbar's character, a man who, like himself, is of no known style and, therefore, uses "no way as way" and has "no limitation" as his limitation, that Lee is up against his toughest foe. Abdul-Jabbar recalls:

I was at the top of the pagoda because, you know, I was the most effective fighter; I didn't have any style. And I was also in a place where my strengths were enhanced by the environment: it was dark. I was supposed to be light sensitive—that was a problem for me—but other than that, I was [supposed to be] an incredible human specimen, etcetera. That was the whole idea about it. And he started knocking out the panes in the walls so that more light came in and I couldn't see, and that's when he got his advantage in the fight.

As Part II of this book explains, the practitioners of the various styles in *The Game of Death* not only represent opponents to be conquered in order for Lee's character

to progress up the pagoda but also serve as metaphors for other challenges in life.

According to Linda Lee Cadwell:

T*he Game of Death* was intended not just to be for a Chinese audience; it was intended to be a statement about martial art, really. And, in being a statement about martial art, it could, in turn, be a statement for any type of pursuit, which is the way Bruce viewed his martial art: as a way of life. Whether you are a martial artist or a writer or a tennis player or whatever, that's your *vehicle*. So, *The Game of Death* was moving in that direction. And by involving the various nationalities of martial artists in *The Game of Death*, Bruce was showing that this was an international film, that the pursuit of a lifestyle is not something that is segmented by race or upbringing.

Through the clever use of symbolism, from costume to choreography, Lee was able to communicate his message of the necessity for freedom of expression in martial art.

The result is three carefully crafted and meaningful sequences that resonate on many different levels—there is philosophy, rich in metaphors, and profound in meaning—as well as the most graceful and dynamic presentation of the human form in hand-to-hand combat ever captured on film.

Daniel Lee, a student of Bruce Lee's, recorded this summary statement of Bruce's sometime around 1972:

Here it is: If you can move with your tools from any angle, then the clumsier, the more restricted, the object is in front of you, the easier it is for you to potshot it. I mean, that's about it!

The student of jeet kune do will see many examples of Lee's art (including his belief in "offensive defense") throughout the battles in *The Game of Death*.

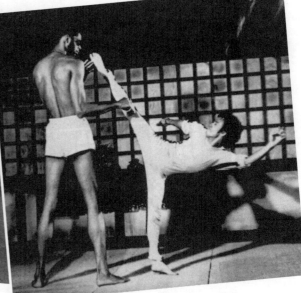

Lee executes a high hook kick that requires him to perform nearly perfect splits as he works out with Kareem Abdul-Jabbar on the set of *The Game of Death*.

PART II

BRUCE LEE—
A CLOSER
LOOK

CHAPTER 7
THE HERO'S JOURNEY

I hope to make multilevel films, the kind of movies where you can just watch the surface story if you want, or you can look deeper into it if you feel like it.
—Bruce Lee

Bruce Lee's films always had something deeper to offer if one was willing to look beneath the surface action.

Ever since the dawn of time, man has told tales of heroes, timeless tales of human beings who had within them the courage to face incredible challenges and who could summon the power necessary to overcome tremendous odds, ultimately to return home from their adventures with new and profound wisdom that would benefit all mankind.

This motif held immense appeal to Bruce Lee ever since he was a young man who sat spellbound in darkened movie houses watching the epic Japanese samurai films. He had been particularly impressed by their presentation of heroism, of courage and honor, and, in films such as *The Seven Samurai* and the *Zatoichi: The Blind Swordsman* series, by their compassion for their fellow human beings.

When Lee began making the films that would establish him as a major cinematic force, he embraced these elements but presented a new heroic archetype: the human being whose weapon was not the samurai sword of Zatoichi or the six-gun of Clint Eastwood, but the individual human body trained to the peak of athletic perfection.

During the final three years of his life, Bruce Lee endeavored to make a film about the "hero's journey," or "vision quest," the individual's personal quest toward enlightenment. The journey would involve the hero's having to pass through a series of trials or tests, each of which would teach him something about himself and, by extension, about life. Finally, at the end of his quest, the hero, now reborn with new enlightenment, would return to where he came from, a better and different being.

The motif for the hero's journey follows a specific format, as described by preeminent mythos authority Joseph Campbell in *The Hero with a Thousand Faces.*

A hero ventures forth from the world of common day into a region of supernatural wonder; fabulous forces are there encountered and a decisive victory is won; the hero comes back from this mysterious adventure with the power to bestow boons on his fellow man.

The hero's journey is an all-embracing metaphor for the deep inner journey of transformation that heroes in every time and place share. Such a journey follows a path that leads them through great movements of separation, descent, ordeal, and return.

According to author Christopher Vogler in his book *The Writer's Journey* there are twelve stages in the archetypical adventure of the hero's journey, consisting of the following:

1. The Ordinary World—in which the audience meets the hero, discovers his or

her ambitions and limitations, and forms a bond of identification and recognition.

2. The Call to Adventure—in which the hero receives a challenge, a quest, or a problem that must be faced.

3. The Refusal of the Call—in which the hero is reluctant to undertake the adventure.

4. The Meeting with the Mentor—in which a mentor provides encouragement, wisdom, or the incentive necessary to motivate the hero to begin his adventure.

5. The Crossing of the Threshold—in which the hero finally accepts the challenge and decides to set off on the adventure.

6. The Discovery of the Tests, Allies, and Enemies to Be Overcome—in which the hero learns about the "cost" of the adventure, its inherent dangers and rewards. He also understands who will be his allies and who will be his enemies.

7. The Initiation of the Adventure—in which the hero approaches the first test or encounter.

8. The Tests—in which the hero must surmount challenges, the central crises, and his or her greatest fear; typically death plays a role.

9. The Reward—in which the hero enjoys the benefits of having confronted fear and death.

10. The Road Back—in which the hero recommits to completing the adventure.

11. The Enlightenment—in which the hero faces the climactic ordeal that purifies, redeems, and transforms the hero prior to the return to the ordinary world.

12. Return of the Enlightened One—in which the hero, now possessed of new insight born of the trials and adventure, returns to the ordinary world a wiser human being.

According to Campbell and Vogler there are also seven character archetypes that typically appear within a hero's journey:

1. The Hero—who undertakes the adventure and is transformed and enlightened for having done so.

2. The Mentor—who motivates the hero to take on the adventure.

3. The Threshold Guardian—who tests the hero and makes sure the person is of the right mettle to continue on the journey and receive the enlightenment.

4. The Herald—who cautions or warns the hero of the dangers of the challenges ahead.

5. The Shape-Shifter—who questions and deceives the Hero.

6. The Shadow—who serves as the ultimate challenge and who seeks to destroy the hero if the hero is ill-prepared for their encounter.

7. The Trickster—who disrupts the hero's adventure but who can also be a catalyst for change.

The stages and archetypes of the hero's journey provide a flexible analytical tool to help understand why any movie's story works or fails. But most important, the paradigm guides us to an understanding of why a story resonates on a universal level.

As Bruce Lee continued to evolve as a filmmaker, he had likewise evolved in his use of film as a tool for allegory, a means through which to craft a work of art that communicated something on many levels. There would be action, by all means, but there would also be something for those who wanted their cinematic experience to include something profound. It was Bruce Lee's intention to use martial art as the vehicle for the hero's transcendence, the vessel that would carry him across the channel separating ignorance from understanding.

He had originally attempted to make such a film in 1970, when he collaborated with screenwriter Stirling Silliphant and actor James Coburn in a never completed project entitled *The Silent Flute*. Lee later wrote another screenplay that also featured the hero's journey motif, entitled *Southern Fist/Northern Leg*.

Both screenplays featured a young seeker of truth who happened to be a martial artist. In the case of *The Silent Flute*, the hero passed through three life tests of "ego," "love," and "death,"—while in *Southern Fist/Northern Leg*, the hero had been fed a steady diet of external masters, teachers, and authorities. In both stories, the hero sets out in pursuit of a book, an object external to himself that he had been told had the "magic answer" he was seeking. And in both stories, after the hero passed through his trials and finally had the object of his quest within his grasp, he understood that the true answer was never in the external object; it was within himself from the very beginning.

During an interview on Radio Hong Kong in 1972, Bruce Lee touched on this idea, revealing how he, too, had once made the mistake of searching externally for an answer that could be found only within:

When I first arrived, I did "The Green Hornet" television series back in 1965, and . . . I was not being myself. I was trying to accumulate external "security," external "technique"—but never to stop and ask "What would Bruce Lee have done if such a thing had happened to me?"

When I look around, I always learn something, and that is: to be always yourself, and to express yourself, to have faith in yourself. Do not go out and look for a successful personality and duplicate him. That seems to me to be the prevalent thing happening in Hong Kong. They always copy mannerism, but they never start from the very root of their being: that is, How can I be me?

It is this germinal idea, this "treasure" of wisdom for personal enlightenment, that the hero brings back into the world for his fellow man. His quest has revealed the possibility of human transcendence and wisdom, the fullness of human strength and possibility.

The Game of Death is a classic example of the hero's journey of world mythology, relating a theme as old as humanity. The ancient Greeks told the tale of Prometheus ascending to the heavens to steal fire from the gods for the benefit of mankind; Jason encountered many adventures and tests en route to capturing the golden fleece; Saint George slew a dragon; David overcame Goliath.

When Lee found himself in a position to make *The Game of Death*, he wanted it to contain this great message of the ages, to reveal that each person has within him the ability to summon the power necessary to overcome his own demons, slay his own dragons, triumph over his own fears, and dare to embrace the adventure of his own life. In other words, he wanted to present an example of a person who had the courage to embrace his own destiny and to realize his full potential as a human being.

In the screenplays that he wrote, he purposely crafted motifs that were not simply about the action of one man overcoming many but that also served as metaphors of man's quest for the ultimate truth of life.

In his own real-life "hero's journey," which was every bit the equal of anything he had ever planned for his films, Bruce Lee embarked on a quest to make a series of films that would educate and enlighten his audience to a message of freedom, self-knowledge, and universal brotherhood. These were messages intrinsic to his personal belief system.

According to the stages and archetypes as outlined, *The Game of Death* can be viewed within the following framework:

STAGES

Part One: The Ordinary World—Bruce, Nora, and boy traveling in Asia.

Part Two: The Call to Adventure—James Tien's phone call at Korean airport.

Part Three: Refusal of the Call—Bruce is offered money to go to the pagoda on a mission; he refuses.

Part Four: Meeting the Mentor—Learning of Wong's prior attempt and visiting him in the asylum.

Part Five: Crossing the Threshold—Abduction of Bruce's sister and brother.

Part Six: Tests, Allies, Enemies—The meeting of allies; the learning of the rules and the lay of the floors in the pagoda and their opponents in the screening room scene.

Part Seven: Initiation of the Adventure—Also occurs at the screening room of the boss's house and on the bus.

Part Eight: The Ordeal—The battles with Dan Insanto, Ji Han Jae, and Kareem Abdul-Jabbar.

Part Nine: The Reward—Bruce defeats Kareem and is free to get the treasure; he receives insight that leads to the defeat of the awesome powers of darkness by realizing that he holds the power to change his environment, by "letting there be light," and by using this change to assist him in his struggle.

Part Ten: The Road Back—Owing to physical exhaustion, Bruce's return is exceedingly difficult.

Part Eleven: The Enlightenment—Bruce and Kareem overcome "attachment" to life by overcoming the fear of death, perhaps a demon that plagued them both; in so doing, Kareem becomes suddenly human and noble and heroic, and Bruce's unwillingness to exploit his natural advantage over Kareem makes him more human as well.

Part Twelve: The Return of the Enlightened One—Bruce returns and is reunited with his family at the airport—the world he left behind.

ARCHETYPES

The Hero—Bruce Lee.

The Mentor—Wong's example warns Bruce of what to expect.

The Threshold Guardians—Dan Inosanto and Ji Han Jae, to see if Bruce and his allies are worthy to pass on to the next level.

The Herald—James Tien's phone call at the airport; Ji Han Jae tries to caution Lee and his allies from proceeding.

The Shape-Shifter—James Tien.

The Shadow—Kareem and the "fear of death" that is overcome by both Bruce and Kareem.

The Trickster—Chieh Yuan, whose antics turn the fourth level into chaos when he knocks over the partitions, and whose comedic gestures help to bring about a change in perception of what the allies are up against before Bruce begins battle.

The Game of Death was the third time that Lee attempted to work in the motif of the hero's journey. The story concerned a treasure kept on the top floor of a pagoda in Korea where martial artists were trained. In the portion of the film that was completed, Bruce and his four accomplices had to fight their way up through the levels, tackling a different martial artist and a different style on each floor. Set within this action was a lesson about total freedom of expression and the limiting nature of styles or methods of martial art.

That Lee's character in *The Game of Death* would be taking on advocates of different styles is significant in a larger context than may be evident initially. Lee was taking on not just the individual exponents of particular styles but the entire concept of "styles" itself. This was the biggest "dragon" that his hero was to slay.

THE METAPHORS OF THE HERO'S JOURNEY

The combative sequences in Bruce Lee's footage from *The Game of Death* contain several lessons that merit closer scrutiny:

- The forces of light or good are pitted against the forces of darkness or evil. It is only when Bruce's character breaks through the barrier that the forces of light come to his aid and the tide of the battle shifts to his favor. While some may interpret the light as the grace of God, or uniting with Tao, or the energy of the universe, it serves by many interpretations as a metaphor for the classic story of the forces of good working through man to triumph over the forces of evil.

- The breaking of the windows is not a technique or style taught in martial art schools; it is the result of being able to think independently and to have the necessary sensitivity to perceive and exploit an opponent's weakness.

- The playing field must be leveled. Bruce is at a distinct disadvantage when he attempts to fight toe-to-toe with the much taller and more powerful character played by Kareem Abdul-Jabbar. It is only when he takes away his opponent's height and reach advantage by bringing him to the ground and essentially leveling the playing field that Lee's character is able to triumph.

- Greed can be a person's undoing. James Tien's character is so caught up in reaching the final level to get his hands on the treasure that he not only willingly endangers the members of his party but also dives headlong into a situation that he is unprepared and ill-equipped to handle. He pays for his folly with his life.

- The pagoda with its various floors and challengers is a metaphor for life. Each of us must face obstacles and challenges as we go through life, and if we approach these challenges with a rigid or inflexible method or way of thinking, we are setting ourselves up for defeat—just as Bruce's opponents are defeated because they "lack the flexibility to adapt." And, at the top of the pagoda, which represents the summit of our life's journey, we must all face the "great unknown," the force of darkness or "death." Lee's character, however, dies to the fear of death, with the result that he is able to transcend its enmity.

- Each challenge that Lee encounters represents the problems that everyone experiences: financial problems, marital problems, and all of the smaller challenges we face every day. These challenges not only help sharpen our problem-solving skills but also prepare us to cope with larger problems with which we may be confronted at any point.

- Lee dressed all of his opponents in the film in the traditional costumes peculiar to each of the styles that they represented. By contrast, Lee's character wears a black and yellow one-piece tracksuit, an indication that Lee is of no established style or system. He is, rather, a human being expressing as completely as possible the personification of the "styleless style" or "formless form" of jeet kune do. He represents freedom from the restricted approaches that encumber all other styles of martial art.

- The opponents he faces are restricted by their "style" or approach and thus lack the flexibility of method to fight "out of the box." Because they lack the flexibility to adapt to changing circumstances and the broken rhythm of the fight, they are defeated.

- The highest level of the pagoda is presided over by the "unknown" style (in essence, jeet kune do), which symbolizes the highest level of martial art. Not surprisingly, it is this least traditional and most liberated art that represents Lee's greatest challenge in the film. As jeet kune do is the art of the individual, Lee's battle with Abdul-Jabbar is nothing so abstract as "style against style," but rather a clash between two human beings who have thrown off the shackles of "ways" and "limitations."

- As other martial art styles did not advocate this degree of freedom, the practitioners of those styles represented not only opponents to be conquered in order for Lee's character to progress up the pagoda but also metaphors for prejudiced or restricted ways of thinking that must be encountered and overcome in order for any hero to continue to progress throughout the journey of his life.

THE LESSONS OF THE HERO'S JOURNEY

1. The Challenge of the Third Level: **You are equal to the task**. You, by the very nature of being a human being, already have weapons that are up to the task at hand (your mind, instincts, etc.) and that are superior to the problem you are facing, no matter how sophisticated or daunting.

2. The Challenge of the Fourth Level: **Learn from your mistakes**. If you make a mistake, learn from it. In *The Game of Death*, after Bruce has been on the receiving end of three debilitating flips at the hands of hapkido master Ji Han Jae, he is given time to reflect on what he had been doing wrong, when his accom-

plice steps into the fray and runs into the same problem. This opportunity to study the situation allows Lee to learn from his mistakes and to figure out a way to counter the problem.

3. The Challenge of the Fifth Level: **The power of patience**. In his battle with Kareem Abdul-Jabbar, Bruce Lee is losing at first and coming off no more than equal by the midpoint. However, because he does not let his emotions or ego rush him into foolhardy decisions, his patience is ultimately rewarded when the key to his opponent's weakness finally presents itself. Lee learns the lesson that if you are patient and diligent, the opportunity for victory or the solution to the problem will present itself.

In Lee's two previous attempts to present the "hero's journey," when the hero finally overcomes his tests and arrives at his goal, he rejects it and leaves, having obtained internally the insight of what is truly valuable: life itself, a treasure of far greater value than the one he was pursuing. Similarly, in the final footage that Lee shot for *The Game of Death*, when the hero finally overcomes the last obstacle to his goal, instead of climbing the final set of stairs to retrieve the prize, he no longer pursues it. Something about his trial caused him to become awakened to a higher truth. He turns and descends the stairs, exiting the pagoda to return to the world, an enlightened and wiser human being.

Lee told the Hong Kong press in 1971 that, through his films, "nation shall speak to nation." He held that martial art could be the perfect vehicle to bring people together if he could present to his audience a "human being" engaged in "the art of expressing the human body," his unique definition of his martial art. If the American audience could see him not as a "Chinaman" or as a "Chinese martial artist," and if the Chinese audience could come to see him not as an "American citizen," Lee believed that would contribute toward uniting people under the umbrella of all humanity.

Another interpretation is that often the object you are pursuing is not as important as you think it is; however, the journey is worth taking, the energy is worth expending, because during the course of your quest you just may catch a glimpse of something of far greater worth than the task at hand.

The external quest for which you are striving is not the meaning of your life; you are not your job, you are not your bank account, you are not your trophies. The quest to discover your true self is, ultimately, the greatest adventure in which you can take part and the most fulfilling one in all of life.

Money, fame, prestige, position, standing, honor—these are not the important things. They hold no intrinsic worth. Seeking those things is significant only if they present you with an opportunity to take part in your own hero's journey and to realize what is and is not truly important. In *The Game of Death*, the treasure at the top of the pagoda proved to be, in the final analysis, only one more of life's distractions. The real treasure lay within the soul of Lee's character of Hai Tien. The point being: Are you going to be distracted all your life, or are you going to live your life fully in the moment? Whatever you think is going to be so great in the future pales in comparison with what is so great right now, just as you are. The secret that some people never figure out is that it doesn't matter what's at the top of the "pagoda." If you are disappointed that Bruce Lee's character didn't proceed to the top of the pagoda to get the treasure, you needn't be, because he understood what's at the top of every pagoda: enlightenment.

In his own life, Lee came to a similar conclusion, telling a reporter in 1971:

Success means doing something sincerely and wholeheartedly. I think that life is a process. Through the ages, the end of heroes is the same as ordinary men. They all died and gradually faded away in the memory of man. But when we are still alive, we have to understand ourselves, discover ourselves, and express ourselves. In this way, we can progress, but we may not be "successful." So, although today I am successful, I will still continue to discover myself. . . .

I wanted all the indirect things—money, fame, the big opening nights. Now that I have it, or am beginning to get it, the whole thing doesn't seem important anymore. I have found that *doing* a thing is more important. I am having fun doing it.

And so the deeper meaning of *The Game of Death* is the eternal conflict of ascending in one's own consciousness. And the metaphor that Bruce Lee utilizes to convey this message is the notion of styles in the martial arts. As Lee stated in an interview in 1971:

That is to me the most important thing, and that is: How can I—in the process of learning how to use my body—come to understand myself?

In the film, Lee begins by overcoming external authority sources—the "ways" of other styles, other people, other institutions. The early levels represent overcoming society's dictates of "what you should do" and "who you should be." They have no regard for you, the individual; they simply want you to fall in line and obey, to become something different from what you are, to become "like them."

The final level of the pagoda can be seen to represent man's greatest obstacle: his ego or excessive sense of self-consciousness, which is what causes suffering and fear—fear of losing the illusion of self, which is the only thing separating man from connecting in a deeper sense with the rest of the world.

This lesson, being fully alive in the moment, is the real treasure the hero had been seeking all along, but it had taken a physical, bodily pursuit to awaken this realization. As Lee once told his student Daniel Lee, "What man has to get over is the consciousness of himself."

This was actually the same lesson he would discuss with the wise old monk in *Enter the Dragon* when he said, "There is no opponent because the word *I* does not exist."

When Bruce Lee leaves the pagoda—a metaphor for his journey through his many layers of self-consciousness, the obstacle to his understanding—and returns to the world, we can almost hear the words he once related to his private student James Coburn, "When you ease the burden of your mind, you just do it."

CHAPTER 8
BRUCE LEE AND THE SCIENCE OF UNARMED COMBAT

For years, martial artists have been told by certain corners of the JKD world that "what works for Bruce Lee will not work for you" and that "because we are all unique as individuals, we all have different martial arts training requirements." This belief strikes me as erroneous on two counts, at least in respect to jeet kune do when Bruce Lee coined the term.

Moreover, in an article titled "Interviewing Bruce Lee: Bruce Lee Tells Us the Secret of Combat," which appeared in *Bruce Lee and Jeet Kun Do* magazine in 1977, Lee himself stated:

Bruce Lee looked to science—not tradition—to determine the most efficient way to deliver maximum impact force to an opponent.

We should regard our martial arts training as scientific, and every energy and capacity can be explained by science. It is not mystical at all. Therefore, everything should be logical.

There exists ample evidence that Bruce Lee considered his martial art to be scientific (i.e., with principles that are universally true). For jeet kune do to qualify as a science, it cannot be as arbitrary or subjective as the "we're all unique" proponents advocate.

In looking over a sampling of Lee's personal papers, one finds statements such as:

- "In any physical movement *there is always a most efficient and alive manner to accomplish the purpose of the performance* for each individual. That is, in regard to proper leverage, balance in movement, economical and efficient use of motion and energy, etc. Live, efficient movement that liberates is one thing; sterile classical sets that bind and condition is another."

- "The students should learn something new in each class period, but one or two new techniques are enough for one session. When the student begins to spar, then he will stop searching for accumulation of techniques; rather he will devote the needed hours of practice to the simple technique for its *right execution*."

- "It is not how much one learns but how much one has absorbed in what he has learned. The best techniques are the simple ones, executed correctly."

- "Students themselves will realize the futile search for more and more new techniques. Rather they will devote the needed hours to practicing the correct execution of simple techniques."

As soon as one makes a distinction about what is right or even "most efficient," one has ceased to endorse subjectivism and instead embraced science. Science is what allows certainty in areas involving correct or efficient action. Let us assume, then, for the sake of argument, that Bruce Lee was of a scientific bent with regard to teaching students his martial art of jeet kune do—during the period in which he classified it as "the way of the intercepting fist."

He wrote several volumes of notes in which he painstakingly detailed how techniques could be "executed correctly." This indicates that he held that there were correct ways to perform techniques that applied to all of his students. In other words, he believed that there are certain universal truths in the realm of unarmed combat. He arrived at this conclusion after spending hundreds, if not thousands, of hours sifting through techniques until he found the ones that were applicable scientifically to all human beings. This belief was echoed in the interview Lee had with Hong Kong–based journalist Ted Thomas, quoted at the beginning of Chapter 6.

If there is a correct way for human beings to fight, there is also an incorrect way. To better our chances of emerging unscathed in a real encounter, it behooves us as human beings to learn how to use our "two hands and two legs . . . to the maximum." In that context Bruce Lee had, and still has, no equal—which is why we continue to look to him as the gold standard of martial art proficiency. Certainly, there are none who have surpassed his skill in this regard. He cultivated this proficiency by constant practice, practice, and then still more practice, in what, to an initiate, may look to be basic—almost rudimentary—techniques. In fact, Lee once made the statement: "Like boxing or fencing, jeet kune do is a step-by-step project, and each maneuver must be repeated many times."

In so doing, Bruce Lee not only became adept at mastering these maneuvers but also discovered much about himself in terms of both his capabilities and his limitations.

While he was open to valid techniques from any so-called style or system, he did not endorse the idea that one had to study the disciplines that contained these techniques in any formal way. For him, it wasn't necessary to study the art of judo "from A to Z" in order to master the principles of leverage and body mechanics necessary to successfully execute an *osoto-gari*, or "outside major reap" takedown, a technique that he found particularly effective in close-quarter combat. In this respect, Lee said:

It is proven more efficient and interesting to devote time to only one or two simple techniques at a one-hour session than to have many unrelated and disorganized techniques crammed into it. . . . A few simple techniques well presented, an aim clearly seen, are better than a tangled maze of data whirling in disorganized educational chaos. . . . The ultimate goal of discipline in JKD is where learning gained is learning lost.

Bruce Lee was not in favor of eclecticism, the arbitrary or whimsical adding of martial techniques to his—or his students'—arsenal, simply for the sake of adding more techniques. He also was not of the opinion that all martial arts had equal value to his own. He once wrote to a friend, "My JKD is something else . . . more and more I pity the martial artists that are blinded by their partiality and ignorance."

There exists further evidence that Lee was not in favor of "style-hopping," a practice that has acquired a certain cachet in martial art circles. During the late 1980s, it was referred to, incorrectly, as cross-training, a fitness term indicating an athlete who mixes cardiovascular training with strength training and/or flexibility training. In response to a letter from one of his JKD students, Jerry Poteet, who had asked Lee if he objected to his teaching a few JKD awareness drills along with some kenpo karate techniques, Bruce Lee stated:

X is jeet kune do. Y is the style you will represent.

To represent and teach Y, one should drill its members according to the preaching of Y.

This is the same with anyone who is qualified and has been approved to represent X.

To justify by interfusing X and Y is basically the denying of Y—but still calling it Y.

A man, as you put it, is one who is noble to stick to the road he has chosen.

A garden of roses will yield roses, and a garden of violets will yield violets.

It is obvious that Lee considered jeet kune do—or "X" in this instance—to be vastly different from any martial art that was not JKD (or "Y"). There exists other evidence that Bruce was not in favor of his students' practicing other arts, particularly once they had been exposed to the verities of jeet kune do. For example, when he learned that one of his private students, Stirling

Silliphant, took up the Japanese art of karate after Lee had left Hollywood for Hong Kong, he told Silliphant that he considered his taking another martial art "a form of treason."

Although Bruce Lee looked at many different arts during the creation of his own, he looked at most of them with a very critical eye, believing the vast majority (if not all) to be too steeped in tradition, convention, imitation, and mysticism to be functional in a real-life encounter. He arrived at this conclusion through his observation of actual street encounters and, later on, through sparring sessions.

Sparring, as anyone who trained with Lee will testify, was to Lee the acid test of a technique's effectiveness. Lee himself sparred frequently and observed others sparring with quiet but highly focused awareness. As a result, he came to the conclusion that only a handful of techniques could typically be employed during a real fight with any degree of success or efficiency, and therefore, to spend one's time engaged in endless hours of drilling in techniques that ultimately would fail the real-world test was counterproductive at best and, at worst, a potentially life-threatening mistake.

Leaving aside the realm of weapons for the moment, since Bruce Lee's martial art focused solely on the discipline of what is commonly referred to as "hand-to-hand combat," we, as human beings possessing "only two hands and two legs," share a commonality irrespective of our differences. That is, while we have differing physical structures (some are tall, others short, etc.), we are all essentially the same.

While this premise may read like a dichotomy, it is the furthest thing from it. The late philosopher Alan Watts once compared human beings to the individual waves that appear briefly and then pass out of existence upon the surface of an ocean; while the waves are different in shape and size from one another, they share a commonality or "sameness" in that they are all composed of the same basic substance—the water of the ocean. This statement, as lyrical as it may sound, is firmly grounded in subatomic physics. At the quantum level, there are no "individuals," no objects or even oceans; there are only wavelike fields or patterns of energy. This image underscores not only our sameness but also the "oneness" of our inner universe with the greater universe without.

Like the water that fills each individual wave on the ocean, our human physiology fills each of us that "peoples" the earth, no matter how tall, short, fat, thin, or ethnically diverse we may be. Bruce Lee held that conventional martial art styles that are founded on tradition or custom and so handed down throughout the ages do not take into account the "oceanlike" common denominator of our species' physiology—our "humanity," in other words. They instead prefer to direct their focus on the "wavelike" individual peculiarities of individuals—or to see the trees but not the forest.

Such a myopic viewpoint is the antithesis of Bruce Lee's perspective of totality. Bruce Lee sought with jeet kune do to create a scientific approach to martial art, to seek a commonality, or "root" denominator that has application to all human beings. He often commented on how unfortunate it was that styles "separate men," dividing them unnecessarily into segments of what should be a totality. These segments are formed by looking so hard at the individual waves (the various nationalities and styles to which martial artists subscribe) popping up on the surface of the ocean that it becomes difficult—if not impossible—to envision the interrelatedness of the waves to the ocean or, for that matter, the vastness of the ocean itself.

Jeet kune do was the first—and, to my knowledge, the only—fighting art based on a quantum perspective; that is, it takes into account our "commonality" as human beings. It represents a scientific approach to martial art in that science seeks to discover principles that apply to broad categories; thus, specific principles have a truly universal application to all individuals. If you're human, then what Bruce Lee taught and what he found valid for himself and his students—more than thirty years ago—will be just as valid for you today as we begin the twenty-first century.

Jeet kune do takes into account such details as "how you are built, how you are structured, and how you are made." In creating it, Lee studied the sciences of human anatomy, physiology, and physics and realized that since fighting, specifically hand-to-hand combat, involves motion, it can be quantified in terms of its techniques by the science of physics, and in training by the sciences of biomechanics and physiology. Therefore, learning to use our two hands and feet to the maximum is an obtainable quest and simply requires a rudimentary study of these scientific disciplines.

Fighting is a physical activity and, as such, is regulated by the various physical laws that govern not only our bodies but also the universe as a whole. To this end, there are appropriate, or valid, physical actions that correspond to these universal rules of science. In as much as our actions are predicated on, and act in accordance with, these universal rules, they are valid and successful. Conversely, they are inappropriate or invalid if they are not predicated on these facts. What this means, then, is that the fat man, the skinny man, the quick man, and the slow man will all be better martial artists when they learn to train or practice utilizing correct, scientifically sound principles that are universal and, hence, valid to our species.

Bruce Lee created what I hold to be the science of martial art, jeet kune do, as a result of attempting to answer his own question: How can we use our two hands and two legs to the maximum? The answer that he discovered is by subjecting all techniques encountered to the litmus test of scientific analysis: physics and its related sciences of physiology and kinesiology. A technique is then accepted or rejected dependent on its correlation to reality (i.e., valid principles).

This is why, for example, the jeet kune do lead punch, thrown semi-extended from the shoulder, will *always* beat the classical karate punch thrown from the hip. It's a simple example of the science of physics (i.e., the shortest distance between two points: being initiated from a semi-extended position in front of the body, the JKD lead punch has a shorter distance to travel than the karate punch, which originates at the hip and must therefore travel almost a foot before it arrives at the starting position of the JKD lead punch). This is a fact of science that is applicable universally—it holds as true for whoever is practicing it (whether fat or slim, tall or short, slow or quick) as it did for Bruce Lee. The lead punch will always be the fastest punch for any individual, and anyone who masters this technique will be a quicker, more effective puncher.

This cuts against the grain of what has become a popular martial art approach which would dismiss the JKD lead punch as simply one of many different types of punches that a martial artist may or may not choose to have in his arsenal. While it's true that many different punches are available for use by the martial artist, the fact remains that none of them is on a parity with the JKD lead punch in speed and efficiency. In terms of scientific fighting, then, the verdict is in. There now exists no reason for the scientific martial artist to continue looking outside of the science of combat that Bruce Lee created for the answer to this particular question of punching supremacy. However, if the martial artist is simply searching for "a new technique" or looking for a little variety, then a different context has been thrown into the equation. All martial artists are, of course, free to do as they choose. They are not, however, free to dismiss reality by granting equality or parity to all punching techniques once having been exposed to Bruce Lee's art.

Some martial artists insist that one must "change all the time" and that this is somehow tantamount to progress. I've never heard an adequate explanation for why such arbitrary change is in any way necessary. While change is a logically desirable occurrence when its alternative is stagnation, it must be remembered that change—in terms of a positive evolution—does not exist in perpetuity. In the context of unarmed combat, human beings are highly complex organisms, and an organism evolves only until it reaches a state of scientific and organic perfection, at which point change is no longer necessary for its survival. Our species reached this plateau approximately one million years ago (and, purely in terms of our bodily development, four to five million years prior). Therefore, to change simply for the sake of change is not only unnecessary but also—when it takes you away from valid principles (which in terms

of science are equated with truth or reality)—potentially dangerous, particularly in a discipline such as martial arts.

If our species ever evolves to the point where we no longer need to use our hands and feet for combative purposes, or, as Lee joked, if we evolve another arm or leg, then there *would* exist a real "need" to evolve martial techniques that are far more expedient and efficacious than what Bruce Lee cultivated for the purpose of hand-to-hand combat. However, given that such an "evolution" has not occurred, and that, if it did, it would require that our future techniques be even more simplistic and economical in structure, delivery, and impact than those that Bruce Lee developed, I'm not sure the individual has yet been born who would have the evolutional wherewithal to "evolve" Bruce's art to such a level.

The problem, as I see it, is that if you subscribe to what was formerly called the "Concepts" viewpoint of JKD, then you cannot claim that JKD is a "scientific martial art," owing to the subjective standards employed (i.e., that all arts are of equal value and must all be examined thoroughly). This particular viewpoint advances the proposal that "because we are all unique, we each require a different martial arts approach"—

in other words, that what Bruce Lee practiced himself is anything but exact, that his method contains no universal truths or principles, and that each one of us has to be our own scientific agent and discover what works best for us. Seen through the filter of this viewpoint, jeet kune do cannot exist as a scientific art under such conditions, as science is an exacting discipline.

While it's true that we all are unique as individuals, this viewpoint fails to take into account the fact that physiologically, we are all essentially the same. It doesn't address the fact that the biochemical changes that resulted in a more powerful punch in Bruce Lee are the same biochemical changes that take place in every human being who wishes to cultivate a more powerful punch. It follows that the stimulus required to induce those specific biochemical changes is also universal. There is, to this end, no mystery surrounding the requirements of muscle contraction, which is the root of force and speed production. The most important factors influencing the rate of improvement in this area are physics, body mechanics (kinesiology), and muscle physiology, which are universal disciplines and not subject to arbitrary change in individuals. If every individual's cells, muscles, and organs were constituted and functioned differently, then a case could be made for such divergent training and combative methods—but then each person would be a unique physiological entity. Doctors would be hard-pressed under such circumstances to make diagnoses, perform surgeries, or prescribe medications.

True, some will develop faster than others due to a greater innate adaptability, but we all become better martial artists when we learn to train scientifically, and this doesn't require studying different arts; it requires studying the human sciences of mechanics, dynamics, and physiology.

Nevertheless, many of the former advocates of JKD "Concepts" claim that each individual martial artist is different and, therefore, that no objective, universal principles of training exist. They imply that the issue of how to best train to maximize one's martial skills is arbitrary and subjective, not rational and scientific. They then contradict themselves by exhorting all of their students in JKD Concepts to train in essentially the same manner: a full complement of classes in the Filipino arts such as kali and escrima, and so on. If we all truly have such vastly different physiological training requirements, the question arises: Why then is the

JKD Concepts curriculum essentially the same for everybody?

A RATIONAL APPROACH TO MARTIAL ART

I would call Bruce Lee's approach to martial art a "rational" approach. The basis of a rational approach to martial arts, or any other arena of human endeavor, is the recognition that only specific, appropriate knowledge can lead one to engage in the purposeful action required to successfully achieve a goal.

An analogy here is the National Aeronautics and Space Administration, better known as NASA. Why have the members of the NASA teams been so spectacularly successful with their manned moon missions? Not because they just whimsically took "a bit of this and a dash of that" and threw it into a quasi-scientific stew. They knew precisely, down to the smallest detail, what was required. They had a firm intellectual understanding of the theory of space travel. They implemented its principles properly, with the result that they have enjoyed tremendous success with their missions.

The purpose of science being to identify the facts of reality and, from those facts, derive a valid theory for successful human action, Bruce Lee succeeded in creating a scientific martial art—one based on correctly identifying the facts of reality and, from those facts, deriving a valid theory or "system" for hand-to-hand combat.

Therefore, to say, "I don't possess Bruce Lee's physical attributes, and therefore, what worked for Bruce won't work for me" is tantamount to saying that what Bruce Lee created with jeet kune do was simply a mishmash of subjective techniques and training beliefs that have no application beyond the person known as Bruce Lee—which is palpably false. After all, Bruce taught the same curriculum, evidently with some degree of success, to individuals of widely diverse physiological makeups. Dan Inosanto, Daniel Lee, Larry Hartsell, Ted Wong, Bob Bremer, Pete Jacobs, Peter Chin, Mito Uyehara, Herb Jackson, Jesse Glover, Joe Lewis, Mike Stone, Taky Kimura, Kareem Abdul-Jabbar, and Stirling Silliphant have all stated that they learned essentially the same techniques and curriculum from Lee, and yet, if ever there was a vast physiological cross section from which to draw for comparative purposes, this would be it.

Following the approach that "since nobody possesses Bruce Lee's capabilities, you must find your own art that suits your attributes," Bruce should immediately have said that there was nothing he could do for a man like Kareem Abdul-Jabbar, who, at 7'2", obviously didn't share Bruce's physical attributes.

Joe Lewis, as another example, did very well with Japanese karate, but he did better with the scientific instruction he received in jeet kune do, admitting to becoming a better martial artist after utilizing it. However, at some three inches taller and forty pounds heavier, Lewis could not be said to have shared Lee's physical attributes any more than did Kareem Abdul-Jabbar, or any of Lee's other students. Neither Stirling Silliphant nor James Coburn was told to investigate other arts to find the truth; history, as preserved in their testimonies and in Lee's private writings, indicates that all of his students were taught the same techniques and combat principles. (See Lee's "Organized Lesson Plan for Jeet Kune Do" and "Bruce Lee's Private Lesson Plan for Jeet Kune Do" in *Jeet Kune Do: Bruce Lee's Commentaries on the Martial Way*, published by Charles E. Tuttle, Boston, for specific evidence.) The reason? Bruce Lee realized that because, physiologically, we are all essentially the same, the

Karate champion Joe Lewis (right) became a better martial artist after Bruce Lee shared with him some of the scientific principles of Lee's approach to martial art.

stimulus that results in quicker and more powerful techniques in Bruce Lee is the same stimulus that results in quicker and more powerful techniques in all other human beings.

In other words, if it involves time, force, speed, or motion, we're talking about science, and scientific principles can be studied, quantified, and measured. And if combat is to be scientific, exacting principles of science must be followed to frame it.

The principles Bruce Lee founded in framing JKD can be looked at as scientific ones that are applicable to the entire human race.

So, say that "it is impossible to teach Bruce Lee's jeet kune do to anyone because nobody possesses Bruce Lee's physical attributes," is inaccurate. Moreover, individual potential is something that can be assessed accurately only in retrospect. You could not know with certainty whether or not you possess attributes like Bruce Lee's unless you train as diligently as he did to cultivate or actualize such attributes. In order to justify such a sweeping statement, you would have to know the individual aptitudes and physiologies of all of your students and potential students. Clearly there is no way of predicting this with any degree of probability, let alone certainty.

ON MOTIVATION

Let's assume for the purpose of discussion that only one in ten thousand individuals has the potential to approach Bruce Lee's level of martial proficiency. Isn't it worth teaching what Bruce Lee did, said, and found to be useful in his training, in the hope of turning out that one rare individual—of providing the tools, as it were, to lay

the groundwork for "another Bruce Lee"? Isn't such a human being to be sought after and held up as the "ideal" to strive for? If instead you're told from day one that you haven't got what it takes to become as good as the best in the world, then what is your motivation for continued pursuit?

Doesn't the best teacher inspire his students to reach for the stars? Doesn't he instill in them the belief that one's limit is exceeded only by one's desire? Shouldn't he teach his students that the excellence they obtain is proportionate to the effort they are willing to expend? And isn't success largely motivational, as opposed to technical? For example, when Roger Bannister broke the four-minute mile, it was broken by eight other individuals within six months afterward. Obviously, their training methods or techniques hadn't changed. There were no nutritional or equipment "breakthroughs" during this period that would account for their improved times. What had changed, however, was their belief that it was now *possible* to break the four-minute barrier. Similarly, if a teacher informs his students categorically that it's impossible for them to study Bruce Lee's art because they're not blessed with the same physical attributes as their hero, he will have effectively killed the very root of their desire and ambition.

On the contrary, they should be told, "Here are the exact methods that Bruce Lee employed to become the greatest martial artist of the twentieth century." And, "If you apply yourself as diligently as Bruce Lee did to the perfecting of these methods and are willing to make martial arts your entire life, at least the *possibility* exists that you can achieve a similar level of greatness and perfection in Bruce Lee's art of jeet kune do." At the very least, such an inspiring approach would allow students to reach a level of excellence that they would have considered to be well beyond their grasp at the present time.

A good teacher inspires students by holding up the possibility for betterment, not by discouraging them from trying. In an article titled "In Kato's Gun Fu Action Is Instant" published in *Black Belt* magazine, Bruce Lee said:

In building a statue, a sculptor doesn't keep adding clay to his subject. Actually, he begins chiseling away at the unessentials until the truth of his creation is revealed without obstructions. Thus, contrary to other styles, being

wise in jeet kune do doesn't mean adding more. It means to minimize. In other words, to hack away at the unessentials. It is not a "daily increase" but a "daily decrease." The way of jeet kune do is a shedding process.

Those who are the future instructors of Bruce Lee's art would be well advised to study all of his surviving writings as their starting point. This is the mountain that Bruce left behind for all of his future "sculptors" to chisel away at, removing the obstructions and the unessentials bit by bit, until they see the same "truth" of martial art that Bruce Lee spoke to us about.

It is relevant that the notes from Bruce's *Commentaries on the Martial Way* were drawn largely from instruction manuals written for the general public: books such as *Championship Fighting* by Jack Dempsey, *Boxing* by Edwin L. Haislet, and *The Theory and Practice of Fencing* by Julio Martinez Castello. These manuals present the correct way to box or fence, respectively, and anyone wishing to learn how to engage in these endeavors correctly can apply the techniques and principles advocated. Lee found that much of what these men wrote was true and recognized the validity and application of the material to his quest of creating a martial art based on pragmatic efficiency.

From a scientific perspective, there is nothing new that has evolved in hand-to-hand combat, and human beings remain tethered to "only two hands and two legs," which would indicate that what was true in 1969–1973, in terms of what Bruce taught about the art, is still true today. (Weapons combat does differ because when our minds learn more about science, we learn to advance our weapons accordingly; however, hand-to-hand combat has experienced no such evolution.)

For a concept to have any meaning, it must have a valid set of principles that underlie it. And if Bruce's principles are valid—which they are—there would exist no reason to alter or "evolve" them.

But while no one would dispute the fact that we have only two hands and two legs, contention arises over the question of "How do we use them to the maximum?" In this regard, Bruce Lee represents the lone individual who actually learned how to use his limbs to the maximum of his ability. Was there an area in his development or bodily expression that was lacking? No. In fact,

we're still talking about his prowess thirty years after his passing because he did develop a unique and still unsurpassed way to "use his tools to the maximum."

Some people have called him a genius; I prefer to think of him as a very dedicated thinker. His insights weren't hot-wired into his consciousness. He had to study, and read, and reread, and comprehend, and make analogies and cognitive connections among diverse disciplines such as nutritional science, strength training, flexibility training, physics, anatomy, kinesiology, and physiology. He availed himself of scientific method and created a form of fighting that is predicated on sound, demonstrable principles that are scientifically valid for everyone.

The principles that Bruce Lee espoused, followed, and passed on to his original students apply to every martial artist—and to every human being. Why? Because the laws of science are immutable. While one martial artist may find that a particular drill or exercise causes him to respond better than another martial artist responds, due to a structural advantage he possesses, both individuals still possess limited physical resources, and both will better simulate the biochemical changes leading to increased speed and strength when they engage in scientific training that is geared specifically for such responses.

No matter what your attributes, you will be a more efficient martial artist when you learn to train and practice scientifically— and jeet kune do, as Bruce Lee taught it, can be viewed as simply science applied to the realm of fighting. It is a way to learn how to use our hands and legs to the maximum.

Cast and crew on the set of "The Story" sequence from the film *Bruce Lee: A Warrior's Journey*. From left to right—front row: Kim Jin-Ho, Kim Kay-Min, Byung Seung, Nam Ju, Kim So Hee, John Little, Kim Hak-Kyu, Lee Taek-Yung. Back row: Lee Hwa-Ryong, Ju Jin-Kwan, Na Yong-Kuk, Hong Ki-Ho, Kim Yong Sing, Han Ki-Up, Lee Hoo-Gon, Lee Kang-Kuk, Jung Hee-Young, Kim Byung-Joo, Park Seung Woo, Jeon Gi-Won.

Director John Little atop the "King Crane" during shooting in Popju-sa, South Korea.

Cinematographer extraordinaire Lee Hoo-Gon puts the Buddha in frame for one of the many artistic shots rendered in *Bruce Lee: A Warrior's Journey.*

Korean actor Kim Hak-Kyu, playing the role of Hai Tien, leads his team (Kim Byung-Joo, Lee Hwa-Ryong, and Park Sung-Woo) toward the pagoda in "The Story" sequence, which brought Bruce Lee's story line to film for the first time. Coproducer Bill Katz (left) doubled as the "American" fighter in the film.

The Buddha and pagoda in Popju-sa that were to be the setting for *The Game of Death*

The production team while in Korea (left to right): assistant director Jeon Gi-Won, actor Kim Hak-Kyu, producer Lee Taek-Yong, producer/director John Little, director of photgraphy Lee Hoo-Gon, coproducer Bill Katz, and assistant director Kim Kwang-Min.

An aerial shot of Popju-sa depicting the ending of "The Story" sequence.

Stills from *The Game of Death*.

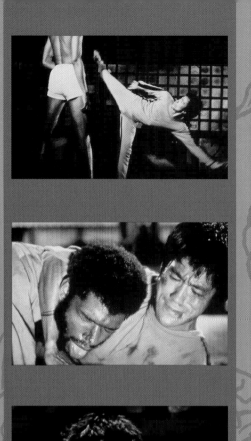

Bruce Lee applies the pressure on Kareem Abdul-Jabbar with a headlock during their climactic battle in *The Game of Death*.

Bruce Lee, the yellow tracksuit, and total freedom of expression—from the set of *The Game of Death*.

BRUCE LEE

& ABDUL JABBAR

李小龍遺作「死亡遊戲」

in "THE GAME OF DEATH"

Bruce Lee and Kareem Abdul-Jabbar reveal the height disparity between the two combatants in a publicity shot taken for *The Game of Death*.

Bruce Lee fires a back kick at Wu-Ngan, one of the extras, on the set of the Warner Bros. smash hit *Enter the Dragon.*

Bruce Lee demonstrates the advantages of "Chinese boxing" in a publicity shot for *Fist of Fury.*

Bruce Lee as Kato in the television series "The Green Hornet."

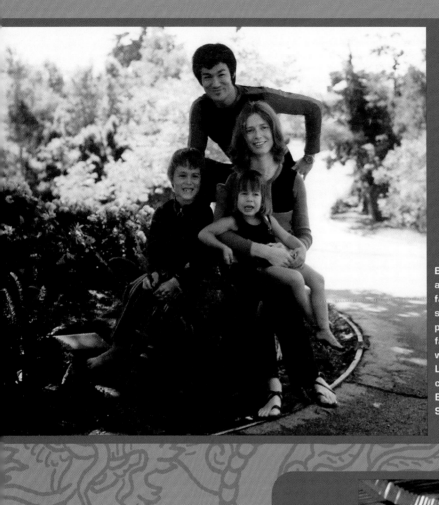

Bruce Lee was a devoted family man, seen here posing for a family portrait with his wife, Linda, and children, Brandon and Shannon.

Bruce Lee with the love of his life: his wife of nine years, Linda Lee.

Bruce Lee (left) and business partner Raymond Chow (middle) scouting locations for *The Way of the Dragon* in Rome in May 1972.

(Left to right): Han Ying Chieh, Maria Yi, Lo Wei, Bruce Lee, and James Tien on the set of *The Big Boss*, a film that rocketed Bruce Lee to superstardom in Asia.

Bruce Lee prepares to team up with John Saxon in the famous courtyard battle of the Warner Bros. 1973 classic *Enter the Dragon*.

A Dragon in Italy: Bruce Lee scouting locations for *The Way of the Dragon.*

Bruce and Linda Lee in the driveway of their home in Kowloon Tong, Hong Kong, circa 1973.

Bruce Lee on the set of *The Way of the Dragon*. Lee's physique has continued to serve as a source of inspiration to millions.

CHAPTER 9
BRUCE LEE AND PHYSICS

You can promote the ability to control the body's action and master your will more easily. **—Bruce Lee**

As an avid student and voracious reader throughout his life, Lee kept a personal library that is now a rich source of insight into the topics that influenced and inspired him. His numerous margin notes and frequent underlining of text offer us a unique sense not only of the great minds that influenced Lee, but of the specific parts of these writings that Lee found most noteworthy. The material in this chapter (and in Chapters 11 and 12) is based on the books and passages that Lee spent many hours pondering, highlighting, and annotating. Full citations can be found in the References.

Bruce Lee's training methods were geared toward one thing: function. And function in the case of martial art concerns movement, or motion.

BRUCE LEE AND SIR ISAAC NEWTON

Recognizing this fact caused Lee to begin to investigate the science of physics. Lee held that "If you understand the root, you understand all of its blossoming," and when it comes to fighting, the science of physics is the foundation of the entire enterprise. He purchased books on kinesiology and physiology and studied the principles of Newtonian physics. He came away with the observation that in martial art, as well as in all other forms of athletics, an athlete's body, a part of the body, or some object of athletic apparatus (such as a pole or shot) behaves in accordance with certain well-settled principles and is subject to the same mechanical laws as everything else on earth, animate and inanimate. (Broer 1960)

TWO TYPES OF MOTION

Motion can be reduced to two types: linear and angular. Linear motion is characterized by the progression of a body in a straight line, with all of its parts moving the same distance, in the same direction, and at the same speed. Angular motion is far more common in all human and animal transport systems and is dependent on a system of levers. Whereas in angular movement, one part of the object—the axis—remains fixed in relation to the others (as when the arm rotates about the shoulder joint, or a discus rotates in the air), in linear motion, every particle of the object travels the same distance simultaneously, moving from one location to another (Broer 1960).

Bruce Lee realized that the best results called for a blending of linear and rotational motion. The martial artist's rotational foot movements, for example, must be coordinated with the linear motion of his whole body; similarly, the hammer thrower's forward movement across the circle must be coordinated with his turns. For most joints to move, we need not only a prime mover (the major muscle that moves the joint) but also some means of maintaining the joint, the pivot point of motion (Kopell and Kester 1969).

VELOCITY VERSUS SPEED

In his study of kinesiology, Lee made a distinction between velocity and speed. Velocity includes the direction of travel as well as the rate. A runner may move at a speed of 24 m.p.h., but to state his velocity, we must find in which direction he is traveling; he may have a velocity of 24 m.p.h. due north. The rate of motion, or the speed of an object, is given in units of length and time. Thus, a speed of 24 m.p.h. may also be stated as 35.2 feet per second. Possessing magnitude and direction, velocity is a vector quantity and can, therefore, be represented diagramatically by straight lines (Broer 1960).

EFFICIENT MOVEMENT

Since the human body is made up of weights (mass of body segments), levers (bones), and devices for producing force (muscles and nerves), it responds to the laws of physics just as any other system of weights and levers. The problem, Lee reasoned, lay in determining how the body weights can be handled so as to maintain stability at rest or in motion (or to use instability to advantage) and to produce and control force, in the performance of various types of combative tasks, so that a desired result can be obtained with the least strain and a minimal expenditure of energy (Broer 1960).

NEWTON'S LAWS

With a desire to maximize his power, speed, and impact force, Lee set about researching the fundamental principles of physics, which led immediately to the laws first noted by Sir Isaac Newton. Lee read that force is the effect that one body has on another and that the main sources of force are (a) internal, or the muscular actions of the individual, and (b) external, the downward pull of gravity, the friction and upthrust of the ground, and the resistance of the air. Newton's laws of motion are fundamental to the whole science of force. Even rocket and missile discoveries are based on his theories.

NEWTON'S FIRST LAW (LAW OF INERTIA)

It was in 1687 that Newton enunciated the first of his three laws in the now famous words:

Every body continues in its state of rest, or of uniform motion in a straight line, except in so far as it may be compelled by impressed forces to change that state.

Expressed in simpler language, everything in the universe is lazy, so lazy in fact that force is necessary to get it to move, when it then travels in a straight line; so lazy that, once it is in motion, a further force must be applied to slow it down, stop it, speed it up, or change its direction. Thus, a shot rolling along level ground would continue to roll forever in a straight line, were it not for ground and air friction. A person moving horizontally through space would continue to travel forever in a straight path, were it not for air resistance and the downward pull of gravity.

Direct proof of the correctness of Newton's assumption is impossible here on Earth, since we cannot remove a body completely from external influences, but in its logical results, the law is never at variance with experience. Inertia, therefore, is concerned with a body's resistance to change in movement.

The claim "To get an object to move, one must overcome its inertia" is based on the common experience whereby it is more difficult to start an object moving than to keep it in motion. This is due to the fact that, to start the object in motion, force must be used against both its inertia and the frictional ground and air forces, whereas to maintain a constant speed, only the frictional forces oppose movement, and less force is therefore required.

Inertia is proportional to mass—the amount of the material of which an object is made. In fact, the terms are often interchangeable. The mass of an object is the measure of its inertia, its resistance to change in motion. The British unit of mass

is the pound (often abbreviated lb.). By way of illustration, if equal forces are applied to a 16-pound shot and a 1-pound, 12¼-ounce javelin, the change in motion of the javelin (i.e., its acceleration) will be much greater. Mass must not be confused with weight; we shall see later that they are not the same (Dyson 1964).

NEWTON'S SECOND LAW (LAW OF ACCELERATION)

By means of Newton's second law we can determine how force can change the motion of an object. It states:

The rate of change of momentum is proportional to the impressed force, and the actual change takes place in the direction in which the force acts.

Momentum is the product of mass and velocity: it can be considered as a measure of the quantity of motion possessed by a body. It is a vector quantity, possessing both magnitude and direction.

A runner having a mass of 140 pounds and a velocity of 30 feet per second has a momentum of 4,200 units, as does a 30-pound object moving at 140 feet per second. Thus, theoretically, a marble may be made to create as much havoc as a cannonball if given sufficient velocity. At a definite time, the moving runner has momentum, and a period of time is necessary for him to change it.

From the law of inertia we know that the velocity of a moving object (i.e., the distance it travels per unit of time in a given direction) remains constant unless a force acts on it. This second law tells us that, provided we consider a definite period of time, any positive or negative change in velocity will be directly proportional to the amount of force used; it will also be inversely proportional to the object's mass. For example, considering a definite period of time of two seconds, the effective force a runner must use to increase his speed in a race during these two seconds is in direct proportion to his speed increase: if he wishes to double this speed increase in the two seconds, he must double the amount of force he exerts.

If there are two runners, one weighing only half as much as the other, and the same effective horizontal force is exerted by each during the two seconds, the lighter athlete will acquire double the speed increase of the heavier one—demonstrating that the change in velocity is inversely proportional to the mass of the object (Dyson 1964).

NEWTON'S THIRD LAW (LAW OF REACTION)

For every force acting anywhere, there is always an equal force acting in an opposite direction. Forces always work in pairs, as "twins" opposing each other. This is the meaning of Newton's third law, which states:

To every action there is an equal and opposite reaction; or the mutual actions of two bodies in contact are always equal and opposite in direction.

The effect upon one body is known as the "action," and that upon the other is the "reaction," but it is often a matter of opinion as to which is which. When a force sets an object in motion, the momentum of that object is altered. According to this third law, forces always work in opposing pairs: a change in momentum of one object in one direction produces a change in momentum of another object in an opposite direction, and the momentum of the system as a whole therefore remains the same. Hence, when a gun is fired, the explosion gives the bullet momentum in a forward direction equal but opposite to the gun's "kick" against the shoulder. It should be noted, however, that to exert a maximum of body force in running, jumping, or throwing, the athlete must be in contact with firm, resisting ground (Dyson 1964).

BRUCE LEE'S APPLICATION

Bruce Lee's notes reveal the following application of Newton's laws to the realm of martial art:

1. A body at rest remains eternally at rest, and a body in motion remains eternally in uniform motion unless acted upon by an external force.

When we stop a push, a blow, or a kick, we receive resistance from them. This resistance is called inertia. (Thus, to give motion to a body at rest or to stop a body in motion, we must overcome the inertia of that body.)

Force—an action to overcome the inertia of a body.

DEFENSE
(a) to lead opponent to the direction of his exertion (harmonious bridging). (b) to be insubstantial to opponent's line of exertion.

ATTACK
Momentum—the product of the mass of an object times its velocity.

(In order to apply a large force, induce momentum in your opponent in the shortest time possible as well as make the weight or power express your "whole weight" and enlarge the velocity so that power and velocity will become greater.)

—The abdominal and waist region coordinate all parts of the body and act as the center or generator. Therefore, you can promote the ability to control the body's action and master your will more easily.

2. The acceleration of a body is directly proportional to the force exerted on

Newton's Three Laws Of Motion

1. A body at rest remains eternally at rest, and a body at motion remains eternally in uniform motion unless acted upon by an external force.

When we stop a push, a blow or a kick, we receive resistance from them. This resistance is called INERTIA. (Thus, to give motion to a body at rest or to stop a body in motion, we must overcome the inertia of that body.)

— Between gap of exertion —

FORCE :— an action to overcome the inertia of a body.

DEFENSE :— a) to lead opponent to the direction of his exertion (bridging harmonious)
b) to be insubstantial to opponent's line of exertion

ATTACK :— MOMENTUM :— The product of the mass of an object times its velocity [In order to apply a large force, induce momentum in your opponent in the shortest time possible as well as make the weight or power express your "whole weight" and enlarge the velocity so that power and velocity will become greater.]

— abdominal and waist region coordinates all parts of the body and act as the center or generator. Therefore you can promote the ability to control the body; action and master your will more easily.

2). The acceleration of a body is directly proportional to the force exerted on the body, is inversely proportional to the mass of the body, and is in the same direction as force. EX.:- The iron and wood ball

To every motion there is a reaction

do not allow force exerted to have a reaction
accelerated force vs. stationary mass (momentum plus muscular force beats muscular force alone)

Bruce Lee's writing on his evolution in martial understanding reveals the profound influence of the principles of Newtonian physics.

the body, is inversely proportional to the mass of the body, and is in the same direction as force.

(e.g.: The iron and wood ball)

3. To every motion there is a reaction.

—Do not allow force exerted to have a reaction.

—Accelerated force vs. stationary mass (momentum plus muscular force beats muscular force alone).

FORCE

As stated earlier, force is the effect that one body has on another. In combat all motion is derived from force: from the muscle contractions, from gravity, from the friction and upthrust of the ground and the resistance of the air. In martial art, we are concerned mostly with the use of force for changing the state of motion of our limbs: slowing them down, stopping, or speeding them up.

However, there can be force without motion. For example, a javelin or pole can be gripped tightly without its moving; a tennis ball can be flattened a little by squeezing.

Force can, therefore, bring about, or tend to bring about, a change of shape in a body, causing stresses within, which are the result of the body's attempt to regain its original shape.

In athletic movement, no muscle—not even a single muscle group—works alone. All the muscles of the body are more or less in constant demand, supporting, guiding, and generally contributing to force and the control of movement (Dyson 1964).

DIRECTION

Bruce Lee believed that combative or martial efficiency is at its best when force has been properly directed both internally and externally. When equal forces are applied against equal masses, they produce the same change in velocity, and experiments prove that accelerations given to a body are proportional to the magnitude of the force. This gives us our measurement of force: *force = mass × acceleration*. Therefore, under otherwise identical conditions, the acceleration of athletes and their apparatus depends on their masses, which, in turn, are measures of inertia, or resistance to motion (Newton's first and second laws).

Frictional forces apart, any force will accelerate any mass. For example, but for the resistance of air and water, a docker leaning against the side of an unmoored Atlantic liner, could give it motion with which to cross from England to America—but he would have to lean in the right direction, and the crossing would take a long time! In practice, of course, liners can be moved only when the force acting on them in a given direction is greater than the frictional and other forces opposing—and so it is with athletes and their apparatus (Dyson 1964).

IMPULSE

Bruce Lee saw that the change in speed of an individual technique or strike depends not merely on the force applied but also on the time for which it operates, its impulse. In throwing a punch, for example, the martial artist should adjust his positions not only to increase his driving force but also to lengthen the time during which it is exerted, thus increasing the starting velocity. An increase in force often requires a more rapid action, resulting in a decrease in time of operation—unless the distance over which the force operates is increased.

EFFECTIVE FORCE

In a kick, top speed is reached when the effective force of the leg drive equals all the opposing forces. In order to accelerate his body, a martial artist must be capable of moving at a greater speed than at rest. And the greater his speed, in comparison, the greater his effective force will be. Thus, the ability of the individual martial artist to apply force depends not only on strength but also on speed (Dyson 1964).

SUMMATION OF FORCES

Where Bruce Lee was concerned, the strongest parts of the body are the heaviest and have a correspondingly greater inertia: consequently, they are less speedy in their movements. With martial artists, it is a question of using the different muscles when they are capable of sufficient speed to apply full force. This calls for a definite sequence and timing of bodily forces. The strong but slower muscles surrounding the body's center of gravity should begin, followed by the trunk and thighs and, finally, the weaker and lighter but faster extremities. When the forces are properly harnessed, therefore, movement flows outward simultaneously from the center of the body (Dyson 1964).

CENTER OF GRAVITY

We know that the Earth attracts every tiny particle of an object with a gravitational force which is proportional to the mass of each particle. If all these separate attractions are thought of as being added together to make one resultant force—the weight of the object—the point where this force acts will be the center of gravity.

In an erect position, with arms to the sides, a man's center of gravity will average 57 percent of his height—approximately one inch below the navel, roughly midway between the abdomen and the back. Children will average a relatively higher center of gravity in such a position, due to carrying relatively more weight in their upper body. A woman's center of gravity in this position will be only 55 percent of her height, on average, because of her smaller thorax, lighter arms, and narrower shoulders but heavier pelvis and thighs, and shorter legs. But the center of gravity lies higher in the body of shorter-legged women than in longer-legged males with correspondingly short trunks—an important point when considering the performances of women in high jumping, hurdling, and the running events.

The location of the center of gravity for any particular person, in any given position, changes with inspiration and expiration, eating and drinking, and increase of fat or age. The center of gravity moves always in sympathy with the movements of different parts of the body. It is, in fact, a most unstable point in the athlete, and yet, despite this almost continuous motion, the center of gravity seldom moves out of the pelvic cavity (Dyson 1964).

MOTION IN CONTACT WITH THE GROUND

Lee observed that by moving when in contact with the ground, an athlete changes the position of his center of gravity in relation to both his mass and the ground itself. This applies whether he is in direct contact (as, for example, when he is actually touching the ground) or vaulting a short wall (when he is in the air but holding the wall) (Dyson 1964).

EQUILIBRIUM OF BALANCE (BALANCE AND STABILITY AT REST)

The first consideration for balance (or equilibrium, as it is called in mechanics) is that the result of the forces acting on the object shall be zero. In all resting positions, the force of gravity pulling the object down is equal but opposite to that of the ground pushing it up. Under such conditions—and this applies to all athletes balanced at rest, too—a plumb line dropped from the center of gravity falls within the base. An object's stability depends on the area of its base, the height of its center of gravity, the horizontal distance between the center of gravity and the pivoting edge, and its weight (Dyson 1964).

BALANCE IN MOTION

Let us consider, for the present, balance in motion to mean that, as a whole, an object or athlete is moving without rotation. If a staff is balanced upright in the palm of a hand, and the hand moves forward, force is applied to the bottom of the staff, causing the staff to rotate backward. On a second attempt, however, the staff is tilted forward as the hand accelerates. The force of the weight of the staff, acting through the center of gravity (now outside the base), tends to rotate it forward, and if the staff leans neither too much nor too little for the force applied by the hand, it remains balanced. Thus, clockwise and counterclockwise rotations cancel out—the second condition for equilibrium. This simple example illustrates an important aspect of the interplay of forces in the maintenance of balance in motion (Dyson 1964).

HOPPING, JUMPING, LEAPING, AND LANDING

There are few sights more impressive than watching the human body performing at the height of muscular coordination, grace, and dexterity. In basketball, it's Michael Jordan slam-dunking a basketball; in ice hockey, it's Wayne Gretzky stickhandling around the opposition to "tuck one upstairs" behind an opposing goaltender; and in martial arts, it's the sight of Bruce Lee leaping through the air like a panther to attack an adversary or an object with a flying kick.

When I was in Hong Kong during the winter of 1994, I had the opportunity to speak with Jon T. Benn, the man who played the evil boss in Bruce Lee's *The Way of the Dragon*. Benn recalled what it was like to witness Bruce Lee in motion:

In one scene, Bruce jumped straight up and kicked a lightbulb out of a very high ceiling light! It was just as high as it appeared on film. It was the first time he'd done it in the film, and we just couldn't believe it. It was a good seven or eight feet off the ground, and he just went—Zoom! Smash!

While one feels the temptation to dismiss such spectacular feats of human move-ment potential as the freakish ability of the genetically elite, the truth is that physiolog-ically, all human beings are the same—which means that the principles of motion under-lying such incredible performances are com-mon to us all.

Scientifically speaking, when the propul-sive force is exerted by one foot, and the body lands on the same foot, the action is defined as a hop. If the landing is made on the other foot, it is defined as a leap. In a jump, the propulsive force may be exerted either by one foot or both feet. In all of these activities, the problem is not only to produce sufficient force to overcome the inertia of the body and gravity's pull, but also to control the angle at which this force is applied so that the desired purpose is ful-filled. The force that projects the body into space must be exerted by the muscles of the body. It is produced by quick contraction of the extensors of the legs, aided by a force-ful arm swing. The faster the leg extension, the more force produced against the floor and the greater the counterpressure which projects the body. In preparation for the production of this force, the hips, knees, and ankles must bend to put the extensors of the legs in position to exert force.

Up to a point, depending on the strength of the legs, the deeper the crouch, the more force obtainable. A deeper crouch gives a greater distance over which acceleration is possible. However, since the body must be lifted through the distance that it is lowered, more work is done when a low crouch is used, and the angle of muscle pull is also changed. The optimal depth of crouch, therefore, depends on the strength of the leg muscles. A deeper crouch is possible if the leg muscles are strong. The crouch of the jump can be likened to the backswing of a throwing or striking action; it is the preparation for the purposeful action.

If the purpose is to gain height, the arms are dropped, with the elbows somewhat flexed, to allow for movement to develop momentum, this time upward. The flexion of the arms makes it possible to swing them more nearly upward in the direction of desired movement and shortens the lever, making it easier to move them rapidly.

Whenever the takeoff is from one foot, as in the flying side kick or a jump preceded by a run, the center of gravity is brought over the takeoff foot at the moment of force application. A preparatory run, which gives the body momentum in the direction in which the action is to be executed, adds force to the final projection. However, in jumping for height, a slow bouncing run, which moves the body up and down, is more effective in producing momentum to aid in gaining height. It keeps the center of gravity more nearly over the feet, and the momentum that is developed is upward.

When height is the objective, the arms are swung upward. It has been suggested that added height can be achieved by swinging one or both arms downward just before the highest point of the jump is reached. It is reasoned that since a given force at takeoff will raise the center of gravity of the body to a certain height, anything that lowers the center of gravity in the body will raise the height to which the head or reaching hand will move. Since the center of gravity is lower in the body when the arms are down, swinging the arms downward should cause the body to rise higher.

The angle of takeoff is very important to the purpose of the jump. The angle at which the force is applied to the body is determined by the line from the center of gravity of the body. In jumping for height, the desired movement is straight upward; therefore, the center of gravity should be directly above the feet at takeoff. The forward lean of the trunk that accompanies the bending of the legs should, therefore, be kept to a minimum (Heidenstam 1963).

BODY MECHANICS

Bruce Lee made a thorough study of body mechanics (kinesiology), which can also be defined as the study of complex muscular movements. Lee soon realized that understanding the basic principles of kinesiology was essential to maximizing his movement potential.

It helps in understanding Bruce Lee's scientific pursuits in this realm to review the fundamentals of this subject and become familiar with the terms and movements.

Muscle Work

Muscles are built up of hairlike fibers which are activated by the nervous system to either shorten, lengthen, or hold a fixed position.

Concentric A muscle is said to be working concentrically when it is actively shortening against resistance. When the body, or a part of the body, is to be raised or when outside resistance has to be overcome, the muscles involved are working concentrically.

Examples: Raising the body from the squat, raising the arms above the head from the sideways position, raising the trunk from the lying position into a sitting position, or raising one leg while standing.

Eccentric A muscle is working eccentrically when it is actively lengthening to permit the controlled lowering of the body, part of the body, or some outside resistance.

Examples: Lowering the arm to the side from above the head, or lowering any weight from any height or position.

Static A muscle is working statically when it is employed to hold a fixed position.

Example: If you stop during any movement, the muscles used to hold that position are working statically. By merely standing to attention, the postural muscles are working statically.

Isotonic muscle work is the same as concentric and eccentric, *isometric* is another term for static work (Heidenstam 1963).

Muscle Action

The muscles can also act for particular movements:

Prime Movers The muscles responsible for producing concentric and permitting eccentric muscle work are known as the prime movers.

Example: When the arms are raised sideways, the abductors of the shoulders (the deltoids) are acting concentrically as the prime movers.

Antagonists The antagonists are the muscles on the opposite side of the joint to the muscles acting as prime movers.

Fixators Muscles act as fixators when they are working statically to fix part of the body in a stationary position while concentric or eccentric muscle work is going on in another part of the body.

Example: When a gardener is bent forward weeding, the hip and spine extensors are acting as fixators to keep the trunk bent forward in a static position while the arms move to pick the weeds.

This is a lot to learn in a short space, but you will find it easier to remember if you consider which muscles are doing what job as you practice your exercises.

Try this exercise—it contains just about all the terms we have covered so far: Place your feet astride, trunk forward at right angles to the legs, arms stretched downward from the shoulders. Raise the arms sideways and

upward to shoulder level, then lower them back to the starting position.

It is simple enough, but a lot of muscles have been in action. The extensors of the spine, hip, and knee have been working statically as fixators to hold the position of the legs and trunk. When the arms are raised sideways and outward, the extensors of the elbow work statically to keep them straight. At the same time, the adductors and refractors of the arms and shoulder girdle (humerus and scapulae) work concentrically as prime movers to raise the arms. During this movement, the abductors of the arms and protractors of the shoulder blades (serratus anterior and pectorals) are the antagonists. When the arms are lowered under control, the same group of muscles responsible for raising the arms now works eccentrically to lower them under control to the starting position (Heisdenstam 1963).

Range of Movement

Most healthy joints have full range of movements: they are able to move from full extension to full flexion (or from full abduction to full adduction). Starting from full extension, the first third of the movement is known as the outer range, when the muscles are working at their longest length. The next third is the middle range, and it is within this range that the muscles are working to their best anatomical advantage. This is because a muscle pulls most strongly when it is working approximately at right angles to the limb or bone that it moves. The final third is known as the inner range, when the muscles are working at their shortest length and closest to full flexion.

It would seem from this that the middle range is the most efficient area anatomically for lifting weights, but this is outweighed by the mechanical disadvantage as the weight arm (that is, the length of the lever from weight to fulcrum) is increased. The reason is that when the weight reaches the center of the middle range (or when the forearm is horizontal), it is at its farthest point from the fulcrum, in this case the elbow. This factor makes the middle range the most difficult of the three for most movements.

The body, however, can be positioned in such a way that any of the three ranges may become the most difficult (Heidenstam 1963).

Levers

Leverage is broken down for study into first class, second class, and third class. We deal here only with the third class, which is the most frequent in the body. From the fulcrum to the point where power is applied is known as the *power arm*, and from the power to the weight is known as the *weight arm*.

When the weight is brought closer to the power, less effort is needed by the muscles that lift or hold it. The line of least resistance is generally where the weight is closest horizontally to the fulcrum. This is an important point to remember when the minimum of effort is needed to provide the maximum efficiency of movement.

In our bodies, joints are fulcrums, bones are levers, and power is supplied by the muscles (Heidenstam 1963).

Balance and the Center of Gravity

When additional weight is being handled by the body, the center of gravity of the weight and body together is referred to as the *combined center of gravity*. It falls somewhere between the center of gravity of the body and that of the weight, the combined center being nearer to whichever is the heavier (Heidenstam 1963).

Joint Actions

The table on page 144 gives the commonly used terms and definitions for the actions of joints.

Term	Definition
Flexion	Bending
Extension	Straightening

(These two movements are the most common and are possible at all major joints.)

Adduction	Movement toward the midline of the body, as in bringing the shoulder blades together.
Abduction	Movement apart from, or away from, the midline of the body, as in jumping astride. The opposite of adduction.
Circumduction	Circular movement of part of the body from a point, such as arms circling from the shoulder joint.
Rotation	Turning outward and inward without changing the position of the long axis of the bone or bones, as in turning the head from left to right; this is rotation of the cervical region.
Elevation	Raising, as in shrugging the shoulders.
Depression	Lowering, as in pulling the shoulders downward.

(Elevation and depression apply to movement of the shoulder girdle, scapula, and clavicle.)

Hyperextension	Extension beyond the normal, as in arching the back in the backlying position.

Source: Heidenstam, Oscar. 1963. *Modern Weight Training*. London: Nicholas Kaye.

CHAPTER 10

BRUCE LEE—THE EVOLUTION OF A MARTIAL ARTIST

Bruce Lee in 1966; even then he was actively refining his approach to martial art.

Bruce Lee shared his teachings with only a select few students, and then, approximately two and a half years before he died, he closed his schools. With his passing, however, a great flower blossomed, and the teachings and wisdom of the man whom history knows as Bruce Lee have spread to the four corners of the earth.

The seed of jeet kune do that Bruce Lee planted has brought forth much fruit. However, it has been poorly cared for over the years (some would say neglected), to the point that a lot of creeping vines and not a few weeds have appeared on the scene.

I would like to attempt a bit of martial horticulture and present an unobstructed view of the fruit that has grown out of Bruce Lee's labors.

In one of his last public statements about jeet kune do, Bruce Lee gave the following answer to the question "What is jeet kune do?" in an article he published in *Black Belt* magazine in September 1971 entitled "Liberate Yourself from Classical Karate":

I am the first to admit that any attempt to crystallize jeet kune do into a written article is no easy task. Do remember, however, that "jeet kune do" is merely a convenient name. I am not interested with the term itself; I am interested in its effect of liberation when JKD is used as a mirror for self-examination.

While this statement may baffle some (particularly those who are not of a philosophic bent), in the proper historical context of the development of his art, it makes perfect sense. Its full significance can be grasped by application to the time line of jeet kune do's growth and development. However it is far easier to define exactly what jeet kune do is if we can first determine clearly what it is not.

WHAT JEET KUNE DO IS NOT

To begin in this vein of negation, and as indicated in the previous chapters, Bruce Lee's art of jeet kune do is not, as some have intimated, merely a synonym for eclecticism; it is not simply an amalgam of many different martial arts. Jeet kune do has its own principles, philosophy, history, and core techniques that separate it from every other martial art and give it its unique identity.

Jeet kune do is also not, as some wing-chun practitioners have implied (both directly and indirectly), a synonym for, or mere variation of, wing chun gung fu. Lee discarded so many "core" essentials of wing-chun methodology (as well as creating enough new and unique techniques, footwork, stance, and combative science research) that looking to wing chun for insight into jeet kune do would be the sociological equivalent of looking to Great

Britain in order to better understand America—after all, America's first exposure to politics was under British rule, wasn't it? However, it quickly developed its own founding principles, methods of justice, charter of individual rights, and political philosophy which created a vast chasm between the two cultures.

Similarly, Lee quickly developed his own principles, unique technical elements, training methods, and philosophy that formed a massive breach between wing chun and do. Wing chun has enjoyed a misbegotten position as the "base system" of jeet kune do. In truth, wing chun is no more the "base system" of jeet kune do (particularly in JKD's later stages) than Oxford University is the "base system" of Harvard University. They are two separate entities.

Wing chun was simply the first art of which Bruce Lee ever made a thorough study, and he practiced its techniques diligently. While it is true that many elements that are part of the wing-chun system Lee continued to practice and teach his students (such as chi sao, or "sticking hands," as well as the centerline and trapping components) right up until the early 1970s, Lee also made thorough studies of Western boxing, European fencing, and even wrestling throughout

this period. They, like wing chun, are simply bricks in the wall of Lee's learning process and total martial arts development.

Third, jeet kune do is not, strictly speaking, either a "Chinese" art or an "American" art, although there are principles and elements from both cultures in its makeup. From the Chinese mind-set, Lee adapted the philosophical principle of the Tao, or the oneness of all things, symbolized by the tai chi, or yin-yang symbol, as well as the philosophical precepts of *wu-hsin* (nonfixated mind) and *wu-wei* (the noninterference with the natural course of things). From the American philosophic tradition, Lee embraced the principles of pragmatism, individualism, and, to a certain extent, empiricism in the sense of accepting as valid only things proved or established by the senses.

But who is to say that the "way of nature," or "Tao," refers to only things Chinese? Certainly the great Tao, as Lao-tzu said in the *Tao Te Ching*, "flows everywhere. All things are born from it." And, on the other side of the coin, it should be obvious to any Westerner that the West holds no monopoly on efficiency, truth, and practicality.

As pointed out in a previous chapter, jeet kune do may be considered a "rational" art in that it is defined by its adherence to humankind's highest nature—the capacity to think, experience, and reason things out. It is not the exclusive property of any particular region, province, nation, or ethnic group. It is the property of all who are willing to put aside their egos, lay bare their souls, and open themselves up to the experience of the reality of combat (and of life itself) without flinching, without prejudices and biases, and without fixed viewpoints, and then to draw their own conclusions based on that unbiased vision of truth.

Related to the subject of what jeet kune do is not, jeet kune do as it existed in 1971 through 1973 was not the same as when Lee began to develop its principles throughout 1965 and 1966, nor as when he first christened it thus in 1967 and as it remained until late 1970. This is not to suggest, as some have done, that it was an art that was "constantly changing." There was change in Lee's approach to martial art, but it was infrequent and sporadic, occurring gradually over a ten-year period, and certain core principles, techniques, and philosophies remained unaffected within the curriculum from the art's inception.

Bruce Lee experienced three epiphanies (the way of gung fu, the way of intercep-

tion, and the way of "no way") during his adult life that had a direct impact on the evolution of his art. Each of these enlightening moments occurred during a period in which he was absorbed in thought regarding the ultimate nature of unarmed combat, and they dramatically affected the format, structure, and metaphysic of his approach to martial arts.

This chapter shines a light on this development so that we may be able to see the true progression, context, and totality of the art.

INCHING TOWARD TRUTH

Accepting the premise that Bruce Lee's art is rational, it must then, by definition, be valid—that is, predicated on an accurate perception of reality or truth as it regards human motion in relation to combat. It is an art, then, that is predicated on truth. As such, it is always in a process of evolution—inching toward truth within the constantly narrowing parameters of context and knowledge. It is thus a process of refinement, as we saw in the earier example of a sculptor carving a statue.

In the 1971 *Black Belt* article cited earlier, Lee reiterated: "In JKD we begin not by accumulation but by discovering the cause of our own ignorance—a discovery that involves a shedding process."

Beyond the stasis of certain core technical aspects of the art (the on-guard position, lead punch, side kick, hook kick, finger jab, backfist strike, etc.), a certain philosophic "constant" or sameness about Lee's art endured from its christening in 1967 through at least 1973. Lee did not switch to a process of adding on or accumulating techniques, methods, or styles.

By way of analogy, when a species evolves, it doesn't "add on" physical material; it refines the genetic raw materials that are inherent. Scientists tell us that, at some point in the evolutionary process, our species had a tail. Now, of course, the tail is gone, but we see its remnants every time we have an x-ray that reveals our "tailbone." And, of course, our appendix is a carryover from days in our species' history when it actually served a purpose. This organ wasn't added to our bodies over time; on the contrary, we've gradually diminished our need for it, and in time, so the physiologists and anthropologists tell us, it too will disappear. Refinement, the process of evolution through the removal of unessentials, is an important concept in the development of jeet kune do.

THREE STAGES OF CULTIVATION

Let us go back to the period before Bruce Lee created jeet kune do. Let us begin at the first stage of Lee's famous "Three Stages of Cultivation," the Stage of First Innocence, or Ignorance. In the Stage of Ignorance, you know nothing at all about the martial arts and, if you seek out an instructor or school, accept unquestioningly the doctrine of the first method to which you are exposed. It is in this context only that wing chun warrants consideration in relation to Bruce Lee's development as a martial artist.

IN THE BEGINNING: WING CHUN GUNG FU

In attempting to trace the evolutionary or refining process of Bruce Lee's art, we must begin where he began, with wing chun gung fu. Wing chun—a Chinese art—was taught to Bruce Lee from the age of thirteen to eighteen while he lived in Hong Kong. Lee remained in the Stage of First Innocence for a relatively brief time, quickly entering into the second stage, the Stage of Art, where he began his first analysis of methods and ways outside of the first art to which he had been fully exposed.

What appealed to Lee about wing chun was that compared with many of the other Chinese arts, it had already been stripped of many inefficient movements, concerning itself with combative practicality rather than ornamentation. It must have occurred to Lee that wing chun, despite this advantage, did not possess all the answers to the reality of combat, given that he sought instruction in several techniques and forms of at least two other "styles" of Chinese gung fu while still in Hong Kong. According to Lee's first student in America, Jesse Glover, Lee continued the practice after he had settled in Seattle.

In fact, by the time Lee reached Seattle, he had added some techniques (namely the *gwa choy*, or backfist) and several kicks and forms that were not from orthodox wing chun. Also at this time and over the next several years, Lee realized and confirmed that wing chun was limited in many respects; most important, it is primarily a passive or receptive art, that you have to have your opponent make contact with your arms in order to execute your counteroffensive or "complete your opponent's attacking force." He wrote in an essay composed in 1961 titled "The Tao of Gung Fu":

Instead of opposing force by force, a gung-fu man completes his opponent's movement by accepting his flow of energy as he aims it, and defeats him by borrowing his own force.

The *bai-jong* (fighting stance) of wing chun gung fu provided an elongated lead arm which is useful for making contact with your opponent's hands by engaging him as soon as he comes in or (as Bruce later implemented) by initiating the contact through advancing and touching your opponent's arms. After studying the mobility and multiple punching geometry of Western boxers, Lee began to experiment and later incorporated "curve" or "hooking" punches into his arsenal. When he learned, through earnest sparring sessions, that these punches could prove very effective in combat, he further realized that this observation negated the concept of wing chun—which utilizes exclusively straight punches—as being a "complete" system. He viewed it as limited in having a "way" or "method" of delivering strikes, standing, balance, and so forth that could not be breached if you wished to call the art you were practicing wing chun.

"TOWARD EFFICIENT STREET FIGHTING"

In time, Lee's study of the attack principles of European fencing and Western boxing taught him that combat needn't be purely passive in order to be effective. Lee reasoned that it made more sense to launch an attack on an opponent when he was least prepared to handle it, rather than waiting for him to attack when he was fully prepared and then attempt to deflect or "complete" his attack, as he had been taught in the wing chun style.

Further, being small, Lee was concerned that if he was in a position where he could put his hands on his opponent, then his opponent could put his hands on him—not necessarily a desirable thing, particularly if your opponent was physically stronger than you and if you had another option. Granted, Lee was particularly powerful and effective in this range, but from a pragmatic point of view, he also realized that much of a person's energy could be utilized here and that the expenditure was not always necessary nor desirable.

This set Lee on a course of thought that caused him to conclude in 1965 that blindly following a method (particularly one that imposed a limited approach to combat: passive/receptive, straight line only, etc.) was not attuned to combative reality. He realized that, in terms of mobility and hand technique, what he was doing now was more like Western boxing than wing chun, although certain principles, techniques, and training methods were retained, such as the centerline, finger jab, *chi sao*, *pak sao*, *lop sao*, *jutt sao*, vertical fist, and four-corner parries. Lee offered a retrospective on this change in a 1969 letter to his old friend, and fellow wing chun student, William Cheung:

I've lost faith in the Chinese classical arts—though I still call mine Chinese—because basically all styles are products of dryland swimming, even the wing chun school. So my line of training is more toward efficient street fighting with everything goes; wearing headgear, gloves, chest guard, shin/knee guards, etc. For the past five years now I've been training the hardest, and for a purpose, not just dissipated hit-miss training. I'm running every day, sometimes up to six miles. I've named my style jeet kune do—reason for my not sticking to wing chun is because I sincerely feel that my style has more to offer regarding efficiency.

And similarly, Lee related to a *Miami News* newspaper reporter: "I favor moving like a boxer; jeet kune do offers more freedom, more self-expression."

Most certainly, wing chun practitioners do not "favor moving like a boxer." By 1966, Bruce Lee was determined that his own research and innovations in the art of unarmed combat should be acknowledged in order to distinguish his approach from other styles of gung fu, particularly wing chun. To this end, he sought to isolate the defining attribute of his new way of think-

ing about combat, and he came up with the principle of *interception*. He began to write about "offensive defense and defensive offense" and to make statements to the press and his students about his art's being 100 percent attack oriented and nondefensive in nature. Witness the following from an article in *Chicago's American* titled "Hornet's Sidekick a Blur on Film":

Gung fu [as I practice it] is more offensive than defensive. At the moment of attack, you intercept the attack and attack in return.

THE CHRISTENING OF JEET KUNE DO

By 1967, Lee had opened his Los Angeles school (Seattle and Oakland had been in operation since 1963 and 1964, respectively). This combative distinction of his art was now in full blossom as its defining characteristic. In the November 1967 article in *Black Belt* magazine, Bruce said:

The main characteristic of this style is the absence of the usual classical passive blocking. Blocking is the least efficient. Jeet kune do is offensive; it's alive and it's free.

Lee had given his art a new name, "Jeet Kune Do," which translates as "the way of the intercepting fist." He specifically chose the word *intercepting* as the art's defining attribute. Along with it, he introduced a series of martial techniques predicated on this principle, such as the stop hit, time hit, and simultaneous hit/block.

What separated jeet kune do from every other combative art, Lee held, was that its emphasis was placed squarely on attack, on intercepting your opponent either during the initiation of his attack or, better still, prior to the initiation. Here is a sampling of his thoughts on this regard from an article published in the *Miami Beach Sun*, October 24, 1969, by Joe Maggio:

- "Of my art—gung fu and jeet kune do—only one of ten thousand can handle it. It is martial art. Complete offensive attacks.

It is silly to think almost anyone can learn it."

- "It isn't really contemporary forms of the art I teach. Mainly that which I work with [is]—martial attack."

- "Unlike other forms of karate, which promote static defense, gung fu and jeet kune do are classically refined for self-defense and offensive aggression."

- "It's really a smooth rhythmic expression of smashing the guy before he hits you, with any method available. Most karate is defensive. You're taught to do something after [something] is done to you."

Lee explained his new system of combat predicated on the principle of interception in the premier episode of the 1971 television series "Longstreet" written in collaboration with his student Stirling Silliphant:

Duke: What is this thing you do?

Bruce Lee: In Cantonese, jeet kune do—*"the way of the intercepting fist."*

Duke: (unimpressed) "Intercepting fist," huh?

Bruce Lee: Or foot—come on, touch me. Anywhere you can. (Duke attempts a punch; Lee intercepts with a lead shin/stop kick.) You see, your attack offers me an opportunity to intercept you. This time I'm using my longest weapon, my side kick, against the nearest target—your knee cap. This can be compared to your left jab in boxing, except it's much more damaging.

Duke: (mad) I see. Well, speaking of a left jab . . . (Duke attempts a left jab; Lee intercepts with a quick finger jab.)

Bruce Lee: Oooh! This time I intercepted your emotional tenseness. You see, from your thought to your hand, how much time was lost?

Silliphant later recounted in the magazine *Martial Arts Legends* how Lee came to refine the art of interception, waiting until the opponent was fully committed before initiating the stop or time hit:

Bruce taught me to dissect time into infinite degrees. It's what he called "playing between the keys" of the piano. It's the understanding that you actually have worlds of time within split seconds to do something else unanticipated while your opponent is committed to his already announced action. Almost to the point where, if his fist is right at the tip of your nose, there's still time to react. Bruce used to say to me: "'Whenever some big guy attacks you, instead of reacting to his ego, teach him to react to yours. You must think to yourself—how grateful I am that this wonderful target of opportunity is presenting itself to me at this moment. Think not that your assailant is going to harm you, but take joy in the havoc you're going to lay on him after he's been so obliging as to put himself in the position where you can reach him." You must do a hell of a lot of work to arrive at this stage of cool thinking. But if you can attain it, you won't be defeated just because an opponent is bigger, stronger, or meaner, but only if he's faster and thinks the way you do.

This, then, was the founding principle of jeet kune do, the principle of interception. However, a new epiphany awaited Lee, the way of "no way."

IMPRISONED BY STYLE

In 1970, Lee's back injury prevented him from teaching or training for six months. With no usual outlet for his energy, Lee channeled it into reading, reflecting, and most important, thinking—in the form of analyzing his art. He came away with the following insight, which appeared in "Liberate Yourself from Classical Karate" from *Black Belt* magazine:

One cannot express himself fully when imprisoned by a confining style. Combat "as is" is total, and it includes all the "is" as well as the "is not," without favorite lines or angles. Lacking boundaries, combat is always fresh, alive, and constantly changing. Your particular style, your personal inclinations, and your physical makeup are all parts of combat, but they do not constitute the whole of combat. Should your responses become dependent

upon any single part, you will react in terms of what "should be" rather than to the reality of the ever-changing "what is." Remember that while the whole is evidenced in all its parts, an isolated part—efficient or not—does not constitute the whole. . . .

There is no standard in total combat, and expression must be free. This liberating truth is a reality only in so far as it is experienced and lived by the individual himself; it is a truth that transcends styles or disciplines.

From analyzing the ultimate or metaphysical nature of combat—and only three years after coining the term and the method of jeet kune do—Bruce Lee discovered that, by creating a method out of the principle of interception, he had imposed a limitation. By creating a distinction, he had denied himself everything that did not fit into the category of "interception." Even by simply stating what jeet kune do was, he had, more important, also stated, through implication, what it was not (i.e., it did not employ methods that were noninterception oriented). This imposition, in fact, is one of the most basic teachings of the Tao. According to Lao-tzu in *Tao Te Ching*:

**When people see some things as beautiful,
Other things become ugly.
When people see some things as good,
Other things become bad.
Being and nonbeing create each other.
Difficult and easy support each other.
Long and short define each other.
High and low depend on each other.
Before and after follow each other.**

By his own definition, Lee had imposed a limit on what he had hoped would be an art of "totality." Instead of presenting the totality of combat, he had created an isolated part or segment—an "efficient" segment, admittedly, but a segment nonetheless. This insight led him to observe: "Any structure, however intelligently designed,

becomes a cage if the student is obsessed with it."

Shortly thereafter, Lee began to regret having given a name to his method, and a "method" to his name. He had now come to view the full metaphysical truth of his credo of "Using no way as way; having no limitation as limitation." This new perspective was reflected in remarks he made in an interview with Hong Kong's TV-B:

Very often when people talk about JKD, they are very much concerned about its title. Actually the title is not important. It's only a symbol for the kind of martial art we study. It's just like the X, Y, and Z of algebra. The emphasis should not be put on its title, but on its effect, because that is a good mirror to reflect the power of JKD.

The beginning of the chapter quoted a passage from "Liberate Yourself from Classical Karate" in which Lee referred to the "effect of liberation when JKD is used as a mirror for self-examination." He continued:

Remember, too, that Jeet Kune Do is merely a term, a label to be used as a boat to get one across; it is to be discarded and not carried on one's back.

Lee had come to see that partialized viewpoints, however well-intended, are by nature restrictive and that "there is no such thing as an effective segment of a totality." While the principle of interception was still effective and, hence, valid, it represented only one method or way of dealing with the issue of combat, and therefore it was restrictive, putting adherents of the style in bondage to the doctrine.

Lee observed that the crux of the problem was the nature of styles. In order for something to be different from something else or unique, it had to have its own defining—and therefore restrictive—characteristics. But what would happen if you had a style that had no distinctive elements, characteristics, or restrictions? The answer: Total freedom in combat. Total pragmatic efficiency.

Combat is fluid and unpredictable, and therefore there could be no one "ideal" way to approach a fight. Rather, there exist instead only possibilities dependent on what options or openings your opponent presents to you during an encounter. Lee, always able to convert a profound thought to the simplest of statements, told journalist Alex Ben Block:

More and more I believe in [the premise that] you have two hands and two legs, and the thing is how to make good use of yourself. And that's about it.

TRAVELER'S AID

Lee realized that how one learns to make "good use" of oneself is a very personal thing. How could Bruce Lee show Joe Public anything other than how Bruce Lee learned to make good use of Bruce Lee? It would be up to Joe Public to learn how to make good use of Joe Public. What Lee could offer was, obviously, not a "system" or a "method," such as they had been conventionally defined—which would be offering the individual only a set of restrictions—but rather a signpost that he hoped would lead the individual to see the same truths that Lee had discovered. This approach would place the student on the correct path toward learning how to make good use of himself.

And what was the signpost that Lee left us? First of all, it was his example of what a man who accepted "no limitation as limitation" could accomplish and achieve, and second, it was his "core" of fundamental techniques and principles of effective combat. However, our success in becoming free-form martial artists is ultimately dependent on how much time we are willing to devote to our personal cultivation, or "homework," in perfecting these techniques and principles. It is up to the student to refine these materials so that they became second nature and reflexive, moving to the target the moment an opening is presented.

This was the underlying message that Lee intended to convey when he wrote the following dialogue scene between his character and a Buddhist monk (played by Roy Chiao) in the film *Enter the Dragon*:

Monk: **Your skill is now not a matter of mere technique but of spiritual insight and training. I would like to ask you several questions.**

Lee: All right.

Monk: **What was your immediate feeling toward your opponent during sparring?**

Lee: There is no opponent.

Monk: **(in a tone of anticipation for more) And why is that?**

Lee: Because the word I *does not exist.*

Monk: **(apparently happy at his student's comprehension) Yes!?**

Lee: When no notion of conflict is stirred in one's thought pattern, when one has forgotten the word mind, then the state of mindlessness is most fluid. When the opponent expands, I contract. And when he contracts, I expand. And when there is an opportunity, "I" do not hit (Lee raises his fist)—"it" hits all by itself.

Lee's focus on cultivating an unconditioned mind meant no restrictions, only a pure and honest reaction to what was unfolding before him from moment to moment—awareness and adjustment. Near the completion of the preceding scene, Lee's character describes the mind-set necessary to allow his hands and feet to move of their own accord:

A good martial artist does not become tense—but ready. Not thinking, yet not dreaming. Ready for whatever may come.

THE STAGE OF ARTLESSNESS

One of Bruce Lee's original students, Bob Bremer, recalls that Lee "knew when my mind became momentarily stopped on something; that's when he reacted." This is precisely in keeping with the reality of combat that Lee sought to embrace. The great Japanese swordsman Miyamoto Musashi, in *The Book of Five Rings* (translated by Thomas Clearly), speaks similarly of this principle of "no-mindedness" that results in

his sword's moving by itself to strike at the opportune moment:

I n the science of martial arts, the mind should remain the same as normal. In ordinary circumstances as well as when practicing martial arts, let there be no change at all—with the mind open and direct, neither tense nor lax, centering the mind so that there is no imbalance, calmly relax your mind, and savor this moment of ease thoroughly so that the relaxation does not stop its relaxation for even an instant. . . .

Let your inner mind be unclouded and open, placing your intellect on a broad plane. It is essential to polish the intellect and mind diligently. Once you have sharpened your intellect to the point where you can see whatever in the world is true or not, where you can tell whatever is good or bad, and when you are experienced in various fields and are incapable of being fooled at all by people of the world, then your mind will become imbued with the knowledge and wisdom of the art of war.

All martial artists who attempt to see the truth or reality of combat free from the bondage of styles and doctrines usually come to the same vision or truth of which Bruce Lee spoke: that there is no "way" of combat, only "ends," and the successful "ends" are determined by the application of successful "means," of "becoming moment to moment."

That's the mind-set, but this mind-set cannot exist in a vacuum; it is the final stage—the Stage of Artlessness—that comes only after countless hours spent in diligent practice in the perfection of one's tools (weapons) of combat, until both the tools and the martial artist's skill in using them are but an extension of the individual martial artist (like his dexterity with his fingers, the beating of his heart, the growing of his hair, and the breathing of his lungs). As Musashi said:

Isubsequently practiced day and night in order to attain an even deeper prin-

ciple, and spontaneously came upon the science of martial arts.

Bruce Lee, writing three centuries later in notes titled "Organized Lesson Plan for Jeet Kune Do," came to see the same combative truth in his own process of martial development:

Jeet kune do is a step-by-step project, and each maneuver must be repeated many times.

He adds to this in a quote from *Fighting Stars* magazine, August 1973:

Some guys may not believe it, but I spent hours perfecting whatever I did.

This final stage of Bruce Lee's Three Stages of Cultivation was, like his art, a "work in progress." It is an experiential process, not an abstract one, and therefore Lee eventually concluded that it was almost impossible for one individual to "give" or teach it to another. As he once wrote in a personal letter:

My experience will help, but I insist and maintain that art—true art, that is—cannot be handed out. Furthermore, art is never decoration or embellishment. Instead, it is a constant process of maturing (in the sense of not having arrived!). You see, John, when we have the opportunity of working out, you'll see that your way of thinking is definitely not the same as mine. Art, after all, is a means of acquiring "personal" liberty. Your way is not my way, nor mine yours. So whether or not we can get together, remember well that art "lives" where absolute freedom is. With all the training thrown to nowhere, with a mind (if there is such a verbal substance) perfectly unaware of its own working, with the "self" vanishing nowhere, the art of J.K.D. attains its perfection.

HOMEWORK AND TRAINING YIELD DISCOVERY

You must be willing to do your homework in this art. You cannot begin to see the truths to which Bruce Lee pointed if you refuse to open your eyes. We can't see through Bruce Lee's eyes, but we can behold the same vision of truth through our own eyes if we are willing to make the effort of adjusting our vision all on our own. All the "sign poles" in the world are useless if you refuse to take the journey. When you begin seeing for yourself, when you begin doing your homework, you will discover things about yourself: your abilities and limitations, new ways to improve the delivery and efficiency of your techniques, and which techniques are critical to your success and which are not.

Although Bruce Lee has been credited with saying, "Research your own experience; absorb what is useful, reject what is useless, and add what is essentially your own," there is no evidence of his authorship of that quote among his personal papers, within the audio record, or among the recollections of his wife and students. However, he did advise: "Shun what is trivial and discard what is ornamental."

This is far more in keeping with Lee's "sculptor" analogy, quoted in Chapter 8:

Contrary to other styles, being wise in jeet kune do does not mean adding more. It means to minimize. In other words, to hack away at the unessentials. It is not a "daily increase," but a "daily decrease."

To "discover" what is essentially your own would be more in keeping with Lee's stated beliefs than to "add what is essentially your own," especially since, as he said in the same context, "the way of jeet kune do is a shedding process."

In *Jeet Kune Do: Bruce Lee's Commentaries on the Martial Way*, Bruce Lee wrote:

To bring the mind into sharp focus and to make it alert so that it can immediately intuit truth, which is everywhere, the mind must be emancipated from old habits, prejudices, restrictive thought process, and even ordinary thought itself.

Here is a way (the core techniques and principles) that is truly no way (do not hold perpetually to the method; allow the art to simply become an extension of you, like the beating of your heart).

And train: learn mobility in order to use your tools effectively from many different angles, which will thereby open up many different attack avenues and options. As Lee, in the video *The Lost Interview*, said about the "it" that "hits all by itself," "You have to train so that when you want it, it's there!"

As noted in Chapter 2, in commenting to Daniel Lee on the philosophical statement that surrounds the symbol of jeet kune do, "Using no way as way; having no limitation as limitation," Lee explained:

That's the most important thing. Because when there is a "way," therein lies the limitation. And when there is a circumference, it traps. And if it traps, it rots. And if it rots, it is lifeless.

Daniel Lee told Bruce Lee that this was the high-water point of philosophy and martial art, and that once a student was exposed to jeet kune do, it would be impossible to then go back to a "way" of doing things. He used the example of kenpo karate, but one could include any other martial art style that limits its adherents to a set "way" of approaching the arena of unarmed combat. To this, Bruce replied:

Man is constantly growing. And when he is bound by a set pattern of ideas or "way" of doing things, that's when he stops growing.

The "way" of jeet kune do is to have no way, using total freedom of movement and expression in combat. This is why Lee's later writings about jeet kune do place more emphasis on honest self-expression than on simple combative "dos and don'ts." Witness the following from his article "Liberate Yourself from Classical Karate":

Knowledge in the martial arts ultimately means self-knowledge. At

this point you may ask, "How do I gain this knowledge?" That you will have to find out all by yourself. You must accept the fact that there is no help but self-help. For the same reason I cannot tell you how to "gain" freedom, since freedom exists within you, I cannot tell you how to "gain" self-knowledge. . . .

While I can tell you what not to do, I cannot tell you what you should do, since that would be confining you to a particular approach. Formulas can only inhibit freedom; externally dictated prescriptions only squelch creativity and assure mediocrity. Bear in mind that the freedom that accrues from self-knowledge cannot be acquired through strict adherence to a formula. We do not suddenly become free; we simply are free.

FULL CIRCLE

We have now come full circle, which is more or less the point of the Three Stages of Cultivation: to return to First Innocence—our stage of initial ignorance. We were ignorant, then we learned the technical aspects of martial art. But we had to shed all of this in order to scale higher up the mountain of self-discovery where true freedom resides.

Because of this reality, it is difficult, if not impossible, for anyone to "give" you jeet kune do, or even certification in jeet kune do, or, more important, understanding of the art. How can someone give you something that you've had within you all along? How can a teacher give you anything that the teacher does not possess (i.e., *your* understanding of truth)? Others can only share their experiences with you in the hope that doing so will serve as an impetus to you to initiate an internal search within yourself for the cause of your ignorance.

We are all ignorant in different areas, and most of us are ignorant of being ignorant, which is the biggest barrier of all and the first one that must fall before we can begin any meaningful process of self-discovery and actualization.

This fact also explains why Bruce Lee felt compelled to close his schools in jeet kune do and why he did away with any type of ranking or grading system after 1968—or at least by 1971, the date that he formally presented this new thesis on the art. Stating that you can get "official" JKD

only from one individual, regardless of who it is, is meaningless. You can get "it" only from yourself.

Bruce Lee's earlier doctrines and beliefs represent only what he himself said they represent: "a sign pole for a traveler" (i.e., a martial artist on the path to self-discovery) or, stated another way, "a finger pointing a way to the moon." And, as Lee cautioned in *Enter the Dragon*, "Don't concentrate on the finger—or take the finger to be the moon—or you will miss all that heavenly glory." The heavenly glory in this instance is your own satori, or personal enlightenment.

In fact, Lee said that the best fighter isn't one who has been schooled in any single method or "way," but rather one who has complete and unrestricted freedom of physical expression and whose mind-set is correct, not rutted or stuck or worried about anything, such as being hit or hurt. Lee once described for a Singapore newspaper, *New Nation*, the worst opponent one could encounter:

One whose aim has become an obsession. For instance, if a man has decided that he is going to bite off your nose no matter what happens to him in the process, the chances are he will succeed in doing it. He may be severely beaten up too, but that will not stop him from carrying out his objective. That is the real fighter.

An individual who has no hang-ups or concerns about what you are going to do to him, and is not worried about the personal consequences of his going after you, has, to cite Lee's phraseology from "Longstreet," learned "the art of dying." He represents the mind-set of the warrior, one who has cultivated a sense of detached awareness and who is firm in his resolve of what he is going to do (i.e., strike or kill his opponent) and is committed to its execution at the cost of all else.

This, then, is the evolutionary process that led to the development and transcendence of jeet kune do. The so-called political problems of the art have arisen only when individuals attempt to posit themselves as "sole authorities." Other problems arise when these same individuals extract one aspect of Lee's evolutionary process and hold it up as the complete and only truth.

This is the equivalent of holding up one frame of a motion picture film and proclaiming that it contains the whole essence of the movie.

Jeet kune do went from being an art predicated on a "way"—the way of the intercepting fist—to an art predicated on the way of "no way," with no limitations or restrictions and complete, unfettered freedom of combative expression. That is the truth that

Bruce Lee demonstrating to hapkido grandmaster Ji Han Jae the effectiveness of "having no limitation as limitation" during *The Game of Death*.

Bruce Lee drove himself to discover. That truth has endured and so too has his "sign pole" of techniques, principles, and philosophy—but extreme caution must be taken in order to see these for what they truly are and not what we would like them to be.

Bruce Lee, in his later writings, referred to jeet kune do as a mirror in which life is reflected and therefore an ongoing process of learning and development. Therefore, any attempt to frame it, or to put the circumference to the circle, is doomed to fail. That is why he told Daniel Lee, in their conversation cited earlier:

There is no such thing as maturity. Because when there is a maturity, there is a conclusion and a cessation.

That's the *end*. That's when the coffin is closed. You might be deteriorating physically in the long process of aging, but your personal process of daily discovery is ongoing. You continue to learn more and more about yourself every day.

Because of this evolution, no one piece of the puzzle, no one frame of the film, and no one individual representative—however knowledgeable—can be said to embody the totality of this art. For Bruce Lee: "There is no such thing as an effective segment of a totality." There is only undifferentiated awareness and spontaneous action in response to the trials and tribulations that life sets before us.

CHAPTER 11
BRUCE LEE
AND BUDDHISM

The closest thing I know to a planetary mythology is Buddhism, which sees all beings as Buddha beings. There is nothing to do. The task is only to know what is, and then to act in relation to the brotherhood of all these beings.
—Joseph Campbell

As in Chapter 9, we now turn to the personal notations and highlights Lee made in the books in his private library. In Chapter 9, these sources offered a unique and intimate glimpse into Lee's thoughts on the complexities of physics, especially as they apply to the marital arts; here they afford similar insights into the nuances and implications of Buddhism. Full citations can be found in the References.

Why Popju-sa? Why, of all the locales in the world, would Bruce Lee choose this remote Buddhist village in South Korea to film *The Game of Death*? One explanation is

While not religious, Bruce Lee was a highly spiritual man who held that "man is a being of self-made soul."

that the giant Buddha figure representing unification of Korea and the harmony of all living beings held particular appeal to Lee.

It may prove fruitful in broadening our understanding of Bruce Lee's journey to explore what influence, if any, the Buddha's life and teachings had on Lee's philosophy. Could Bruce Lee be said to be a Buddha in the purest sense of the term: one who has had his consciousness finely tuned or "awakened" to the facts of reality? Or, perhaps it would be more accurate to consider him a *bodhisattva*. Literally a bodhisattva is an "enlightened being" who, having attained the insight, compassion, and understanding that attends the realization of ultimate truth, then renounces *nirvana* in order to help all other beings toward their own personal enlightenment.

Before we can make such assessments, we need to learn a little something about the Buddha and his doctrine.

THE CORE PRINCIPLES

According to Buddhist tradition, in approximately 560 B.C., at the age of twenty-nine, a young prince named Siddhartha Gautama left his wife, child, and social caste and became a begging monk in a local ascetic order that traveled throughout Nepal.

It wasn't that he was immoral or was shirking his paternal, marital, or royal duties but that, through meditation, he suddenly had become profoundly affected by the fact that people were suffering in this world—right outside of his splendid palace—and that this suffering was a terrible thing that should be stopped, if at all possible. Gautama then set out to learn all that he could about human suffering and to explore all of the possibilities open to a human being's highest faculty—the mind—in attempting to eradicate it.

After some six years, Gautama experienced *bodhi* (the "awakening" or "enlightenment") regarding the subject of suffering and, as a result, became the Buddha. The term *Buddha* which derives from the Sanskrit and is akin to *bodhi*, applies to anyone who experiences such an awakening or enlightenment. A Buddha is an individual who has awakened from the dream of life as we ordinarily take it to be, who has seen through the illusory image of self, or ego, to discover who he truly is (Watts 1996).

This "awakening" delivered to the Buddha a new state of mind or, more accurately, new state of consciousness. It proved to be a way of liberation from the ordinary way in which people typically view themselves and the world. The Buddha then set down his insights much as a physician may set down a prescription: by ascertaining first what the particular ailment is that is afflicting the patient, then its cause, its cure, and the prescription necessary to realize its cure. He called this four-tiered observation the Four Noble Truths, which have since become the cornerstone of all Buddhist belief.

THE FOUR NOBLE TRUTHS

1. The world (life) is suffering.

The Sanskrit word is *duhkha*, which is most commonly rendered into English as "suffering." This is comparable to the initial stage in which the disease being treated is identified by the physician. Suffering would include moral as well as physical suffering and, perhaps more accurately, the frustration that attends the longing for something unattainable, the anguish of thwarted desires. According to the Buddha, suffering is "being born, aging, falling sick, being tied to what one does not love, being separated from what one does love, and not realizing one's desire."

2. Suffering is caused by desire.

This truth corresponds to the identification of the disease. The Sanskrit word for this is *trishna*, which translates into English as "the futile desire to attempt to clutch at or grasp hold of something that is impermanent." It is an attempt to make permanent that which is not, such as trying to catch a river in a bucket; what you end up with is simply a pail of water, not the river.

3. It is possible not to suffer.

The third noble truth corresponds to the physician's prognosis. What mankind suffers from is curable, and the cure is called *nirvana* (from the Sanskrit, meaning "to blow out," as in heaving a sigh of relief). The message here is that it is possible to attain a sense of release from the desire to be bound up in the ways of the ego or the world. If, upon learning that having air is a good thing, you therefore decide to hold your breath in an attempt to "hold on to" your air, the only thing you succeed in doing is passing out. In much the same way, the third noble truth responds that letting go, detachment, or "emptiness" is not only all right but also absolutely essential to effecting the cure. One must be empty in order to become fulfilled.

4. There is a way to prevent suffering.

The fourth noble truth is the Buddha's "prescription" to end suffering, which is called in Sanskrit *marga*. *Marga* means the path that leads to awakening, and according to the Buddha, it consists of eight steps. It expresses the "middle way," which is often misinterpreted as a form of compromise but is in reality an enlightened position of centeredness or "balance" between all extreme points of view. It is the avoidance of extremes in life. The Buddha found that both hedonism (or extreme indulgence of the sensual pleasures such as eating and sex) and self-mortification or strict asceticism (such as long periods of fasting, or lying on beds of nails) were unnecessary to enlightenment. What was necessary was neither extreme but a more moderate approach to our appetites and our denials.

THE EIGHTFOLD PATH

According to the Buddha, the eightfold path consists of:

1. Right understanding
2. Right thought (or resolution)
3. Right speech
4. Right action
5. Right livelihood
6. Right effort
7. Right mindfulness
8. Right concentration

The term *right* in this context means total, or nonpartialized.

Initially, the Buddha was convinced that his insights could not be passed on and that, even if they could, the vast majority of people, assuming they accepted them at all, would be doing so in an experiential vacuum, not really understanding the nobleness behind the truth. Nevertheless, he decided that if even some individuals could be influenced to make the effort to become enlightened or to understand his doctrine, it would be worth his labors in attempting to communicate it. So, rather than keeping his newfound enlightenment and prescription for total peace of mind to himself, the Buddha elected to encourage his fellow men to walk the path of truth (dharma), or eightfold path, so that they, too, might be relieved of the yoke of their emotional and spiritual burdens, thus becoming Buddhas themselves.

The Buddha's decision to help his fellow man led him to become a bodhisattva. He began his ministry at Sarnath, near Varanasi, and continued for the remaining forty-five years of his life to try to enlighten his fellow men to "wake up." He died at the age of eighty in the forest of Uparvarta near Kusinagara.

ZEN BUDDHISM

Buddha's disciples would repeat his teachings orally, handing them down for a period exceeding 100 years. In time, two main branches of Buddhism arose: the Hinayana (little vehicle) and the Mahayana (great vehicle), with the former emphasizing the original, this-worldly teachings of the Buddha, and the latter applying the fundamental principles to areas such as metaphysics (whereas the Buddha himself had formerly kept a "noble silence" on such topics).

In time (thirteen centuries ago), a branch of Buddhism came into being in China as the result of the commingling of Mahayana Buddhism and Taoism. This branch of Buddhism was originally called *Ch'an* by its Chinese progenitors and later *Zen* by its Japanese inheritors.

ENTER BRUCE LEE

It was Zen Buddhism that held Bruce Lee's interest (although he had more than 130 titles in his personal library dealing with all aspects of Buddhist history, practice, and philosophy). To understand what aspects of Zen attracted and influenced Bruce Lee, it behooves us to first examine the history of this school.

History reveals that the Zen school of Buddhism came into being largely due to the fact that contemporary Buddhism 1,300 years ago had become too scholarly and largely a matter of scriptural mastery, with little practical significance to the vast majority of people seeking enlightenment.

Members of the Zen sect maintained that they were more closely following the original—if less ethereal—form of Buddhism practiced by the Buddha himself, and they reemphasized the practice of meditation (which is roughly the meaning of *Ch'an* and *Zen*) as the indispensable heart of the Buddha's way. After all, they reasoned, it was through seated meditation under the bodhi tree that the Buddha was able to obtain his enlightenment about the human condition.

According to the doctrine of the Zen school (which is actually a doctrine of no doctrine), becoming a Buddha is not a very exclusive club, as every human being has a "Buddha-nature." The Zen Buddhists advocate *za-zen* (seated meditation) as one of the more effective means of actualizing our inalienable Buddha-nature, although not a "core essential" to enlightenment, and hold that the insight *za-zen* fosters is capable of bestowing upon its practitioner inner liberation or true freedom.

While Zen claims to be a teaching "outside the scriptures," its philosophical roots lie in the Mahayana precepts of "emptiness" and scriptures such as the Heart and Diamond Sutras. The following description of Zen Buddhism is attributed to Bodhidharma (circa A.D. 500), the sage reputed to have brought the Zen mind from India to China and the monk whom legend also credits as the founder of the branch of gung fu taught in China's renowned Shaolin Temple:

A special tradition outside the scriptures;
No dependence upon words and letters;
Direct pointing at the mind;
Seeing into one's own nature, and the attainment of Buddhahood.

How Bruce Lee came to embrace Zen, or at least be profoundly influenced by its precepts, is not altogether clear, but there is ample evidence that the seeds of receptivity were sown during his formative years. Lee's father was a Buddhist, which means that the son would have received some exposure to the tenets of this belief system. However, both his mother and his upbringing were Catholic (it was well known that the Catholic schools in Hong Kong at the time had the highest standards of education), which made for an interesting balance between Eastern and Western spiritual traditions in the young Bruce Lee's life.

The fact that Bruce Lee embraced certain Buddhist principles and insights while rejecting the orthodoxy and doctrines of its clergy or priesthood, and saw not diversity but common ground among all of the great spiritual traditions of the world, no doubt availed him of a deeper insight that in time allowed him to formulate his theorem of "root" as it applied to the understanding of martial art:

I hope martial artists are more interested in the root of martial art and not the different decorative branches, flowers, or leaves. It is futile to argue as to which single leaf, which design of branch, or which attractive flower you like; when you understand the root, you understand all of its blossoming.

Lee posed for pictures inside a Buddhist temple in Hong Kong, and certainly the insights of the Buddha as revealed through the written word stayed with him during his early years in America and, indeed, throughout his life. He came in time to read voraciously on the subject of Buddhism and to see that the "root" truth of martial art was also the "root" truth of spiritual insight as evinced through Zen Buddhism. According to his essay "The Ultimate Source of Jeet Kune Do":

L earning of the techniques [in jeet kune do] corresponds to an intellectual appreciation in Zen of its philosophy, and in both Zen and jeet kune do a proficiency in this does not cover the whole ground of the discipline. Both require us to come to the attainment of ultimate reality, which is the emptiness or the absolute. The latter transcends all modes of relativity. In jeet kune do, all the technique is to be forgotten and the unconscious is to be left alone to handle the situation, when the technique will assume its wonders automatically or spontaneously—to float in totality; to have no technique is to have all technique.

In Lee's private writings and public teachings, many attitudes of the Buddha and Lee are found to be similar, if not exact fits. For example, both emphasize in their teachings the higher aspect of spiritual realization. In fact, according to Lee, this was precisely the aim of jeet kune do, which he defined as being "ultimately, not a matter of technology, but of spiritual insight and training."

Bruce Lee was using martial art as a bridge, or "vehicle" (a popular Buddhist metaphor), to allow him to come to a fuller awareness and understanding of spiritual matters. The fertile garden of his mind—a mind that cultivated the future blossoming of JKD—was tilled and nourished by the spiritual teachings of the Buddha and Lao-tzu, who some historians claim was the Buddha (Grigg 1994). He wrote to a friend in Hong Kong:

All in all, the goal of my planning and doing is to find the true meaning in life—peace of mind. . . . In order to achieve this peace of mind, the teaching of detachment of Taoism and Zen proved to be valuable.

It was the spiritual aspects (i.e., soulful, universal reality) that most interested him. In the same letter Lee quoted electrical genius Charles P. Steinmetz:

When man comes to a conscious, vital realization of those great spiritual forces within himself and begins to use those forces in science, in business, and in life, his progress in the future will be unparalleled.

Although he never felt the necessity of sitting under a bodhi tree, Bruce Lee nevertheless became "awakened" through a long process of self-questioning and self-exami-nation, once telling Hong Kong broadcaster Ted Thomas: "My life [is] a life of self-examination, self-peeling bit by bit, day by day."

This process of self-questioning allows us to, in Lee's opinion:

Scratch away all the dirt our being has accumulated and reveal reality in its is-ness, or in its suchness, or in its nakedness, which corresponds to the Buddhist concept of emptiness.

A "SIGN POLE" FOR A TRAVELER

Like the Buddha, Bruce Lee recognized that the truths that his profound introspection had revealed to him about his true self, life, and reality could not simply be "given" to another human being. All that he could do as a teacher was point out the means that had served to bring about his own awakening; it would be up to each individual to experiment with these means to see if they would yield similar spiritual insights. As to this, the Buddha had said:

One is one's own refuge. Who else could be the refuge?

He admonished his disciples to be a refuge unto themselves and never to seek refuge in or help from anybody else. He taught, encouraged, and stimulated each person to develop and to work out his or her own emancipation, believing that each individual man and woman has the power to liberate himself or herself from all bondage through personal effort and intelligence. The Buddha pronounced:

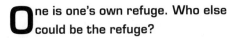

You should do your work, for the Tathagatas ("ones who have come to truth") only teach the way.

In fact, according to Dr. Walpola Rahula, a Buddhist monk and scholar who wrote *What the Buddha Taught*:

If the Buddha is to be called a "savior" at all, it is only in the sense that he discovered and showed the path to liberation, Nirvana. But we must tread the path ourselves.

This point was underscored by commentator Bill Moyers in an interview with Joseph Campbell published in *The Power of Myth*:

Like all heroes, the Buddha doesn't show you the truth itself; he shows you the way to truth.

To which Campbell responded:

But it's got to be *your* way, not his. The Buddha can't tell you exactly how to get rid of your particular fears, for example. Different teachers may suggest exercises, but they may not be the ones to work for you. All a teacher can do is suggest. He is like a lighthouse that says, "There are rocks over here; steer clear. There is a channel, however, out there."

The Buddha's perspective parallels Bruce Lee's own thoughts on the matter, which are beautifully reflected in writings such as the following from *The Silent Flute*:

Each man must seek out realization himself. No master can give it to him.

And this one from "Zen," Lee's notes published in *Commentaries on the Martial Way*:

There is no fixed teaching. All I can provide is an appropriate medicine for a particular ailment.

And again in this quote from the typed version of the essay "Jeet Kune Do: Toward Personal Liberation":

A teacher, a good teacher that is, functions as a pointer to truth, but not a giver of truth.

The problem for many martial artists is that they seek to derive their sense of security and fulfillment from external sources, such as their teachers, which draws them in the opposite direction from where they need to seek—internally. According to Bruce Lee:

The secondhand artist, in blindly following the *sensei* or *sifu*, accepts his pattern—and as a result, his action and, above all, his thinking become mechanical, his responses automatic, according to the pattern—and thereby ceases to expand or to grow. He is a mechanical robot, a product of thou-

sands of years of propaganda and conditioning. One must be uninfluenced and die to one's conditioning in order to be aware of the totally fresh, totally new. Because reality changes every moment, even as I say it.

During the time that he was most active as a teacher, Lee constantly strove to have his students look beyond the simply physical. As he wrote in a paper titled "Economical Expressing—a Way of Liberation," he sought "ways to raise the pupils' minds above duality, to the absolute awareness which transcends it."

As indicated in his writings, he realized that the most enlightened form of teaching is to serve not as a "giver of truth" but rather as "a pointer toward truth," to point one in the direction of one's own process of discovering truth. Lee believed that the road to truth, and from that truth to satori, had no particular path—out of necessity. People, spiritually speaking, as Lee noted earlier, are different, with different wants, desires, and aspirations. And while we all share a common biological root, the individual expression of our personalities and true selves is tremendously diverse.

After Bruce Lee had conceived of the vision of totality that he called jeet kune do, he came to understand that the name of the art was not the important part of it. In fact, a name, being a word or a symbol, is by definition a limiting factor, restricting and imprisoning the essence of what it seeks to represent. To Lee, whether it came from *za-zen*, Buddhist meditation, Taoist detachment, modern dance, or a JKD side kick, the important thing was how the individual used this "vehicle" to understand himself.

As we saw earlier, Lee even made use of the Buddhist metaphor of the raft to better explain the liberating and spiritually rewarding aspect of jeet kune do:

Remember too that JKD is just a name used, a vehicle to carry you over obstacles, like a boat used to get one across a river. Once across, it is to be discarded, not carried on one's back.

The metaphor of the "boat used to get one across a river" is one of the earliest teachings of the Buddha with regard to liberation.

Bruce Lee held that one's personal experience is the core of jeet kune do. In "Economical Expressing—a Way of Liberation," he wrote:

Jeet kune do's first concern is about its experience, and not its modes of expression.

He cautioned his students not to attach too much importance to the vehicle that provided the means to the experience, nor, particularly, to the name of the vehicle of deliverance. He even mentioned that he wished he had never coined a name for his art, since, in so doing, he had set up a limitation of sorts. Similarly, in Buddhism, "sectarian labels are a hindrance to the independent understanding of Truth, and they produce harmful prejudices in men's minds" (Rahula 1959).

The cynics among us may be tempted to say, "Oh, Bruce Lee simply copied the Buddha's doctrines!" Not so fast. As each of us is a product of our conditioning (i.e., the forces that work to shape our thought processes), very few thoughts that we have are unique or exclusive, and fewer still are profound. Bruce Lee, however, had both unique and profound thoughts through the genius of being able to recognize causal connections between all effective patterns of motion for human beings, from dance to combat, and from the physical sciences of motion to the zenith of spiritual insight.

Lee studied the science of motion and discovered spiritual truths that are eternal and, therefore, have been in existence since long before any of us came into being. All great spiritual leaders have had such insights. They didn't invent them; they simply experienced them and then chose to share their experiences with all who had ears to listen. According to Walpola Rahula:

To the seeker after truth it is immaterial from where an idea comes. The source and development of an idea is a matter for the academic. In fact, in order to understand Truth, it is not necessary even to know whether the teaching comes from the Buddha, or

**from anyone else. What is essential is
seeing the thing, understanding it.**

Mark Watts, the son of the late philosopher Alan Watts, the renowned popularizer of Buddhism, Zen, and Taoist philosophy, recently made this point about Bruce Lee's teachings in the book *The Warrior Within*:

One will find essential ideas once expressed by Alan Watts, Krishnamurti, both Suzukis, Joseph Campbell, and many others—and long before by Lao-tzu, Chuang-tzu, Buddha, and Shankara. Although many of these ideas are not new, their expression embodies a living art that points to a way of liberation my father once described as the "religion of no religion."

In the final analysis, it doesn't matter whether you extinguish egoism through meditation or a side kick. The jar that contains the medicine for your suffering is not as important as the medicine itself. The spiritual truths of which both the Buddha and Bruce Lee were aware are eternal and profound, such as the Buddha's realization that "nothing is stable forever" (Carriere 1994).

Or, as Bruce Lee said in "The Tao of Gung Fu":

Nothing is so permanent as never to change.

Another truth acknowledged through the teachings of both Buddhism and Bruce Lee is the universal brotherhood of all mankind. For example, Tenzin Gyatso, the fourteenth Dalai Lama, the spiritual figurehead of Tibetan Buddhism, stated, "Although the peoples and nations of the world are so different, they are all made up of human beings" (Ellinger 1996).

For his part, Bruce Lee commented to Canadian journalist Pierre Berton:

You know how I like to think of myself? As a human being. I don't want to sound like "As Confucius say," but under the sky, under the heavens, there is but one family. It just so happens that people are different.

Further, both great teachers stressed the absolute necessity of never taking enlightenment on faith—but rather, only on one's own personal experience. The Buddha, as quoted by the Dalai Lama in Jean-Claude Carrier's *Violence and Compassion*, recommended:

As you test gold by rubbing it and cutting it and melting it, so judge my words. If you accept them, don't let that be out of mere respect.

Bruce Lee's beliefs parallel this notion perfectly:

Truth is never a set idea and definitely not a conclusion. Styles and

methods are conclusions, but, like our life, the truth of martial art is a process. All I can offer is an experience but never a conclusion, so even what I have said needs to be thoroughly examined by you.

French filmmaker and longtime student of Buddhism Jean-Claude Carrier, author of *Violence and Compassion*, pointed out:

As long as the internal awakening, the fruit of a strictly personal experience, has not been granted us, we will be living in ignorance. It is our nature and our prison, and everything must be done to destroy it.

That statement is simply a more dramatic expression of Bruce Lee's belief that each individual must "seek out realization himself. No master can give it to him" (Lee circa 1970).

Both Bruce Lee and the Buddha also emphasized the same method or manner of arriving at deeper spiritual insights: the removal of ego, or self-image, which obstructs the path to our true, universal self. According to Alan Watts in his landmark book *The Way of Zen*:

All ideas of self-improvement and of becoming or getting something in the future relate solely to our abstract image of ourselves. To follow them is to give ever more reality to that image. On the other hand, our true, nonconceptual self is already the Buddha, and needs no improvement.

Lee, of course, wrote volumes on this subject, in his notes titled "Buddhism's Eightfold Path":

The one-ness of all life is a truth that can be fully realized only when false notions of a separate self—whose des-tiny can be considered apart from the WHOLE—are forever annihilated. . . . Jeet kune do is fitting in with one's opponent, but there is no path, no self, and no goal.

And in "Zen," from *Commentaries on the Martial Way*:

The consciousness of the self is the greatest hindrance to the proper execution of all physical action.

Additionally, both the Buddha and Bruce Lee held that enlightenment further consists of realizing the interrelatedness of all things. According to Alan Watts in "The Wisdom of the Mountain" from *Buddhism: The Religion of No-Religion*:

Buddhist enlightenment consists simply in knowing the secret of the unity of opposites—the unity of the inner and outer worlds—and in understanding that secret as an adult rather than as a child. It means, really, to finally grow up.

Bruce Lee's thoughts in this regard are substantially similar as is reflected in this quote from his essay "Living: The Oneness of Things":

The world is seen as an inseparable, interrelated field, no part of which can actually be separated from the other. That is, there would be no bright stars without dim stars, and, without the surrounding darkness, no stars at all. Oppositions have become mutually dependent instead of mutually exclusive, and there is no longer any conflict between the individual man and nature.

This is exactly in keeping with the Buddhist perspective. According to the Dalai Lama:

The notion of interdependence . . . has been a part of Buddhist thought from time immemorial. . . . Nothing exists separately. On the contrary, everything is connected to everything else. . . . No species, not even the human species, can place itself outside the world, outside the wheel of the universe. We are one of the cogs in that wheel.

And, as the Buddha's teachings emphasize "the middle way," as Herbert Ellinger describes in his book *Buddhism*:

Time and again in his teaching he emphasizes the "middle way" which cannot be either turning away or the unconditional and exclusive worship of the earthly (samsara).

. . . so, too, did Bruce Lee in "Our Marriage Brought Us a Miracle of Love" from *TV and Movie Screen* magazine:

O nly sober moderation lasts, and that persists through all time. Only the midpart of anything is preserved because the pendulum of life must have balance, and the midpart is the balance.

And again in his interview with Pierre Berton:

H ere is natural instinct, and here is control. You are to combine the two in harmony. If you have one to the

Bruce Lee viewed martial art as a vehicle to carry one from the ground of ignorance to the heights of transcendence.

extreme, you'll be very unscientific, and if you have the other to the extreme, you become all of a sudden a mechanical man, no longer a human being. So, it is a successful combination of both. Therefore, it is not pure naturalness or pure unnaturalness. The ideal is unnatural naturalness or natural unnaturalness.

This interrelatedness takes place in what the Buddhist scholars call the "void." Bruce

Lee offered this description in "Buddhism's Eightfold Path" in 1970:

Voidness is that which stands right in the middle between this and that. The void is all-inclusive; having no opposite, there is nothing which it excludes or opposes. It is living void, because all forms come out of it, and whoever realizes the void is filled with life and power and the love of all beings.

And then there are the more obvious indications of Lee's research into the teachings of the Buddha. Here is another excerpt from "Buddhism's Eightfold Path":

The eight requirements that will eliminate suffering by correcting false values and giving true knowledge of life's meaning have been summed up as follows:

1. First, you must see clearly what is wrong.

2. **Next, decide to be cured.**
3. **You must act.**
4. **Speak so as to aim at being cured.**
5. **Your livelihood must not conflict with your therapy.**
6. **The therapy must go forward at the "staying speed," the critical velocity that can be sustained.**
7. **You must think and feel about it incessantly.**
8. **Learn how to contemplate with the deep mind.**

In his essay titled "Zen" Lee quoted Master Lin-Chi of the T'ang Dynasty:

In Buddhism there is no place for using effort. "Just be ordinary and nothing special. Eat your food, move your bowels, pass water, and when you're tired, go and lie down. The ignorant will laugh at me, but the wise will understand."

BUDDHA OR BODHISATTVA?

Certainly the case can be made for Bruce Lee having "awakened" to his own Buddha-nature and, perforce, having become enlightened, or a Buddha. But then there are his writings that indicate that he viewed himself more as a "sign pole for a traveler," as a teacher (through his writings, films, and martial arts classes) not only of martial art but of the art of life as well. In a note titled "What Is an Actor" he wrote:

Many of you know that I am a martial artist by choice, an actor by profession and, toward daily actualizing my potentiality through soulful discoveries and daily exercising (in my case) to become also an artist of life.

In this respect, it may be said that Bruce Lee was a bodhisattva of sorts; that is, a being who has had his eyes opened to reality but, rather than dwell eternally in such a state (i.e., to remain a Buddha), he opts to renounce any exalted spiritual position in order to help his fellow men seek out enlightenment.

Consider this passage from "The Ultimate Source of Jeet Kune Do":

Leave sagehood behind and enter once more into ordinary humanity. After coming to understand the other side, come back and live on this side. After the cultivation of noncultivation, one's thoughts continue to be detached from phenomenal things and one still remains amid the phenomenal, yet devoid of the phenomenal.

And then there is the artwork and statuary that decorated the home of this learned man and his family: little Buddha statues, incense as found in Buddhist temples, and even a large statue of the Buddhist bodhisattva Avalokiteshvara, known in China as Kwan-yin, the god (India) or goddess (China) of compassion and/or mercy, which Bruce Lee had placed in the living room of his Hong Kong home in Kowloon Tong (he even had a bust of Kwan-yin in his garden).

Lee looked to Kwan-yin as representing the ideal mind-set for the martial artist and, in fact, cited a passage written by Daisetz Suzuki, the great Zen scholar, in Lee's introduction to *The Silent Flute*:

Kwan-yin, the Goddess of Mercy, is sometimes represented with up to 1,000 arms, each holding a different instrument. If her mind stops with the use, for instance, of a spear, all the other arms (999) will be of no use whatsoever. It is only because of her mind not stopping with the use of one arm, but moving from one instrument to another, that all her arms prove useful with the utmost degree of efficiency. Thus the figure is meant to demonstrate that when the ultimate truth is realized, even as many as 1,000 arms on one body may each be serviceable in one way or another.

In concluding his introduction, Lee points out:

True mastery transcends any particular art. It stems from mastery of oneself—the ability, developed through self-discipline, to be calm, fully aware, and completely in tune with oneself and the surroundings. Then, and only then, can a person know himself.

When the foregoing insights are compared with Buddhist precepts, not to mention the cultivated insights of no-mindedness, detachment, and nonaction, the line separating the teachings of these two great teachers becomes less distinct.

Additional parallels are found in Bruce Lee's carefully cultivated views on the inter-relatedness of being and beings (that is, human beings and their relationship with one another and with the universe that sustains them), on transcendence and self-knowledge, and in Lee's love of water as educator, which parallels the learning process of the young Siddhartha Gautama (the Buddha) as related by Hermann Hesse, one of Bruce's favorite writers, in the novel *Sid-*

dhartha, in which the protagonist receives his "satori" after watching a river.

Looked at in this light, it could be argued convincingly that Bruce Lee was not only one of the greatest martial artists of all time but also, given the scope, breadth, depth, and enduring impact of his words on such matters, one of history's greatest spiritual teachers—or bodhisattvas.

And finally, the words of Stirling Silliphant:

Bruce's philosophy seemed always to be going back to Zen origins, where contradictory advice states the simplest of all truths. Bruce's lessons were lessons without being lessons; he was not a teacher, yet he was the greatest teacher I've ever known (Tugend 1974).

CHAPTER 12
BRUCE LEE'S TAO OF PHILOSOPHY

Philosophy will tell you what man lives for.   **—Bruce Lee**

Bruce Lee was well-versed in both the Eastern and Western philosophic traditions, viewing himself as a "citizen of the world."

As we have seen from other chapters in this book, Lee had a lifelong interest in the philosophies of Eastern and Western cultures. Although many of today's readers have been exposed to the basic tenets of Eastern philosophies, concepts such as *chi*, *Tao*, and *yin* and *yang* were relatively unknown in the West during Lee's lifetime. Even today, Lee's thoughts on the fundamentals of Eastern philosophy warrant close examination and shed light on Lee's own life and work. In this chapter, we turn our attention to Lee's thoughts on Eastern metaphysical traditions, as evidenced by his own words and writings. As we will see, his insights are as informative today as they were a generation ago.

EMPTYING THE CUP

In order to understand and experience an Eastern viewpoint, you must first empty your mind of all of the preconceived Western opinions and beliefs that you may have accumulated regarding nature, reality, and existence. As Bruce Lee pointed out in his 1971 essay "Jeet Kune Do: Toward Personal Liberation," you cannot force new knowledge into a brain that is already full any more than a full cup can receive new tea:

A learned man once went to a Zen master to inquire about Zen. As the Zen master talked, the learned man would frequently interrupt him with remarks like, "Oh yes, we have that, too," etc. Finally the Zen master stopped talking and began to serve tea to the learned man; however, he kept on pouring until the teacup overflowed. "Enough, no more can go into the cup!"

the learned man interrupted. "Indeed, I see," answered the Zen master. "But if you do not first empty your cup, then how can you taste my cup of tea?"

The need for an empty cup—or empty mind—is the first requirement in coming to understand Bruce Lee's metaphysics. The mind must be pure; that is to say, our thoughts must be unobstructed by the intrusion of an existing value system or filter of judgment.

This emancipation or freeing of the mind, emptying it of prior knowledge, was referred to by Bruce Lee as *wu-hsin* or no-mindedness. It is a frame of mind that Lee wrote a great deal about, particularly in the early 1960s. His most in-depth dissertation on the subject is found within the pages of his essay "The Tao of Gung Fu," in which he wrote the following:

The phenomenon of Wu-hsin or "No-mindedness" is not a blank mind that shuts out all thoughts and emotions; nor is it simply calmness and quietness of mind. Although quietude and calmness are necessary, it is the "nongraspingness" of thoughts that mainly constitutes the principle of no-mind. A . . . man employs his mind as a mirror—it grasps nothing and refuses nothing; it receives but does not keep. As Alan Watts puts it, the no-mindedness is "a state of wholeness in which the mind functions freely and easily, without the sensation of a second mind or ego standing over it with a club."

What he [Watts] means is that we should let the mind think what it likes without interference by the separate thinker or ego within oneself. So long as it [the mind] thinks what it wants, there is absolutely no effort in letting it go; and the disappearance of the effort to let go is precisely the disappearance of the separate thinker. There is nothing to try to do, for whatever comes up moment by moment is accepted, including nonacceptance. No-mindedness is not an absence of emotion or feeling, but rather [a state in which] feeling is not sticky or blocked. It is a mind immune to emotional influences.

Like [a] river, everything is flowing on ceaselessly. [To practice] no-mindedness is to employ the whole mind [in the same way that] we use the eyes when we rest them upon various objects but make no special effort to take anything in. Chuang Tzu, the disciple of Lao-Tzu, stated:

The baby looks at things all day without blinking, because his eyes are not focused on any particular object. He goes without knowing where he is going, and stops without knowing what he is doing. He merges himself with the surroundings and moves along with it. These are the principles of mental hygiene.

Therefore, concentration . . . does not have the usual sense of restricting the attention to a single sense [or] object but is simply a quiet awareness of whatever happens to be here and now. Such concentration can be illustrated by the audience at a football game; instead of a concentrated attention on the player who has the ball, the audience has an awareness of the whole football field. . . .

This is possible only when the mind moves from one object to another without being "stopped" or arrested by anything. . . . [The] mind is present everywhere because it is nowhere attached to any particular object. And it can remain present because, even when related to this or that object, it does not cling to it. The flow of thought is like water filling a pond, which is always ready to flow off again. It can work its inexhaustible power because it is free, and be open to everything because it is empty.

This can be compared with what Chang Chen Chi called "serene reflection." He wrote:

> Serene *means tranquility of no thought, and* reflection *means vivid and clear awareness. Therefore,* serene reflection *is clear awareness of no-thought.*

NO-MINDEDNESS AND CHOICELESS AWARENESS

From this mindset of no-mindedness we are able to look out upon the world and witness it with a sense of unprejudiced detachment, a detached or "choiceless awareness" of which Lee wrote:

Choiceless awareness [means that you] do not condemn, do not justify. Just watch choicelessly and in the watching lies the wonder. It is not an ideal, an end to be desired. The watching is a state of being already, not a state of becoming.

Lee concluded that this direct and untainted awareness of "what is" (i.e., reality) was the starting point of metaphysics, since such perception contains tangible, existential reality. In a 1971 essay titled "Additional Notes on Jeet Kune Do," Lee wrote:

The direct awareness [is that] in which is formed the "truth that makes us free"—not the truth as an object of knowledge only, but the truth lived and experienced in concrete and existential awareness.

___

As our survival depends on our ability to process facts or truths, the closer our metaphysics is to truth, the better will be our chances of coping successfully in this world. To Lee, metaphysics was all about truth—ultimate reality or "ultimate truth"—whether of martial art or of the way of nature. As a result, he employed the word *Tao* as a synonym for the ultimate truth of an object, be it his martial art of jeet kune do or the ultimate reality underlying the way of nature. In "The Tao of Gung Fu," circa 1963, Bruce Lee makes it clear that only the broadest definition of Tao is adequate:

The word *Tao* has no exact equivalent in the English language. To render it into "Way," "Principle," or "Law" is to give it a too narrow interpretation. . . . Although no one word can substitute its meaning, I have used the word "Truth" for it.

___

YIN-YANG

The energy through which the Tao expresses itself is symbolized in yin and yang, a pair of mutually complementary forces that are at work in and behind all phenomena. The famous yin-yang symbol (also known as the tai chi symbol or Grand Terminus symbol) was first drafted more than three thousand years ago by Chou Chun-I (who also penned the Yung Shu, which explained the theory of yin-yang). In "The Tao of Gung Fu," Lee provides a wonderful description of the nature and significance of the yin-yang symbol:

The *yang* (whiteness) principle represents positiveness, firmness, masculinity, substantiality, brightness, day, heat, etc. The *yin* (blackness) principle is the opposite. It represents negativeness, softness, femininity, insubstantiality, darkness, night, coldness, and so forth.

The basic theory in tai chi is that nothing is so permanent as never to change. In other words, when activity (yang) reaches the extreme point, it becomes inactivity, and inactivity forms yin. Extreme inactivity will, in the same way, return to become activity, which is yang. Activity, then, is the cause of inactivity, and vice versa. This system of complementary increasing and decreasing of the principle [of yin-yang] is continuous. From this one can see that the two forces (yin and yang), although they appear to conflict, are mutually interdependent; instead of opposition, there is a quietude, a shrinking from action, an appearance of inability to do so.

The common mistake of the Western world is to identify these two forces as dualistic; that is, yang being the opposite of yin and vice versa. At best, [Westerners] see the two forces as cause and effect, but never paired like sound and echo, or light and shadow. As long as this "oneness" is viewed as two separate forces, realization of the Tao . . . cannot be achieved. In reality, things are whole and cannot be separated into two parts. When I say, "The heat makes me perspire," the heat and perspiring are just one process and the one could not exist but for the other. Things do have their complements, and complementary things coexist; instead of [being] mutually exclusive, they are mutually dependent and are a function each of the other.

In the yin-yang symbol there is a white spot on the black part and a black spot on the white one. This is to illustrate the balance in life, for nothing can survive long going to either extreme, be it pure yin (passiveness) or pure yang (activeness). Notice the stiffest tree is most easily cracked, while the bamboo or willow survives by bending with the wind. Extreme heat kills and so does extreme cold; no violent extremes can endure [for] long. Therefore, positiveness (yang) should be concealed in negativeness (yin) and vice versa.

In martial art parlance, this is the foundation of Lee's maxim that the martial artist who is in tune with the Tao is "soft, yet not yielding; firm, yet not hard." In other words, he embodies the totality of yin-yang, and not simply one aspect (i.e., hard or soft) of its totality. From Bruce Lee's perspective, Tao, or truth, reveals that there exists no such thing as separation. And, moreover, no distinction can be made between the observer and the observed—each is but one half of the other, and the whole is formed only when they are joined. The world that is observed and the person observing it are engaged in what Lee calls in his essay "Living: The Oneness of Things" an "active correlation." The person is that entity that sees the world, and the world is that which is seen or perceived by the entity.

LIVING: THE ONENESS OF THINGS

In Western philosophy, the prevailing metaphysical viewpoint is predicated on pluralism—the notion that the world contains many kinds of existents, which in their uniqueness cannot be reduced to just one. Renowned philosophers Bertrand Russell (1872–1970) and Ludwig Wittgenstein (1889–1951) both offered canonical works on this viewpoint, although both men later abandoned it. Apart from pluralism, the West also advanced the philosophical position of dualism, asserting that substances are either mental or material, with neither being

reducible to the other. The outstanding exponent of the dualistic position was René Descartes (1596–1650).

Bruce Lee, however, recognized that to be aware necessarily implies the existence of awareness, that is, the existence of a state of consciousness, or thought. In turn, this implies the existence of the remaining three axiomatic primaries: Existence, Interdependence, and Identity. Lee confronts the Western metaphysical dualism of René Descartes head-on in his brilliant essay "Living: The Oneness of Things," reprinted here in its entirety:

Many philosophers are among those who say one thing and do another, and the philosophy that a man professes is often quite other than the one he lives by. Philosophy is in danger of becoming more and more only something professed.

Philosophy [to such individuals] is not "living" but an activity concerning theoretic knowledge; most philosophers are not going to live things, but simply to theorize about them, to contemplate them. And to contemplate a thing implies maintaining oneself out-side it, resolved to keep a distance between it and ourselves.

In life, we accept naturally the full reality of what we see and feel in general with no shadow of a doubt. [Western philosophy], however, does not accept what life believes and strives to convert reality into a problem. Like asking such questions as: "Is this chair that I see in front of me really there?" "Can it exist by itself?" Thus, rather than making life easy for living by living in accord with life, philosophy complicates it by replacing the world's tranquility with the restlessness of problems. It is [like] asking a normal person how he actually breathes! That will immediately choke the breath out of him when he consciously describes the process. Why try to arrest and interrupt the flow of life? Why create such fuss? A person simply breathes.

The Western approach to reality is mostly through theory, and theory begins by denying reality—to talk about reality, to go around reality, to catch anything that attracts our sense-intellect and abstract it from reality itself.

Thus philosophy begins by saying that the outside world is not a basic fact, that its existence can be doubted and that every proposition in which the reality of the outside world is affirmed is not an evident proposition but one that needs to be divided, dissected, and analyzed. It is to stand consciously aside and try to square a circle.

René Descartes (1596–1650), the great French philosopher and mathematician, raised the above problem. Since [the] existence of anything, including my being, is not certain, what is there in the universe [that is] beyond any shadow of doubt? When one has

The young student of philosophy in 1964, while enrolled at the University of Washington.

doubts about the world, and even about the whole entire universe, what is left? Let's stand outside this world for a moment, follow Descartes, and see what is actually left.

According to Descartes, the doubt itself is left because for something to be doubtful, it must seem to me that it is; and the whole universe may seem to me doubtful, except for the fact of its seeming to me. To doubt is to think and thought is the only thing in the universe whose existence cannot be denied, because to deny is to think. When one says that thought exists, it automatically includes saying that one exists because there is no thought that does not contain as one of its elements a subject who thinks.

In Chinese Taoism and *Ch'an* (Zen), the world is seen as an inseparable, interrelated field, no part of which can actually be separated from the other. That is, there would be no bright stars without dim stars, and, without the surrounding darkness, no stars at all. Oppositions have become mutually dependent instead of mutually exclu-

sive, and there is no longer any conflict between the individual and nature.

So if thought exists, I who think and the world about which I think also exist; the one exists but for the other, having no possible separation between them. Therefore, the world and I are both in active correlation; I am that which sees the world and the world is that which is seen by me. I exist for the world, and the world exists for me.

If there were no things to be seen, thought about, and imagined, I would not see, think, or imagine. That is to say, I would not exist. One sure and primary and fundamental fact is the joint existence of a subject and of its world. The one does not exist without the other. I acquire no understanding of myself except as I take account of objects, of the surroundings. I do not think unless I think of things—therefore on finding myself.

It is of no use to talk merely about objects of consciousness, whether they are thought-sensations or wax candles. An object must have a subject, and subject-object is a pair of complementaries (not opposites), like all others, which are two halves of one whole and are a function each of the other. . . . I do not experience; I am experience. I am not the subject of an experience; I am that experience. I am awareness. Nothing else can be me or can exist.

Thus we do not sweat because it is hot; the sweating is the heat. It is just as true to say that the sun is light because of the sun. This peculiar Chinese viewpoint is unfamiliar because it is our settled convention to think that heat comes first and then, by causality, the body sweats. To put it the other way round is startling, like saying "cheese and bread" instead of "bread and cheese." This shocking and seemingly illogical reversal of common sense may perhaps be clarified by the following illustration of the moon in the water.

The Moon in the Water

The phenomenon of moon-in-the-water is likened to human experience. The water is the subject, and the moon the object. When there is no water, there is no moon-in-the-water and likewise when there is no moon. But when the moon rises the water does not wait to receive its image, and when even the tiniest drop of water is poured out the moon does not wait to cast its reflection. For the moon does not intend to cast its reflection, and the water does not receive its image on purpose. The event is caused as much by the water as by the moon, and as the water manifests the brightness of the moon, the moon manifests the clarity of the water.

Everything does have a real relationship, a mutuality in which the subject creates the object just as much as the object creates the subject. Thus the knower no longer feels himself to be separated from the known; the experiencer no longer feels himself to stand apart from the experience. Consequently, the whole notion of getting something out of life, of seeking from experience, becomes absurd. To put it in another way, it becomes vividly clear that in concrete fact I have no other self than the oneness of things of which I am aware.

Master Lin-Chi of the T'ang Dynasty said, "Just be ordinary and nothing special. Eat your food, move your bowels, pass water, and when you are tired, go and lie down. The ignorant will laugh at me, but the wise will understand." A person is not living a conceptually or scientifically defined life; for the essential quality of living life lies simply in the living. Do not, as when in the midst of enjoying yourself, step out for a moment and examine yourself to see if you are getting the utmost out of the occasion. Or not content with the feeling happy, you want to feel yourself feeling happy—so as to be sure not to miss anything.

Living exists when life lives through us—unhampered in its flow, for he who is living is not conscious of living and, in this, is the life it lives.

Life lives; and in the living flow, no questions are raised. The reason is that life is a living now! Completeness, the now, is an absence of the conscious mind to strive to divide that which is indivisible. For once the completeness of things is taken apart, it is no longer complete. All the pieces of a car that has been taken apart may be there, but it is no longer a car in its original nature, which is its function or life. So, in order to live life wholeheartedly, the answer is: *life simply is.*

THE DEMISE OF DUALISM

This sense of "an absence of the conscious mind to strive to divide that which is indivisible" is the mind-set of wu-hsin that is expressed through yin-yang, which we touched upon earlier. From this unencumbered viewpoint, we are able to more clearly see the world as it is, and therefore observe the interdependency of all things—rather than the separation. Thus, dualism is revealed to be existentially false, while the monistic perception is revealed to be accurate—even from a modern scientific point of view. According to Lee in his note titled "Yin-Yang" from 1963:

The dualistic philosophy reigned supreme in Europe, dominating the development of Western science. But with the advent of atomic physics, findings based on demonstrable experiment were seen to negate the dualistic theory, and the trend of thought since then has been back toward the monistic conception of the ancient Taoists.

In atomic physics, no distinction is recognized between matter and energy; nor is it possible to make such a distinction, since they are in reality one essence, or at least two poles of the same unit.

In the same way, the Taoist philosophy . . . is essentially monistic. The Chinese conceived [of] the entire universe as activated by two principles, the yang and the yin, the positive and negative, and they considered that nothing that exists, either animate or so-called inanimate, does so except by virtue of the ceaseless interplay of these two forces. Matter and energy, yang and yin, heaven and earth, are conceived of as essentially one or as two coexistent poles of one indivisible whole.

Here, Lee clearly makes the case for the interdependency, or oneness, of all things as being the correct metaphysical viewpoint. Growing up in Hong Kong, where the influence of the great Chinese belief systems such as Confucianism and Taoism is still strong, Lee naturally was exposed to both systems of thought and, by his own admission, was influenced by them.

However, rather than simply adopting the tenets of either system, Lee opted instead to run both systems through the filter of his axiomatic primaries, with the result that only those principles that were—at a root or metaphysical level—true, were accepted as valid.

At this point, it is important to note that Lee did not consider these philosophical tenets to be true simply because they were held to be so by traditional Chinese culture. Rather, Lee adopted them because he saw and understood the reasons they were true. Lee discovered that the theory of yin-yang fit perfectly with both his metaphysical and axiomatic viewpoints, allowing him an unsegmented view of the totality of existence. As he wrote in his paper "The Union of Firmness and Softness":

Once distinction is made on something, that certain something will suggest its opposite. On the surface, [for example] softness and firmness appear as opposites, but in reality they are interdependent—the complementary parts of a whole.

Their meaning (softness/firmness) is obtained *from* each other and they find their completion *through* each other. This "one-ness" of things is a characteristic of the Chinese mind.

In the Chinese language, events are looked on as a whole because their meanings are derived from each other. For example, the Chinese character for "good" and the Chinese character for "not good" when combined together will reflect the "quality" of something (whether good or not good). Likewise, the Chinese character for "long" and the Chinese character for "short" when brought together means "length," and the character for "buying" when combined with the character for "selling" forms the new word "trade."

All these examples show us that everything has a complementary part to form a whole. Now we can look at the "one-ness" of firmness and softness, without favoring too much on either side so that we can truly appreciate the "good/bad" of them. Not only does everything have a complementary part, but even within that "one" special thing, it, too, should have the characteristic of the other part. In other words, softness is to be concealed in firmness, and firmness in softness. In either case, be it softness or firmness, it should never stand alone; for standing alone will lead to extremes and going to extremes is never best.

This last point gave rise to one of Lee's most famous maxims, taken from "The Tao of Gung Fu":

Nothing is so permanent as never to change.

And as this process of change is, to use Lee's word, "incessant," it is itself unchangeable. Which, in turn, gives rise to another of Lee's most famous dictums:

To change with change is the changeless state.

As we've established, Lee's metaphysical viewpoint of monism is an outgrowth from what he took to be the axiomatic principle of Interdependency, which is symbolized in the yin-yang. Lee's metaphysics rests on his conviction that picking and choosing, differentiating and discriminating, conceals the truth of the oneness of life. As he said in "Zen," a handwritten note found in *Commentaries on the Martial Way*:

The perfect way is only difficult for those who pick and choose. Do not like, do not dislike—all will then be clear. Make a hair's-breadth difference and heaven and earth are set apart. If you want the truth to stand clear before you, never be *for* or *against*. The struggle between "For" and "Against" is the mind's worst disease.

THE LIVING VOID

The yin-yang energy that forms everything under the stars emerges from a source that Lee refers to as "the void." However, unlike nothingness, such as empty space, Lee, in his notes titled "Buddhism's Eightfold Path," describes this primary energy as a "living void":

Voidness is that which stands right in the middle between this and that. The void is all-inclusive, having no opposite; there is nothing that it excludes or opposes. It is [a] living void because all forms come out of it, and whoever realizes the void is filled with life and power and the love of all beings.

In another writing on the void, Lee describes it as a synonym for our unconscious mind, which many great religions credit for such things as revelation, satori, *tun-wu*, and great spiritual insights.

Lee noted that conflict is the result of opposing thoughts that we allow to enter our consciousness. These thoughts often contradict the spiritual truths as revealed through the void or our unconscious mind. However, if we do not allow our viewpoint of reality to be disrupted by illusory, consciously held thoughts of division, we will be privy to great spiritual insights. In a letter dated September 1962 to family friend Pearl Tso, Lee makes the case for the conscious mind attuning itself to the great internal energy of the unconscious to serve as an impetus for all great human accomplishment:

I feel I have this great creative and spiritual force within me that is greater than faith, greater than ambition, greater than confidence, greater than determination, greater than vision. It is all these combined. My brain becomes magnetized with this dominating force that I hold in my head.

When you drop a pebble into a pool of water, the pebble starts a series of ripples that expand until they encompass the whole pool. This is exactly what will happen when I give my ideas a definite plan of action. . . . I am not easily discouraged; [I] readily visualize myself as overcoming obstacles, winning out over setbacks, achieving "impossible" objectives.

Whether it is the God-head or not, I feel this great force, this untapped power, this dynamic something within me. This feeling defies description, and [there is] no experience with which this feeling may be compared. It is something like a strong emotion mixed with faith, but a lot stronger.

All in all, the goal of my planning and doing is to find the true meaning in life—peace of mind. I know that the sum of all possessions I mentioned does not necessarily add up to peace of mind; however, it can be if I devote to real accomplishment of self, rather than neurotic combat. In order to achieve this peace of mind, the teaching of detachment of Taoism and Zen proved to be valuable.

SPIRITUAL AND METAPHYSICAL AWARENESS

Spiritual awareness is, in effect, metaphysical awareness; that is, making the mind conscious of matters that transcend the physical and to realize that, on a metaphysical level, there is no separation between matter and mind. In other words, in metaphysical reality, there exist no "mental" dividing lines, in much the same way that a map itself is not the reality of a country.

Separation, division, segregation, and dissecting lines are simply products of our imagination that we have imposed on metaphysical reality. Our planet is vast, certainly far greater than what we can directly perceive, and hence we rely on the constructed crutch of mutually exclusive distinctions (east/west, black/white, male/female)—and suffer the consequences.

Bruce Lee has demonstrated that these dividing lines are entirely illusory. We've merely accepted them as reality because that is what we have been taught to do. Most of us rarely, if ever, question this metaphysical viewpoint—we simply accept it as Truth. Because of this largely unconsidered view, we are unaware of what reality "really" is. In contrast, Lee questioned what he had been taught, wanting to see reality with his own eyes and to honestly report on what he saw. He then built the rest of his philosophy upon the foundation of "what is"—as opposed to what should be. As is only proper, the final word on this matter, from the essay "In My Own Process," belongs to Bruce Lee:

Oh, I know we all admit that we are intelligent beings; yet, I wonder how many of us have gone through some sort of self-inquiries and/or self-examining of all these ready-made facts or truths that are crammed down our throats ever since we acquired the capacity and the sensibility to learn. Though we possess a pair of eyes, . . . most of us do not really see in the true sense of the word. True seeing, in the sense of choiceless awareness, leads to new discovery, and discovery is one of the means to uncovering our potentiality.

CHAPTER 13
BRUCE LEE AND ART

The artistic activity does not lie in art itself as such. It penetrates into a deeper world in which all art forms (of things inwardly experienced) flow together, and in which the harmony of soul and cosmos in the nothing has its outcome in reality. —**Bruce Lee**

The above quote may sound somewhat esoteric to those of us who have tended to view the "art" of martial art as simply a better way to dominate an opponent. However, the highest goal of the martial artist is not simply combative efficiency, although this is a means to the highest goal, in much the same way that a ladder is a means to get you from the ground to the roof of your house.

There is a higher purpose to the arts. Bruce Lee speaks of "self-knowledge" and the need to "express yourself" and to acquire "personal liberation," but what does any of this mean? Unless you are well read

Bruce Lee studied the Roman ruins during a break in filming *The Way of the Dragon* in 1972. Lee had a deep and abiding interest in the art of all cultures.

in philosophical method, these high-level intellectual abstractions may well be meaningless to you. However, even lofty philosophical concepts can be understood by anyone when the message is conveyed through a common mode of communication that is intelligible to all of us. And the machine that can decode this message is art.

The novelist and objectivist philosopher Ayn Rand stated, "The basic purpose of art is not to teach, but to show—to hold up to man a concretized image of his nature and his place in the universe." By this definition, since the function of art is to bring man's concepts to the perceptual level—the level of immediate comprehension—the task of the artist is not to present conceptual information but to provide man with a definite experience. It is the experience not of thinking but of seeing, as we contemplate the artistic concrete, that "this is what reality is like."

Art is the great interpreter; it communicates directly to the perceiver the honest feelings of the artist with regard to some aspect of life. Lee said of it:

The aim of art is to project an inner vision into the world, to state in aesthetic creation the deepest psychic and personal experiences of a human being. It is to enable those experiences to be intelligible and generally recognized within the total framework of an ideal world.

And once you see what creative vistas are open to you when you understand the meaning and potential of art for communicating and expressing yourself, you realize what a potent educator and liberator it is.

A NET OF GEMS

In Hindu mythology there exists a fable regarding a vast net of gems, and other cultures have similar fables; the Japanese, for example, speak of a spiderweb covered with dew and shimmering in the morning light, much like the gems in the Hindu story. This is an example of art as metaphor; the universe is seen as a great net with a gem at every joint, each gem not only reflecting all the others but also reflected in all of them. This powerful metaphor reveals how the flavor of the ocean is contained within every drop of water, or the whole mystery of life within a DNA coil.

James Joyce once said that art "is an image that hits one where it counts," and noted:

It is not addressed first to the brain, to be there interpreted and appreciated. On the contrary, if that is where it has to be read, the symbol is already dead. Art speaks directly to the feeling system of the body and immediately elicits a response, after which the brain may come along with its interesting comments.

Art contains a method whereby mental imagery can directly communicate to us a moral precept that is visual and therefore immediately understood. Or, as Bruce Lee said:

Art is the way to the absolute and to the essence of human life. The aim of art is not the one-side promotion of spirit, soul, and senses, but the opening of all human capacities—thought, feeling, will—to the life rhythm of the world of nature. So will the voiceless voice be heard and the self be brought into harmony with it.

The example of the net of gems truly does, as Lee said earlier, "state in aesthetic creation the deepest psychic and personal experiences of the human being." It relates a profound moral truth that is applicable to all human beings, to the planet on which we live, and to the universe that sustains it all. It also relates a perspective that allowed Bruce Lee to liberate himself from looking at only one segment or component of life—ruthless fighting efficiency—to its totality. As he once said:

To obtain enlightenment in martial art means the extinction of everything which obscures the "true knowledge," the "real life." At the same time, it implies boundless expansion, and indeed, emphasis should fall not on the cultivation of the particular department which merges into the totality, but rather on the totality that enters and unites that particular department.

That is the first statement recorded in Lee's 1975 book *The Tao of Jeet Kune Do*, and it refers specifically to this matter of totality, how all things are interconnected and interdependent. To refer to our earlier analogy, the web and net are symbols of this interdependence of life.

The beauty of art is that it can lead you on a journey from one thing to many things, only to lead you back to the one thing all over again, but with a better sense of the "way" behind it all. It can further be utilized to represent the most abstract or profound ideas symbolically or metaphorically, in a manner that can be readily understood by the beholder, irrespective of the era in which the work of art is viewed. Thus art is transcendent. According to Lee:

Art is an expression that transcends both time and space. We must

employ our own souls through art to give a new form and a new meaning to nature or the world.

Martial art—or any other art for that matter—can be used as a means of employing or expressing your soul in a manner that will provide a new meaning or understanding of nature or the world. This is, in fact, where the significance of the net of gems analogy lies. In the gem of martial art is reflected the gem of yourself; you are a gem that reflects the gem of the world in which you live; the gem of the world in which you live contains within it a reflection of the gem of the galaxy that houses it; in which is reflected the gem of the solar system that sustains it; and so on in an infinite expansion covering the breadth and depth of the universe and everything in between.

To be an artist requires that you look into your subject matter deeply, and the more deeply you look into anything, the more you can learn about everything, including the fact that you are part of a vast, universal process that is intricately and magnificently interconnected.

Art, then, is a communicator of truths, an educator. It's not just something pretty that hangs on a wall, but a vital facet of our everyday existence. However, most martial artists don't see themselves as artists—and in most cases, rightly so. It would be more accurate perhaps to call them martial practitioners. And yet, the martial arts qualify as art in every sense of the word. Once we recognize this fact, to neglect to cultivate this higher capacity in favor of developing solely combative efficiency is akin to a master carpenter's being concerned only with chopping down trees.

Art can therefore be viewed as a vehicle or process through which artists are able to relate or communicate the totality of their essence and feelings directly to another human being. A great painting, for example, will stir in viewers some profound and powerful feelings—and can continue to do so over hundreds or thousands of years.

Bruce Lee was able to connect and communicate similar feelings through his films and writings. Viewers of Lee on the big screen often feel a "connection" with him—as an antenna receives a transmitted signal—on an emotional level. An artist is, first and foremost, a communicator, or what Lee called "a competent deliverer," and the message that he delivered was the honest expression of his soul—from him to you. He was able to accomplish this because of what he learned from initially looking into that one gem called martial art.

The closer Lee looked into this gem, the more clearly he saw the reflections of all of the other gems in the net of life. He quickly realized that it was impossible to be truly a master or a guru, because such titles indicate that you've learned all there is to know about everything—but the web of life goes on into infinity, with gems too numerous to count. There isn't enough time in a person's life to become a "master," because martial art is a reflection of life, and life is an ongoing process that has no end or limit. Bruce once wrote in the margins of page 186 in *On Becoming a Person*, by the American psychotherapist Dr. Carl Rogers:

- A "good" martial artist, not a "master"

- A maturing martial artist, not a matured artist

- An actualizing artist, rather than an actualized master

These thoughts on maturity clearly echo Lee's comments to his student Daniel Lee in 1972 quoted in Chapter 10.

He realized that this gem into which he had looked and had polished to such a high point of refinement for so long was, to use his terms, like a mirror in which to reflect himself. He began to see that martial art was the key that could unlock the door of life. As he said:

Basically, I have always been a martial artist by choice, and an actor by profession. But, above all, I am hoping to actualize myself to be an artist of life along the way. . . . Therefore, to be a martial artist also means to be an artist of life. Since life is an ever-evolving process, one should flow in this process and discover how to actualize and expand oneself.

And the way to look at martial arts with an eye toward discovering how to actualize and expand oneself is by first recognizing that it involves far more than the domination of an opponent. It is about developing the skill to master your own limitations. Defeating an opponent has to be viewed as simply an exercise in self-knowledge. It is to be used to develop yourself into a better person in the same way that you may work out for exercise. It is the benefits brought by working out that you are ultimately seeking: longer life, increased energy, better health, and so on. Exercise is simply a means to the achievement of higher goals.

The true martial artist—with the emphasis on *artist*—does not fight with an opponent in order to see him defeated; he does it as a means to achieving his own higher goals, as a tool to reach an honest understanding and expression of the self. So, while the martial art may provide the tools necessary to master oneself, it is up to the individual to learn to use them for this purpose.

Bruce Lee said that "all knowledge is self-knowledge," which again harks back to the net of gems and the fact that you are part of everything. If you look into any one area of existence, you will come to see in it a reflection of the fact that you are part of this vast, universal process of life. It is up to you to learn the correct application of your observations.

ART AS MEANS TO SELF-KNOWLEDGE

"Art," Bruce Lee once said, "is the music of the soul made visible." And the way to hear the music of your soul—"the silent flute"—is through a thorough and relentless dedication to discovering the real you, refusing to accept anything less than 100 percent of who you really are, and then communicating or "expressing" it. That journey to self-discovery begins, according to Lee, with the individual's acknowledging his or her humanity and saying, "Here I am as a human being; how can I honestly express myself?" This, Lee discovered, was accomplished by reducing everything about you to its core, by asking the simple question "How can I be me?"

The one obstacle to progress in this regard is self-consciousness. You must learn to put aside your image of yourself because image is largely an illusion—a scrap heap of unwarranted assumptions and generalizations that does not even begin to represent

the real you and what your feelings and actual potentials are. Bruce Lee pointed this out in one of his last essays:

Most people only live for their image. That is why, where some have a self, a starting point, most people have a void. Because they are so busy projecting themselves as "this" or "that," they end up wasting and dissipating all their energy in projection and conjuring up a facade, rather than centering their energy on expanding and broadening their potential or expressing and relaying this unified energy for efficient communication.

Efficient communication, as we've seen, is the essence of art. However, before you can efficiently communicate your feelings through the artistic process to another human being, you need to get in touch with the real you. This requires a similar process of communication: first with yourself and then later, if you're truly an artist, of yourself with others. According to Lee, this latter component, once mastered, creates an individual who is a "master of life," for the artist is then able to share the total of everything that he is and is becoming:

When another human being sees a self-actualizing person walk past, he cannot help but say: "Hey now, there is someone real!"

All of this Lee learned by first looking into that reflective gem, or mirror, of martial art—as he states in the sentence that opens the film *Bruce Lee: A Warrior's Journey:*

As an actor, as a martial artist, as a human being—all these—I have learned from martial art.

From the utilization of his body in the practice of martial art, Bruce Lee was able

to learn the best way to relate to life, which he believed lay in trying to abide in the process of becoming, moment to moment. This means learning about yourself—your true potentials and limitations, joys and fears, hopes, desires—and then expressing them to the best of your ability, and to the root and marrow of your existence.

The questions that Lee asked himself along the path of self-knowledge were simple, but they were questions that needed to be asked constantly:

1. What is this [feeling]?

2. Is it true or is it not true? (i.e., Is this your true feeling in this regard or an emotion falsely held?)

3. Do you really mean it or not mean it? (i.e., Are you honestly expressing what you feel or are you expressing something different from what you are actually feeling?)

Once he was able to determine the appropriate responses to these questions, he had his answer. This is what being a true martial artist entails. The ultimate aim of the artist is, according to Lee:

To use his daily activity to become a past master of life, and so lay hold of the art of living. Masters in all branches of art must first be masters of living, for the soul creates everything.

He explained:

Art is never decoration, embellishment; instead it is work of enlightenment. Art, in other words, is a technique for acquiring liberty.

In his personal practice of martial art, in his movies, and in his writings, Bruce Lee revealed, in masterly form, his own vision of the world and the content of a noble soul. He revealed to all of us who understood his message what heights are possible for a human being to ascend if we allow the winds of honesty to lift our wings.

To his students, he was a person who was able to explain his art while creating it. It saddened him to see martial artists bickering over the "truth" of particular leaves in their own backyards when there were vast forests of discovery that he wished to take them to.

Once Bruce Lee looked deeply into that individual gem of martial art, he saw a reflection of himself—and within himself, a reflection of the universe and the fact that that same universe is reflected within us all as part of a vast net or web that interconnects all people as brothers and sisters.

"Under the heavens, there is but one family," he once said. So too in martial art, since martial art is not something set apart from life but is part of it.

How often are we told by different "Sensei" or "Masters" that the martial arts are life itself? But how many of them truly understand what they are saying?

We are wise to remember that two words make up the term *martial artist*—

martial and *artist*. We cannot place disproportionate emphasis on the former and thereby engage in battles for the sake of battles, allowing perceived martial diversity to separate us from the fact that we are all related.

Bruce Lee often commented on how unfortunate it was that styles separate people, dividing them unnecessarily into segments of what should be a totality. These segments are formed by taking only superficial notice of one gem, of being partial or segmented in one's view of the art of combat, blind to the reflection of the other truths contained within it.

The Chinese, of course, have their own renowned counterpart to the gem symbol, which they call the yin-yang or *tai chi* symbol. The yin-yang symbolizes that all things are not only interconnected but also interdependent. Nothing can exist but in the form and nature that it does, and all things depend upon every other thing to remain true to its nature in order for them to express its own. In this way, all things are dependent on all other things for their sustenance and existence. In relating this principle to combat, Bruce Lee taught that the firm seeks out the soft to "complete" the opponent's attack and/or defense. There is a constant flux in combat as each participant struggles through a natural process of transformation—full to empty, forceful to passive—and then transforms back again in perfect complement to the opponent's actions.

One of the highlights of reading Bruce Lee's writings is being able to partake of a feast of truths—not only of combat, but also of life—that Lee set out for both his own edification and that of his students as a means to enhance their quest for self-discovery. It is at that summit that he found the unique form of nourishment for the soul that is jeet kune do—a source of nourishment that has sustained thousands, if not millions, of individuals from all walks of life through the end of the twentieth century and now into the twenty-first. That's quite a banquet by any standard.

CHAPTER 14
QUESTIONS AND ANSWERS

Bruce Lee's philosophy stressed independent judgment over herd mentality, and self-expression over the perpetuation of systems and dogma.

As a recognized expert on Bruce Lee, I am frequently asked to give presentations and lectures on Lee's life, philosophy, and training methods. At the end of each presentation, I open the floor for questions from the audience. Over the years, people of all types have asked some very insightful questions. This chapter shares some of those questions and responses.

LEARNING BRUCE LEE'S MARTIAL ART

Q: What would be your advice to the person who wants to study JKD and to truly understand all of its origins and foundation?

A: Someone who wants to study JKD the martial art as opposed to the philosophy—

which, in pure yin-yang fashion, are different and yet interrelated—should contact the Bruce Lee Educational Foundation (www.bruceleefoundation.com) for referral to a local recognized instructor.

The Nucleus is a group of devoted first- and second-generation students that was formed in 1996 under the auspices of Bruce's widow, Linda Lee Cadwell, and daughter, Shannon Lee Keasler. Members of the Nucleus are devoted to the preservation and perpetuation of Bruce Lee's art of jeet kune do. In fact, they've rechristened the art "Jun Fan jeet kune do" in deference to Bruce, whose Chinese name was Lee Jun Fan. The Nucleus sponsors annual public seminars and contributes articles regularly to the martial arts mainstream press. Some of the members who are excellent teachers of Bruce Lee's art are Taky Kimura and his son, Andrew Kimura, Ted Wong, Daniel Lee, George Lee, Allen Joe, Chris Kent, Bob Bremer, Tim Tackett, Richard Bustillo, Herb Jackson, Steve Golden, Greglon Lee, Jerry Poteet, Pete Jacobs, Tommy Gong, and Cass Magda.

Dan Inosanto, who was Bruce's assistant instructor at his Los Angeles school, is also very knowledgeable about the art and philosophy of jeet kune do and would be very helpful to any individual wanting to fully understand the breadth and scope of Lee's art. At present, I am the only one focusing primarily on Bruce Lee's philosophy and approach to life, but I hope that more people will spread the word about his thought so that others might benefit.

WESTERN PHILOSOPHICAL INFLUENCES

Q: It's clear that there were many Eastern influences in Lee's personal philosophy. Were there many Western philosophical influences?

A: Many Western philosophers contributed in varying degrees to Lee's philosophical outlook. In reviewing his philosophical papers, including those from his days at the University of Washington (where he majored in philosophy), I see plenty of notes on people such as Socrates, Plato, Descartes, the Scottish empiricist David Hume, and John Locke, in addition to books Lee purchased for his personal library by learned men such as Bertrand Russell and Will Durant. Lee was also influenced by the less academic Western thinkers such as the novelist Hermann Hesse—who stressed the idea of the self-willed man—and the more popular self-help authors such as Napoleon Hill, who himself synthesized the success-oriented philosophies of men such as Henry Ford and Thomas Edison.

In Lee's notes, there are plenty of quotations—often contrasted with the Eastern perspective—from these individuals, and his philosophical notebooks are loaded with information on categories such as free will, philosophical analysis, and the various forms of religious arguments, such as those postulated by Saint Anselm and Saint Thomas Aquinas, covering the ontological argument, the cosomological argument, and Cartesian dualism.

In addition, he had written copious notes on the use of logic; the law of identity, particulars, and universals; a posteriori—or the argument from effect to cause, or knowledge based on experience; a priori—or the argument from cause to effect, or knowledge acquired independently of experience; the use of human reason; the relation of cause and effect; ethics—including the consequential theory, the motivational theory, and the objective theory; and the nature of truth. I can go on and on—

Lee also explored the philosophical problem of perception, the distinction between negation and privation.

THE INFLUENCE OF KRISHNAMURTI

Q: In what ways was Bruce Lee influenced by Jiddu Krishnamurti?

A: Lee was not so much influenced as he was delighted to have found a kindred spirit. Many of the truths that Krishnamurti expressed were truths that Lee had come to behold independently. Krishnamurti was such an eloquent speaker and author that his words served to echo truths that Lee had thought only he had experienced. And then, of course, Bruce Lee was particularly influenced by certain extrapolations of these truths by Krishnamurti. Bruce had an audiotape of Krishnamurti speaking on meditation that he listened to from time to time, and he read many of Krishnamurti's books and made notations such as:

- "To think about oneself all the time is to be insensitive, for then the mind and heart are enclosed and lose all appreciation of beauty."

• "The poorer we are inwardly, the more we try to enrich ourselves outwardly."

Certainly the two men shared a profound belief that truth is outside of all organizations, systems, and methods.

Q: I've heard that Bruce Lee never said anything original; that he simply parroted what Krishnamurti said. Is this true?

A: No, it is not true. Anyone who is willing to devote some time to examining the beliefs of these two great thinkers will see that there existed many points on which their thoughts diverged. There are also many points on which both men agreed: the autonomy of man, the need to remove the sense of self (only in combative situations, Lee believed, as thinking required time, which was not a luxury a fighter had).

It must also be remembered that much of what has been published under Lee's name are simply his notebooks; he did not own a photocopier or a computer database, so he read books and wrote down observations that he considered to be important. These books were for his personal edification, but his marginalia tell us something of his views on a wide range of topics. That his notebooks have been published was not Lee's choice, and he never attempted to appropriate another's thoughts as his own. However, like the books in his library, Lee's journals shed significant light on his thoughts on a given subject; he often made reference to various works of like-minded thinkers.

Although Lee's influences were many, his thoughts were always his own. The conformist declares, "I believe it because others do." The noncomformist declares, "I don't believe it because others do." But the individualist, the rarest of all human beings, declares, "I believe it because I see for myself the reasons that it is true."

PRAGMATIC, NOT ECLECTIC

Q: Was it inevitable that such an eclectic form of philosophy would lead to Lee's eclectic style of martial art?

A: It was more of Krishnamurti's influence that led to what some people have called Lee's "eclectic style of martial art." Lee actually would deny that what he offered was a "style," as he believed that styles tend to separate people and place tradition over pragmatism.

Lee really wasn't eclectic either, in the sense of how that term is typically defined. He was, however, pragmatic; that is, if an exercise, belief, or combative technique was functional and refined, or reduced to the very root of what made it an efficient entity, then Lee would incorporate it into his arsenal, regardless of its source. He didn't simply view the martial arts as a smorgasbord from which you were to sample "a little of this and a bit of that." Instead, he viewed all ideas, techniques, and principles as hypotheses that had to be tested before adopted through empirical—a Western concept, by the way—research and testing.

The Eastern viewpoint was, however, entirely supportive of this position because of its monistic perspective: that such things as East and West are mutually interdependent, part of one universal process, and that therefore, one should not be closed-minded to only one segmented, nationalistic, or philosophical way of looking at things.

THE CHALLENGE TO LIVE IN THE MOMENT

Q: Did Bruce struggle with his own ability to "live in the moment"?

A: Constantly. He was forever jotting down notes in an attempt to honestly communicate to himself his genuine feelings or beliefs at the moment. As Linda Lee Cadwell observed in her introduction to my book *The Warrior Within*:

His journey was a constant process of evolving, one step at a time, with the object being not to reach a state of perfection, but to experience life with every nerve exposed, fully in touch with gut-level feelings and cerebral senses. To this end, Bruce delved deeply into his psyche to define and refine his own philosophy of life.

For him, the key to living life is being able to simply do that—to *live* it, not conceptualize about it, not deal with abstractions, but experience it in full. You're given only one spin of the wheel, so take in as much of the game as possible while you're here.

One of Bruce's jottings to himself reveals him trying to just drop his ego and let his

Bruce Lee's thought ignored race, sex, and class distinctions, focusing instead on the common denominator of our shared humanity.

honest emotions flow forth without pausing to analyze what he's saying; it's just an honest form of self-communication. Remember, these notes were his personal writings, not statements intended for other people, but hearing them may prove helpful to people who wish to attempt a similar mode of getting in touch with their inner selves. Bruce wrote this sometime in 1973:

I don't know what I will be writing, but just simply writing whatever wants to be written. If the writing communicates and stirs something with someone, it's beautiful. If not, well, it can't be helped. Among people, a great majority don't feel comfortable at all with the unknown; that is, anything foreign that threatens their protected daily mold. So, for their sake of security, they construct chosen patterns to justify. Granted, unlike the lower animals, human beings are indeed intelligent beings. To be a martial artist means and demands absence of prejudice, superstitions, ignorance, and all that. [Seek for] the primary, essential ingredient of what a quality fighter is and leave the circus acts to the circus performers. Mentally, it means a burning enthusiasm with neutrality to choose to be.

There are so many notes like this one that are both fascinating and revealing, particularly regarding his total commitment to honest self-expression.

Q: Is the concept of "effortlessness" necessarily anti-intellectual? That is, if it involves "not thinking," is it purely emotional?

A: "Effortless" doesn't mean shutting off your mind. It's more of a case of not letting your ego, or sense of self, get in the way of your experiencing life to the fullest. You are still capable of learning and reasoning, but in a more pragmatic, immediate sense of the *now*. You're not in abstract; you don't lose yourself in thought, like the centipede considering how it walks with so many legs—until it gets so mired in cerebral gymnastics that it trips and falls.

It has to do with the concept of *wei*, which means "forced," strained or unnatural. *Wu-wei* is the removal of artifice, putting on the corrective eyeglasses that will allow you to view reality in its proper light. So, it's not purely emotional. In fact, that would set up a false dichotomy of intellectual versus emotional, as if they were opposites, when in fact they are interdependent poles of the same process. Your emotions are simply the effect of the cause of your intellect.

That's why people with varying degrees of knowledge will have extremely different emotional reactions to the same stimulus: those who have a broader base of knowledge are usually calm because they're aware of what the stimulus represents, while those with lesser knowledge will not be so calm,

owing to the "mysterious" element they are observing and—depending on their personal experience—will either fear it or simply feel uncomfortable with it. (You can find more on this in Chapter 2 of this book and in *The Warrior Within*.)

PHILOSOPHY AND COMBAT—A CONTRADICTION?

Q: With Bruce Lee's belief in such concepts as yin and yang, is it contradictory that he devoted much of his life to physical combat?

A: Not really. After all, physical activity is simply the yang counterpart to the yin aspect of mental activity. His writings and interviews are testaments to Bruce's devotion to mental cultivation, and the physique he had is, obviously, testament to his devotion to physical cultivation. Bruce Lee represented the perfect balance of the physical and the mental. His journals are full of references to his setting aside specific times during the day for exercise and other times for mental cultivation, in the form of translating Chinese poetry, reading philosophy books, writing about philosophy or martial arts, and so on. In fact, much of his physical training was simply the physical application of the mental insights that came to him during such periods of reading, writing, and contemplation.

RACISM FROM THE WEST

Q: Bruce had a very progressive, optimistic outlook on racism, but wasn't it a blow to him to lose the lead role in the "Kung Fu" TV series to an Occidental?

A: Bruce Lee was the eternal optimist. He could turn stumbling blocks into stepping-stones. When the door to Hollywood was closed to him, like water, he simply flowed on to Southeast Asia and became such a success overseas that the door to Hollywood had to reopen. His belief was that if you concern yourself with being a quality human being and work as hard as you can to create quality products by making them honest reflections of how you express yourself, then you will succeed. It is a formula that has proved itself time after time for many different individuals, male and female—and from all races.

RACISM FROM THE EAST

Q: To what extent was Bruce Lee vilified by his own race for teaching the martial arts to Westerners?

A: Among the Chinese people who truly understand the Taoist perspective, he wasn't vilified at all, because they understood the truths of which he spoke. However, those who did not comprehend the full significance of yin-yang and the interdependency of apparent opposites couldn't bridge the chasm of the cultures and saw him as giving away "secrets" to foreign devils.

"Martial art has a very deep meaning as far as my life is concerned. As an actor, as a martial artist, as a human being—all these—I have learned from martial art." —Bruce Lee

These people didn't understand what Bruce said about the yin-yang principle as it applies to cultures. Bruce said, "There are good points in Chinese culture; there are good points in Occidental culture," and "they are not mutually exclusive, but mutually dependent." He noted, "Neither would be remarkable if it were not for the existence of the other."

So, he was vilified to a certain extent, but only by those people who were—or who remain—philosophically ignorant of the true ways of the world.

LEE VIS-A-VIS ALI

Q: **What is the deeper significance of Bruce Lee's real-life fight for the right to teach non-Chinese people the art of gung fu? In particular, how would you contrast or compare Lee's standing up for his rights to what Muhammad Ali did in refusing induction into the army?**

A: Many people view this piece of Bruce's history as simply an interesting "fight"—an exciting display of martial skill against a worthy adversary. Others look a little bit deeper than that and recognize within the incident a principle of "standing up for your

beliefs." Some have even gone so far as to compare Bruce to Muhammad Ali in this regard, but I think that Bruce's example transcends Ali's—at least in one respect: Bruce stood alone. Remember that Ali had the support of half of the country, his race, and the Muslim community behind him in the Nation of Islam. He was a hero to them because of what he did, and rightly so. But Bruce Lee stood alone. The Asian community resented his lack of tradition.

In American culture it's very easy to do pretty much as you please, and to look at something and improve it, no matter who invented it, if you have the insight. In fact, this is actually encouraged. But the Chinese culture and tradition is one in which the veneration of ancestors and the acceptance of ancient teachings for the sake of the preservation of the tradition is encouraged. It's hard, therefore, for the Western mind to appreciate the enormous pressure Bruce Lee was under when he stood up to say, "There's a better way to do this," and, "I'll live my life—and teach whom I choose—on my own terms."

And, lest we forget, Bruce married a Caucasian woman in the 1960s—something Ali said he would never do, by the way. A mixed-race marriage brought even more disdain to Bruce from bigoted Asians and Americans who had some traditions of their own they didn't want challenged. Consider the kind of discipline of character that it takes to go against everyone—absolutely everyone—around you, without support from any quarter, because of a principle that you believe in.

Also don't forget that Bruce wasn't a world champion like Ali, with a large following and money in the bank. He was an unknown with no money and no connections. And yet in the end, he won. He was proved correct and his ideas and his new martial art not only prevailed but also have endured for more than thirty years.

I don't believe there is a fighter who could better represent that one aspect of being a true individual, a true champion of the human spirit. What other athlete had to stand alone against sacred ancestors, revered elders, orthodox tradition, his own race, the belief system of another culture, his colleagues in his sport, and even against racism itself—and then was proved right? Totally vindicated for his beliefs on all counts?

And to top it off, immediately after his fight with the martial artist, rather than crow about his triumph (the way many lesser martial artists would), Bruce was able

to step back and recognize a personal weakness—and then devise new training and combative methods to correct it. That, to me, is the sign of the true individual—a man of totality.

THE DISTINCTION BETWEEN DISCOVERING AND ACCUMULATING KNOWLEDGE

Q: To Bruce, what was the distinction between "accumulating knowledge" and "discovering the cause of one's ignorance"?

A: The distinction would be this: The person who attempts to understand himself or herself through accumulating knowledge is piling up sandbags of information. He or she goes to school, say, reads countless books, and solicits and collects the opinions of various informed individuals; that is simply an accumulative process. Discovering the cause of ignorance—with emphasis on "cause"—is an internal method of peeling away the superficial layers.

For example, if you were to sit down now and make a note of what it would take to truly make you happy—eliminating survival necessities such as rent and food—you'd probably discover that it is not "accumulating" anything, not buying a new car or building a bigger house, but something intrinsic to yourself or your family. It's a self-discovery process and a whittling away of the unessentials until the real you—with all of your likes, wants, and dislikes—is revealed to you. Once this is done, the peeling away of the artificial layers of you, you will have also peeled away the "cause" of your ignorance.

What you gain once this has been accomplished is a very personal discovery, and my personal discovery may be completely different from yours, but the process of removing the psychic layers of falsehood is the universal way to this ultimate and very moral destination.

TRANSLATION IN THE GAME OF DEATH

Q: I understand that for the "thought dialogue" sections of the film <u>Bruce Lee: A Warrior's Journey</u>, Bruce wrote some of the dialogue in English and other passages in Chinese. Given the diversity of the languages, did you find that rendering Bruce Lee's Chinese dialogue for <u>The Game of Death</u> in English lost anything in the translation?

A: In some respects, it did, although nothing that would impact his message or intent. In some instances, the literal translations of the Chinese characters were not comprehensible because they were missing context that Bruce doubtless would have provided had he lived to complete the film.

As an example, during Hai Tien's first "thought dialogue," the literal translation of what Bruce Lee wrote in his shooting script is:

The best advantage of Mantis is that he does not bother with the characters of life and death and has no distracting thoughts and can concentrate on fighting against the attack from outside.

For months I puzzled over this phrase and the reference to "Mantis." It didn't make sense that Hai Tien, in the midst of a life-

and-death battle, would lapse into a philosophical abstraction about the thought processes of an insect, nor did it make sense in reference to the style of praying mantis gung fu—as he had just defeated a praying mantis stylist on the second floor of the pagoda with his "formless" approach of jeet kune do, thus proving his point about the effectiveness of having "no style."

However, if the name of Kareem's character was Mantis (in his story line there was an oblique reference to "Mantis" as a name), then the sentence made sense contextually, as his greatest attribute was, in effect, the highest level of jeet kune do: the loss of any sense of "self" and any fear of death. Just as in "Longstreet," when Lee says, "Like everyone else, you want to learn the way to win—but never to accept the way to lose. To accept defeat, to learn to die is to be liberated from it. So, when tomorrow comes, you must free your ambitious mind and learn the art of dying."

Therefore, to capture the essence of Lee's statement in a manner that would more accurately reflect Lee's beliefs, I consulted with three Cantonese authorities, who concurred with my thoughts on the intent of the excerpt. The result is that the sentence was rendered:

His [Jabbar's character in the film] big advantage is that he gives no thought to life or death. And, with no distracting thoughts, he is therefore free to concentrate in fighting against the attack from outside.

I removed the "Mantis" reference, since it would have confused the audience. Hai Tien didn't yet know the name of his opponent. Also, in the actual English dialogue that follows this "thought dialogue," both combatants state that they "do not let the word *death*" bother them, so the "art of dying" reference is more in keeping with what the mind-set of both individuals would be.

A similar situation occurred with another piece of thought dialogue that Bruce had written in Chinese:

The bigger the body of the giant, the more difficult for me to prevent being crushed when he falls every time I knock him down!

Two Chinese-language experts told me that this statement is, in essence, a cross between the English colloquialism "The bigger they are, the harder they fall" and, more precisely, "With his great size, he is going to find it difficult to keep getting up each time I knock him down!" I opted for the latter because, according to the linguistic experts, it's more in keeping with Lee's original intent than the literal translation would have been.

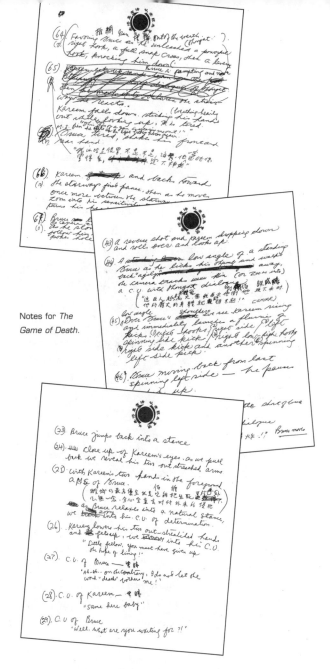

Notes for *The Game of Death.*

MISSING DIALOGUE IN <u>THE GAME OF DEATH</u>

Q: I greatly appreciated seeing Bruce Lee's footage for <u>The Game of Death</u> in the manner that he had intended in your film <u>Bruce Lee: A Warrior's Journey</u>. However, I noticed that the dialogue at the very end of the movie, where Bruce Lee yells out the window to the locksmith, is not included with his choreography writings and also that one dialogue scene in the film has no sound. Does that mean you somehow obtained the necessary dialogue for the end of the film but not for the earlier passage?

A: It's true that Bruce Lee did not write the final dialogue in which his character yells out the window to the locksmith down below or, at least, if he did write it down, it was subsequently lost. As what he was yelling was in Cantonese, I consulted with several Chinese-language experts as well as with specialists in lipreading to determine what Lee was saying. Factors such as whether he was speaking Cantonese or Mandarin (the dialects in which the film was to be originally dubbed) were considered, as well as the story line that Bruce wrote. In addition, individuals who were on the set when that scene was shot, such as Kareem Abdul-Jabbar, recollected that Bruce had yelled down to tell the remaining member of the team to "come on up."

Lipreading indicated that Lee's next response was "Yes!" Lee walks down the stairs and goes down to the last level, where he pokes more holes in the window and yells again, "Help me!" ("*Cul man*"—in Can-

tonese). Another response is heard, and then he exits the pagoda.

Paul Li, a Bruce Lee historian in Hong Kong, relayed to me that Lee had told someone in the Hong Kong press that when his character reached the bottom of the pagoda, he would have his exit way obstructed by a wing-chun man who assumed the *tong sao* position. Lee would then draw himself together and fix the man with a deadly stare, causing the man to stumble backward in fear and trip and fall. Bruce would then roll his eyes and leave the pagoda. However, as I could find no evidence of such a scene in Bruce's writings, I declined to film it while filming the story line sequences in Korea.

I was less fortunate in being able to get an English-language lip-reader to determine what Bruce Lee's character says to Dan Inosanto's character just prior to Inosanto's throwing away his last escrima stick and pulling out his nunchaku. The sound people suggested that I "just fudge something" so that there would not be a gap in the dialogue. However, that would have defeated the purpose of the film, which was to present Lee's vision the way he wanted. He would not have wanted some improvised dialogue passage that might not have accurately reflected his original statement. Since we do not know with certainty what he was saying in this passage, I thought it best to simply admit to that and let it go without dialogue. It rings truer this way and also serves to remind us that this was not a finished film, thereby adding to the authenticity and historical accuracy of the project.

ESCRIMA

Q: I had always thought that Bruce Lee was a practitioner or, at the very least, a supporter of the Filipino martial art of escrima. In fact, my instructor in JKD teaches escrima as part of his jeet kune do curriculum. However, after seeing all of the footage—particularly the dialogue passages between Bruce Lee's character and Dan—in The Game of Death, it strikes me that Lee did not support any kind of style—including that of escrima. How do you explain this apparent contradiction?

A: While much has been said in favor of many of the Indonesian and Filipino martial art methods, it remains true that very little of this was said by Bruce Lee. And, if the

recollections of certain of his students are accurate, what Bruce Lee did say about them wasn't all that complimentary.

This is as you would expect from an enlightened being who saw beyond the confines of "styles" and "nationalities." Lee was

In his fight with Dan Inosanto, Bruce Lee's character teaches the lesson of "using no way as way" and the advantage of "having no limitation as limitation." It marked the first cinematic presentation of his personal belief of jeet kune do, an art predicated on total freedom for the individual practioner.

While Bruce Lee choreographed the escrima routines that Dan Inosanto employed in their battle in *The Game of Death*, in real life, Inosanto recalls, Lee "took a pretty dim view" of the art when he first introduced it to him in 1964.

not interested in the "ways" or "styles" of others. As he said himself, he no longer believed in styles, which he saw as one-dimensional approaches to an activity that is multidimensional. Lee was interested in the "root" truth underlying efficiency in movement in human combat. So, it is ironic that his name has been attached—incorrectly—to many Filipino martial arts by proxy: one of his higher-profile students, Dan Inosanto, happens to be one of the art's biggest boosters. The public seemed to assume that because Dan had been one of Bruce Lee's students, anything he teaches has to have some connection to what Bruce Lee taught—which clearly is not the case.

One finds next to nothing in Bruce Lee's writings about the Indonesian or Filipino arts—as contrasted with, say, the disciplines of Western boxing and European fencing, or, for that matter, even wrestling and wing chun gung fu methodologies. Apart from one two-sentence statement about the attributes of a penjat-silat master (quoted from a book that Lee had in his library) which was simply transcribed by Bruce Lee—in an era before photocopy machines were readily available—Lee made no reference to escrima or penjat-silat at all in any of the 3,000-plus papers he left behind. The influences of western boxing, fencing, wrestling, judo, and wing chun gung fu are obvious even in a cursory scanning of his writings. The same cannot be said of the Filipino arts, and yet, owing to Inosanto's connection to Bruce Lee, the Filipino arts are often held to be synonymous with Bruce Lee's art.

The supreme irony in all of this is that Inosanto—utilizing escrima—took part in the one sequence in *The Game of Death* in which Lee set up a contrast and battle between escrima and his own "formless" art of jeet kune do. Lee's character, representing jeet kune do, was dressed very nonclassically in a yellow and black tracksuit, since he needed to adapt instantly to whatever combative situation beset him—from an expert joint grappler, personified by hap-kido expert Ji Han Jae, to a 7'2" giant of no discernible style, as personified by Kareem Abdul-Jabbar. Inosanto portrayed a Filipino escrimador, and Lee had him dress very traditionally, right down to the Muslim head-band. The fight sequence that followed revealed that escrima was too formalized and patternized to keep up with the more "elusive" art of jeet kune do.

In fact, after watching Dan's character's rhythmic twirling of the escrima sticks, Hai Jien, utilizing a bamboo whip (which also symbolizes the flexibility, speed, and dexterity of JKD—*The Game of Death* was to be loaded with such symbolism), says:

Y**ou know, baby, this bamboo is more lively, flexible, and longer than yours, and when your flashy stick routine cannot keep up with the speed of this elusive weapon, all I can say is that you will be in trouble!**

The two combatants clash, with Dan coming away the worse in the exchange, to which Bruce comments: "I'm telling you, it's difficult to have a rehearsed routine to fit in with broken rhythm!" They clash again, with Dan taking another hit. Bruce comments: "See? Rehearsed routines lack the flexibility to adapt."

Clearly, Bruce Lee was setting up a contrast between a patternized style (as represented in this instance by escrima) and jeet kune do, with escrima losing because it lacks the flexibility and adaptive capacity necessary to evolve and adapt to the broken rhythm and elusiveness of jeet kune do. It is not that Lee was "anti-escrima" nor "anti" any art; in fact, he had many friends in the martial arts community who practiced a wide range of arts. Personally, however, he was not in favor of any type of style, and escrima, with its distinctive patterns and methods, falls into the category of "style." In Bruce Lee's eyes, any style is patternized and made up of "rehearsed routines."

Near the end of the fight, Lee wrote, "Dan, in disgust, throws away his escrima"—not that he threw away simply his escrima sticks, but actually threw away his entire "style," indicating that it wasn't working against Lee's jeet kune do.

To my knowledge, and to his credit, Inosanto has never claimed that Bruce Lee was influenced by the art of escrima in any way, shape, or form. And when he teaches the various martial art styles that he does, Inosanto always makes it a point to keep the other arts separate from the elements of Bruce's art that he teaches.

The only references attributed to Bruce Lee with respect to the Filipino arts are anecdotal and, again, from Dan Insanto. In his book *Jeet Kune Do: The Art and Philosophy of Bruce Lee* (now out of print), on page 149, Dan says:

As early as 1964 at the first Internationals, I had introduced Bruce to the art of escrima. At that time, however, he took a pretty dim view of it.

He adds:

Then later when I visited him in Hong Kong, he told me what he liked and what he didn't like about escrima.

What Bruce liked, apparently, is what he referred to as the "flashy stick routine," which he thought looked good for use in movies, much like the staff and nunchaku that he utilized. This is a far cry from a blanket endorsement of the Filipino arts, and yet, again, many people today assume that these arts were either part of Bruce Lee's jeet kune do curriculum or somehow a positive influence in his martial development, when in fact they played no meaningful role.

PENJAT-SILAT

Q: A Jeet Kune Do Concepts instructor recently told me that Bruce Lee had a penjat-silat instructor. Have you found any evidence of this among Bruce Lee's appointment books or correspondence? What does Linda or any of Bruce's closest students recall about this?

A: I've asked Linda, Taky Kimura, Ted Wong, Wally Jay, and Jhoon Rhee, in addition to other students, all people who knew Bruce Lee well, and they have no idea where this rumor originated. I even consulted Bruce Lee's daytime diaries from 1966 to 1973 for the name of this instructor and found no mention of this person. I'm told that there is a photograph of Bruce Lee standing with this man. Even assuming this photograph does exist, there apparently is no evidence that this man was Bruce Lee's instructor in anything. Lee, being a celebrity and in the public eye, had his photograph taken with plenty of individuals, martial artists and otherwise.

When the issue of "Bruce Lee's instructor" comes up—and the martial arts being also a business for many people these days, the issue comes up frequently—you would do well to remember that Bruce Lee had only one martial art instructor, Yip Man, and he studied with him for only five years. Bruce Lee's best instructor was Bruce Lee, and it was only when he stopped seeking out "masters" and "teachers" and started to seek out the truth for himself that his talent as a martial artist hit full bloom and he revolutionized the martial arts. Anyone who makes such claims is looking to attach himself to Bruce Lee's accomplishments or to use Bruce Lee's credibility to prop up his own particular approach to martial art.

A page from Bruce Lee's choreography for *The Game of Death*, in which Lee's character explains the limitations of a "flashy stick routine."

FOUNDATIONS OF LEE'S WESTERN PHILOSOPHY

Q: Like Bruce Lee, I, too, am a philosophy student in America. I would

(47) Bruce's M.S. of twirling the
23 stick going into his C.U. "It's diff
    stick adjusts to the wooden rhythm, you know"
(48) C.U. of Dan's puzzlement
24 back to M.S. as he twirls his
    stick.
(49) favoring Bruce into another
25 more complex combination and
    gets Dan as he get back into he
    open stance.
(50) Dan's M.S. as he gets into
26 some strong combination.
(51) Bruce M.S. as he fits in
27 Calmly
(52) Dan, in disgusted, throw away
28 his escrima and immediately
    gets his two sectional staff.

Bruce Lee's choreography notes depicting the battle between escrima and jeet kune do.

like very much to see his philosophy taught to students in universities one day. However, how would you summarize what his philosophy is—and is it possible to break it down into the five traditional categories of Western philosophy?

A: I share your desire to see Lee's philosophy taught at the academic level. I think it represents the perfect bridge between East and West, being both purposeful and practical. The philosophy that forms the basis of Bruce Lee's films (and all of his other work) offers each individual an alternative to living the same day over and over again for the rest of your life. It is a means by which people can fully realize their innate potential in all aspects of their humanity: physical, emotional, and spiritual. Lee's philosophy celebrates the best that is within each of us as human beings. It is a philosophy of purportful productivity and achievement.

Bruce Lee's teachings present a rich alternative to the prevalent ideas dominating today's culture and academic institutions, which tend to offer a cookie-cutter system for education and learning without consideration of students' uniqueness as individual human beings. As Lee said with regard to such methods:

It doesn't matter what you are, who you are, how you are built, how you are structured, how you are made. You just go in there and be that product. And that, to me, is not right.

From his perspective, such methods, perforce, take no account of the potential inherent in the human spirit. Lee's philosophy is predicated on personal and unconditional liberation from all that would limit or bind us from becoming all that we are truly capable of. Lee's teachings stress independent judgment over herd mentality; self-expression over perpetuation of systems; and the primacy of our humanity (including our physiology and conscious and subconscious cognition systems) above all other issues such as ethnicity, social status, and institutions.

Lee challenged more than 2,000 years of tradition and provided the basis for a new renaissance of the human spirit. His philosophy is at once both highly integrated and free-form, providing a set of consistent fundamental principles which the individual is free to adapt to his or her own life situation, without becoming a prisoner to the edicts and dogma that compose so many of our institutionalized belief systems.

Bruce Lee never wanted to create a system of thought, nor to put a name on his personal philosophy. Names or symbols he viewed as potentially restrictive agents, limiting the scope of one's thought to only those areas that fall within the general definition of the symbol or words used to denote it. The menu is not the dinner and the map is not the tree, the soil, the water of the territory.

He had named the martial expression of his philosophy jeet kune do but later commented: "It is only a name; please don't fuss over it." Adding:

The title is not important. It's only a symbol for the kind of martial art we study. It's just like the X, Y, and Z of algebra. The emphasis should not be put on its title.

Freeing his thought of such restrictive encumbrances, Bruce Lee's philosophy was geared for living life fully, with every nerve exposed to the dynamic of life. It was also integrated, explicitly and implicitly including all five of the major branches of philosophy: metaphysics, epistemology, ethics, politics, and aesthetics. He first presented his philosophy in the form of the heroes he created for his hit films *The Way of the Dragon* (1972) and *Enter the Dragon* (1973) as well as the premier episode of the American television series "Longstreet" (1971), entitled "The Way of the Intercepting Fist" (the literal English translation of jeet kune do). He also presented his philosophy many times throughout his life in nonfiction form.

When asked how he planned to teach his children about life, his answer was:

Through all [my children's] education will run the Confucianist philosophy that the highest standards of conduct consist of treating others as you wish to be treated, plus loyalty, intelligence, and the fullest development of the individual in the five chief relationships of life: government and those who are governed, father and son, elder and younger brother, husband and wife, friend and friend. Equipped in that way, I don't think [they] can go far wrong.

From Lee's writings and discourses, we learn that the foundation of his philosophy is openness and brotherhood. He believed that it is best for individuals to remain free to see and interpret the truth for themselves, without shutting off their minds and becoming dependent on another individual's (or institution's) approach and interpretation of life.

The basic principles of Bruce Lee's philosophy can be categorized into the five traditional branches of Western philosophy as follows:

METAPHYSICS

- Axioms: existence, awareness, interdependency, identity

- Yin-yang and Tao as attempts to symbolize the ultimate reality of the axioms for purposes of communication

- The void—the fundamental energy source of the universe (the "living void")

EPISTEMOLOGY

- The nature, role, and effectiveness (and limitations) of logic

- The successful combination of the mechanical (linear thinking) and the instinctive (creative, artistic thinking)

- All types of knowledge ultimately mean self-knowledge (as extension of axioms of interdependency and existence)

- The "Three Stages of Cultivation"

ETHICS

- Treating others as you wish to be treated

- The fullest development of the individual in the five chief relationships of life: government and those who are governed, parent and child, elder and younger sibling, husband and wife, friend and friend

- The values: openness, brotherhood, intelligence, truth, sincerity, quality, self-actualization, honesty, integrity, compassion, equality, love, benevolence, loyalty, productivity, creativity

POLITICS

- Individual freedom

- Freedom of individual expression

- Society as the extension of individual rights

- The proper role and nature of trade (i.e., money)

- Having no limitation as limitation

AESTHETICS

- Art as the honest expression of one's soul

- Art as means of communication

- Self-actualization versus self-image actualization

- The human being as the creating individual

- Using no way as way

In summary, Lee's philosophy was not something geared to recruit fragmented "followers," or "secondhand artists," as Bruce referred to them, but rather to develop individuals—people of totality—as the self-actualizers and true individuals that the example of his life has revealed it is possible to become.

MARTIAL ART AND SELF-KNOWLEDGE

Q: What is the basis of Bruce Lee's belief that knowledge in martial art ultimately leads to a knowledge of self?

A: Bruce Lee sought out the ultimate truth of martial art, but he discovered that he could do this only by acknowledging that he was simultaneously learning about himself. He discovered that as you pursue the mastery of the martial arts, you will inevitably encounter barriers to your progress toward this goal. These barriers are your limitations, both perceived and physical: your physical ability, your problem-solving ability, your reasoning, how you handle defeat and success. All of these experiences teach you as much about yourself as about the goal you are pursuing.

PERSONAL FREEDOM

Q: The notion of achieving personal liberation is intriguing. How can Bruce Lee's teachings lead one to become free of psychological limitations?

A: The fundamental touchstone of Bruce Lee's martial art is freedom—not freedom from without to within, but rather from within to without. Many people speak of freedom in, say, the political arena as being simply "less government": fewer restrictions on *me*," "fewer demands on *me*," "less taxation on *me*."

As noted in the book *Bruce Lee: Artist of Life*, Lee saw that if we focus solely on external entities, the result is that we would "see ourselves as instruments in the hands of others and thus free ourselves from the responsibility for acts that are prompted by our own questionable inclinations and impulses."

Bruce Lee saw a more immanent freedom that we need to acquire: freedom from ourselves—from our expectations of ourselves, from all of the events and experiences that condition and mold us into who we *think* we are. We drag these overly self-conscious attitudes around with us like a ball and chain: our fears, our hang-ups, our insecurities, our fear of being different from the group. "What man has to get over is the consciousness of himself"—so said Bruce Lee.

As society is the projection of the individual upon the group, we can change society, government, policies, and so forth only by first changing the "root" on which society is based. If you wish better society, first have better citizens. "We start by dissolving our attitude—not by altering outer conditions."

How do we do this? By applying the tool of JKD, the "search for the ultimate truth," only this time to the "root" of our being, which, according to Lee, was to ask the question "How can I be *me*?" This internal search leads you to search within your heart and soul to discover that you are your own source of ultimate authority:

It is not a question of developing what has already been developed, but of recovering what has been left behind—although this has been with us, in us, all the time and has never been lost or distorted except for our misguided manipulation of it. . . . Scratch away all the dirt our being has accumulated and reveal reality in its is-ness, or in its suchness, or in its nakedness, which corresponds to the Buddhist concept of emptiness.

Bruce Lee used martial art as a means to honestly express himself and believed that to be a man of freedom is more important than to be a great fighter.

Bruce Lee's philosophy accepts you as you are. It does not seek to change you; it seeks to help you explore yourself—admittedly, a deeper self than your ego may now allow you to believe exists. For this reason, it is not a philosophy or belief system "on the make." It is, instead, a mirror in which is reflected the real you.

The bottle that contains the medicine, Lee stressed, is not as important as the medicine itself. The instructor's role is like that of any good physician: to help you get better:

The medicine for my suffering I had within me from the very beginning,
But I did not take it.

My ailment came from within myself,
But I did not observe it.
Until this moment.

Now I see that I will never find the light
Unless, like the candle, I am my own fuel,
Consuming myself.

It was this understanding that made Bruce Lee decide to close his schools: the ultimate authority on everything in life, including martial art, is *you*. You empower the art; the art does not empower you. After all, you, the human being—the creating individual—are always more important than any established style or system.

As Bruce Lee said:

With all the training thrown to nowhere, with a mind (if there is such a verbal substance) perfectly unaware of its own working, with the "self" vanishing nowhere, the art of JKD attains its perfection.

THE NEED FOR JEET KUNE DO SCHOOLS

Q: If the ultimate authority in jeet kune do is the individual practitioner, why are there so many schools teaching JKD?

A: In one respect, there exists no need for a school. If *you* see this truth—and can apply it on your own—then all is well. But what of those who cannot? What of those who still experience a gnawing feeling of personal unfulfillment? What of those who have lost their way and can't get back in touch with themselves? Or those who want to fully actualize themselves in all aspects of their humanity—mental, physical, and spiritual?

Training is required as the trigger mechanism for the internal process of discovery and self-knowledge—like the Buddhist ferryboat that is necessary to get one across the river, if only to be discarded on the other side. And, in truth, all of us are subject to the vicissitudes of life that can from time to time erode our more powerful insights—unless we are able to keep ahead of the curve, to keep pace with life's changes so that we can "change with change." Even the Buddhists have their *sanga* (or brotherhood) where they strive for, and seek to maintain, the transcendental state that led them to the experience of satori or *bodhi* or nirvana (enlightenment).

I liken Bruce Lee's art and philosophy to the methods of the optometrist, rather than, say, the guru. The guru tries to procure members for his organization. Members help to support him financially, pay off the mortgage on an expensive building, and keep the Lear jet fueled up, and they generally "belong" to the guru, boosting his membership and thereby proving by sheer weight of numbers the veracity of his creed. The optometrist, on the other hand, hopes to cure you of your dependency upon him; to get you, through the use of a corrective lens, to see reality more clearly. Bruce Lee's art is like the corrective lens in the refractor, or eye-testing machine, in the optometrist's office. The practitioner sits you down in the chair and asks you questions about yourself: Does it look clearer with this lens or with this lens? Looking at life from this perspective or that perspective? Looking at combat from the part—or from the whole?

And guess whose answer is the deciding one? *Yours. You decide.* And once you see things more clearly, you're on your way.

Similarly, Bruce Lee's art doesn't seek to "own" you, nor to "possess" you. It seeks only to help you to explore yourself physically, mentally, and spiritually, by correcting the astigmatism of self, or ego, that is blinding you to seeing and actualizing your true potential as a human being. That accomplished, you have no further need of the so-called ferryboat that has brought you from the shore of ignorance to the shore of transcendence.

Using Bruce Lee's words and teachings as a touchstone in our lives, we are inspired to question, to form our own judgments, and to set our own standards of truth. We have before us the example of how another human being was able to avail himself of a fuller, richer, more meaningful existence on this planet through altering his level of perception and looking at life in a new and exciting way. That is where training in Bruce Lee's art can prove to be very helpful.

Unlike other arts, JKD bears in mind that the end is not "mechanical efficiency" or the ability to "fill time and space through some sort of organized movements." As Lee pointed out, "Machines can do that." JKD realizes that your physical movement is your soul made visible. "Martial art," Bruce Lee said, "is the expression of the human soul."

He emphasized in *Artist of Life*, "There is no sets or form, for JKD is not a method of classified techniques, laws, and so forth, that constitute a 'system' of fighting." What confuses people is that "It does employ a sys-

tematic approach to training, but never a method of fighting."

A good JKD instructor is one who dispenses this systematic approach to training and, therefore, is a guide to his students, not the "keeper of secret information." There is no secret information. How can there be when the "secret" to the whole thing is within you and not your instructor? The instructor knows this only too well, having awakened to that fact himself after many years of training, and so he sees himself as a midwife to the birth of your discoveries and growth toward personal freedom as a fully actualized human being.

So, you can see that it's about much more than fighting; it's to round you into a complete and total person, a man or woman who is self-actualized and totally free. As Bruce Lee said: "To be a man of freedom is more important than to be a great fighter."

CHAPTER 15

FIRSTHAND ACCOUNTS OF BRUCE LEE

Bruce Lee touched the lives of many people through his art, his philosophy, and his friendship and love. Following are memories of Bruce from the people who were closest to him.

TAKY KIMURA, BRUCE LEE'S HIGHEST-RANKED STUDENT

Mine was a unique situation, a unique friendship with Bruce. I had spent a little over four years in a prisoner of war camp in America during the Second World War because of my ancestry. The basis for the frustration that I had fallen into was the fact that I was raised in an all-white community up in the tip of the Olympic Peninsula. Until I was about twelve years old, I thought I was just as white as my friends, but when I became a teenager, all of a sudden the young girls and the friends that I had—they still loved me, but it was something a little bit different. I could feel it. It wasn't discrimination; it was just something that was innate there, and I began to feel a little bit more insecure with myself.

And, of course, then the war came along. Because of the war in Europe, and because of my ancestry, they took all of us Japanese and put us into internment camps. Even the president said it was a concentration camp, actually, but I suppose that's neither here nor there. I spent a little over four years in there, and when I came out, I was a devastated person. I felt less than human. When I walked down the street, if a white person was walking behind me, I felt so inferior that I made myself stop walking and let the person pass me. Couple that with walking into a restaurant and having people just ignore you and not wait on you, and walking into a barbershop and they tell you they're closed. When I'd try to get on a Greyhound Bus, they would shove me back to the end of the line. I went through all of those things, much like the black people in this country have. It devastated me.

But then I met Bruce, and he picked up my spirits. He could take a look at you and see what was bothering you. He was only eighteen, but he had the unique knack of being able to read people. I was Japanese American, and coming from Hong Kong, he had been raised with the same resentment toward the Japanese that my American

friends possessed. Despite coming from that background and sharing those frustrations watching the Japanese soldiers come into Hong Kong, Bruce was able to look beyond that, to look at me as a human being. He didn't size me up, or say "He's Japanese— I'm not going to help this guy."

I think that was one of the wonderful things about Bruce: he had this inner desire to create equality among people and to try to bring the best out of people. So, he picked me up there and started working on me. He kept telling me that I was "just as good as anybody else," but I couldn't buy it at first because I just couldn't *feel* it.

As time went on, he started telling me to shape up: to get my hair cut differently and wear clothes that were not so depressing. He said, "Geez, Taky, you're dressing like an old man! Let's get you into something more modern!" He just started working with me to feel better about myself. I fought it for a while, but I finally gave in and started going with his advice. Then as I became more proficient with my physical appearance, I'd look in the mirror and I'd see something staring back at me that was somewhat more than insecure. I was able to lift myself up and recognize that because he kept telling me, "You're just as good as me—no better, no worse." That had a big effect on me. So, that's how Bruce shaped me up.

I've been categorized as "the keeper of Bruce's grave" here in Seattle. I try to make it up to the cemetery at least once a month. Often I may go four or five times during the month, depending on who comes in from other parts of the world. Many people who come are not even martial artists. You would expect the people who come to be into the martial arts and hoping to have some of Bruce's ability rub off on them, but that's not the case. These people often tell me, "I'm not even into martial arts. I just came to have some of that inspiration of his come into my life. I'm in a place where I need something."

Because of Bruce I've been able to help several young people to find themselves, to get out of the drug scene and things like that. I don't take credit for that; it's Bruce, but it's coming through me because I was his close friend.

The goal in life is to try to leave a legacy that helps people. There's an inscription on a bench by Bruce's grave that says, "The key to immortality is to live a life that is worth remembering." I think that we have not traveled and lived our life in a worthwhile manner unless we can leave a legacy behind us so that somebody can say after you're gone, "Boy, that guy was a really great guy." Bruce's personality and the positive nature of his character is an example of that. He was a man who left a mark.

KAREEM ABDUL-JABBAR, BRUCE LEE'S PRIVATE STUDENT

When you're formally studying any martial art, you get caught up in what the rules and regulations are and how to get there, how to achieve mastery of yourself and the art. Then, at a certain point, you don't need the art anymore to express yourself. You have to move beyond that. That was something that Bruce felt very strongly about.

Once he pointed out to me this great text from Miyamoto Musashi's *Book of Five Rings* on how to go out and deal with one-on-one combat, but Bruce then turned to me and said, "When you learn this, all you know is how to beat people up." He said that all you know is how to overwhelm people physically—and that does not make you an evolved human being. You must evolve so much beyond that in order to use that knowledge in the best and most productive way.

When you understand the nature of physical conflict, you also understand that between human beings it should be useless. We can achieve so much more and settle so much more using our brains and common respect and decency. The things that make us civilized and cultured serve us a lot more than martial art.

Sometimes you have to take the negative approach in order to understand where the positive side is. People who get too caught up in morality and those types of things end up being goody-two-shoes, and people who get too caught up in physical power and the ability to control others reflect a Fascist tendency—they have to deal with everything in terms of power. Bruce taught that we have to guard against those extremes and seek the middle path. That is the essence of it all: a balanced approach to what happens and how to deal with what happens.

When I was teaching my children about martial arts, I was confronted by people who said, "Why are you teaching them violence?" That's not what I was teaching them. I was teaching them how to cope with people who *use* violence. You also have to make the distinction clear to the people you're teaching and make sure that they incorporate it into their life view. If they don't have that view, they missed it, and they're going to end up punch-drunk prizefighters. It just gives you a negative end to that path—and Bruce understood that.

LINDA LEE CADWELL, BRUCE LEE'S WIDOW

Bruce was a man who never wasted a minute. In thirty-two short years, he lived every minute of his life fully. He spent great amounts of time not only studying his martial art and writing his film scripts and choreography notes but also in introspection, looking inward and at what the work he was doing meant to his personal growth. Fortunately, he actually wrote down on paper what he learned about life, which has been of such great benefit to all of us.

In the early years after Bruce passed away and *Enter the Dragon* came out, followed by Bruce's earlier movies, I received letters mainly from either the martial arts groups, who appreciated his tremendous martial arts skill and how that came across on screen, or from people who appreciated his acting. And that was great; that was wonderful. We thought, "That's really super that people realize that he was a super martial artist."

But then as the years went on and Bruce's popularity continued to grow, the tenor of the letters I started receiving indicated that people were seeing more to Bruce than just this martial arts skill. And through small indications in his films—maybe the insert of some philosophical saying—the people started to want to know more about Bruce Lee the human being.

So, over the last three decades, the appreciation for Bruce as more than a martial artist, as a man of many aspects and great depth, has grown among the viewing public. People now want to know what this man was all about. It's not just that he made fighting films that they happened to like the action in; they've realized that there is more about Bruce, more about a man, than what comes across on a film, and this initiates an interest in finding out more about him. That leads to their reading more of his writings, such as in The Bruce Lee Library Series, which contains all of his works, and being

able to apply what Bruce did or believed to their own lives.

That cuts across all races, cultures, nationalities, and economic strata: people see in Bruce's work and in his life something that they can apply to their own lives. So, a person who is poor can relate to Bruce in that way, because there were many years when we were just scraping by. Bruce was working arduously toward his goal, but financially we were just barely making it. They can relate to that, being persistent in a goal. Or, if they are physically inclined and want to be in good shape, they can use Bruce as a model because not only was he a martial artist, but also he was in superb physical condition. They can study his exercise methods, his training routines, his nutritional habits, and, again, his persistence to carry through—his discipline, which, of course, is something you learn so well through the study of martial art.

As far as his actual martial arts way, which he called jeet kune do, he often said, "This is not a Japanese art, it's not a Chinese art, it's not a Western art—it is my art; it is my self-expression." In that way, he lets people know that they need not learn just from a certain style or a certain master or a certain nationality of martial arts.

That's why I say that in so many respects, Bruce cuts across the barriers of race, age, gender, and nationality, and there is something that appeals to him for all levels of people. I get letters now—twenty-seven years after he's been gone—from people who weren't even born when he was alive, and they're telling me how he has motivated them to be a better person, to achieve their goals, to be in better physical condition, to live their own life from their own heart, rather than just following or emulating somebody else. It really does my heart good, and I think that Bruce would be smiling down to know that his work and his art have continued to benefit people all over the world.

APPENDIX A

BRUCE LEE'S CHOREOGRAPHY WRITINGS FOR <u>THE GAME OF DEATH</u>

The following is a verbatim transcription of the handwritten choreography notes that Bruce Lee composed and used in the final fight sequences shot for *The Game of Death*. They include multiple versions, or drafts, of the fight scenes and underwent additional revision when Lee got before the cameras. Note the numbers in square brackets after certain shot numbers in Lee's notes; these are alignment numbers in order to bring the shots more in line with what was actually shot that day, rather than simply going by the shot numbers on Lee's rough notes. At other points Lee has discarded papers that continued a combative sequence

and has rewritten the shot sequences, resulting in a break in numbers (for example, shot number 42 jumps to shot number 30).

Note also that Lee referred to Ji Han Jae by an alternate phonetic spelling of "Chi" and occasionally refers to his friend and student Kareem Abdul-Jabbar as "Lew" in deference to "Lew Alcindor," which was Abdul-Jabbar's name prior to his conversion to Islam. I have added certain words or points within square brackets to clarify a point, as many of Lee's notations were quickly dashed off and, in truth, were for his own private use rather than being notes for publication.

Being not only the star of the film but also its producer, director, and cinematographer, Bruce Lee made many technical references throughout his notes with regard to camera shots, angles, and production methodology. The following key may prove helpful:

ECU—Extreme Close-Up Shot

MCU—Medium Close-Up Shot

CU—Close-Up

M.S.—Medium Shot

OS—Off Screen (refers to a subject or sound that is outside of the camera frame)

WS—Wide Shot

LS—Long Shot

ELS—Extreme Long Shot

BG (bg)—Background

FG (fg)—Foreground

OTS—Over the Shoulder Shot

P.O.V.—Point of View Shot

CUT—A single shot inserted into a sequence that momentarily interrupts the general flow of action. Usually inserted to introduce a pertinent detail.

TRACKING SHOT—A shot taken from a camera mounted on a dolly that moves along a track to follow action or to "walk" with a character (typically it represents one character's point of view).

REVERSE ANGLE—A shot that is turned approximately 180 degrees in relation to the preceding shot.

TOP SHOT—A high-angle shot of a subject, taken from a crane or stationary elevated camera position.

DAN INOSANTO'S FIGHT WITH TIEN AND CHIEH YUAN

1. Tien and Chieh jump up [the stairs] and both look.

2. Dan sits on chair and gazes coldly. He has a bag alongside of him.

3. From M.S. Two-man shots of Tien and Chieh; we zoom in to a two-close-up stare.

4. P.O.V. scanning shot of Dan as we zoom/pan down to his bag close to him.

5. Tracking two-man M.S. as they shift their looks.

TIEN (TO CHIEH YUAN)

"Prepare our weapons."

(But Tien has not taken his out. Pause, both are looking)

TIEN (TO CHIEH YUAN)

"You have a longer weapon than his. You go first."

As the camera moves back, Chieh moves forward.

6. A [tracking-] in shot forward toward Dan as Dan reaches for his two sticks and slowly stands up as he coolly bangs his staff (teasing beat) and never changes his gaze as camera motion stops.

7. A M.S. of Chieh as we zoom in to his eyes (close-up).

8. A pan from sticks as we zoom back in to his M.S. with Dan banging his sticks and staring (banging with teasing beats).

9. Chieh M.S. as he twirls his staff with screams and shouts.

10. Same M.S. as number 8: Dan in his same teasing beat.

11. Close-up of Chieh turning around to look at Tien.

12. Tien's close-up as he encourages Chieh.

13. Close-up of Chieh as he turns back and looks at Dan. Then he screams toward screen.

14. As Dan twirls some fancy moves [with his sticks] toward camera and ends up with a cross [formation with the sticks].

15. Chieh backs up and looks back at Tien.

16. Tien's close-up

TIEN

"Don't let him psych you out!"

17. With [Dan's] crossed sticks in foreground, Chieh turns back to look at Dan.

18. Close-up of Dan with sticks crossed in front.

19. A low shot of [the] two men circling.

20. Favoring Dan as Dan knocks [the] hell out of Chieh.

21. Chieh's M.S. of his painful experience as he decides to go at it again.

22. Favoring Dan in another longer combination, again knocking hell out of Chieh.

23. [nothing written]

24. Down by kenpo and up.

25. #1: Front kick, lunge punch, and the dance of death. Dan looks at Tien.

26. #2: Dan looks at Tien.

27. Tien pulls out his short stick.

....

1. Bruce rushes up [the stairs], stops and looks.

2. P.O.V. favoring Dan; Tien is being pressed backward.

3. Bruce interferes, Dan stops, Tien falls on his ass.

4. M.S. of Dan looking with sticks in ready position.

5. Close-up of Bruce looking at Dan, then he turns.

6. Tien is on the ground, pissed and embarrassed about his [being] on the ground.

7. Bruce shifts his look—after reacting to Tien's posture—to Dan.

LEE
"Do you speak any English?"

DAN
"Of course I speak English!"

8. Bruce's M.S. as Tien comes up from the shot. After a gesture, [Bruce says]:

LEE
"I hope you don't mind us moving our man so that the two of us will have more room to groove."

9. M.S. of Dan after a gesture of approval.

DAN
"*But*, have your men stay as far away (pointing) from that stairway as possible."

10. Tracking out and in. Bruce's gesture of agreeing. Then motions the now confused Tien to do the job. Having brought back the unconscious Chieh, Bruce never takes his look from Dan.

11. Dan, with a smile, goes into his cocky combination of twirling.

12. Zoom close-up of Bruce's reaction to the above; we pull back as Bruce hands the double-jointed stick [i.e., the case containing his nunchaku] to the now wrecked Tien. After asking them to go to a far corner, Bruce then adjusts his bamboo staff.

13. M.S. of Dan as he gets into his teasing beat.

14. Close-up of Bruce while observing the above.

LEE
"You know, baby, this bamboo is longer, more flexible, and very much alive. When your flashy routine cannot keep up with the speed and the elusiveness of this thing here, all I can say is that you will be in *deep* trouble."

15. M.S. of Dan.

DAN
"That we will have to find out!"
    (Immediately he gets into some fancy movements)

16. From a nonchalant way, Bruce adjusts his sticks then gets into his wired open stance.

17. Dan's close-up as he fixes his glance into Bruce's stance.

18. Favoring Bruce as Dan attempts a shin lead hit, which Bruce backs way [from] with control, matching his movement, at the end of which he whips Dan right on the face.

19. Close-up of Dan's face with slash.

20. Zoom over the shoulder. Close-up of Bruce.

LEE
"I'm telling you, it's difficult to have a rehearsed routine to fit in with broken rhythm!"
    He immediately launches a few fakes and hit, tying Dan in knots.

21. Dan gets into his twirl, though his forehead wound forms a cross.

22. Bruce again gets into his wired stance.

LEE
"See? Rehearsed routines lack the flexibility to adapt."

23. Zoom into his close-up, favoring an angry Dan as he attacks, while Bruce's stick never engaged (active/passive both).

24. Bruce gets him with advanced targets of wrist, shin, etc.

25. Over-the-shoulder M.S. of Bruce, as Dan attempts something. Bruce's quick reaction stops him (cool reaction with above).

26. [1] M.S. of Dan, in disgust, throws away his escrima and whips out his two-sectional staff, twirls, and gets into his stance.

27. Bruce observes, then snaps his signal [snaps his fingers and motions for his nunchaku].

28. Tien disgustedly hands the bag to Chieh! Chieh comes forward with the bag.

29. Close-up of Dan's reaction.

30. M.S. of Bruce.

LEE
"Surprised?"
(He twirls and starts circling)

31. A top shot of a snap routine.

32. Dan's getting back into stance.

33. Bruce's getting back into stance.

34. Dan hits [toward] camera.

35. Continue with last move. Bruce snaps back and hits [toward] camera.

36. Observation of Tien and Chieh.

37. Tracking in to M.S. of Bruce in his "brand" stance.

38. M.S. of Dan in his slingshot.

39. Favoring Bruce—work out combination (longer).

40. Dan's getting hit in last [exchange] and recovers. Twirls and gets back into stance.

41. Bruce appears complacent and gets back into stance, and we zoom in to a close-up.

42. Close-up of Dan.

....

30. Favor Bruce—another sequence: Bruce fake (Dan snaps); Bruce lead hook kick to calf—immediately Bruce jabs Dan.

31. Dan's getting it but immediately gets into stance again. Pan him starting to circle.

32. Bruce's casual open stance after twirl.

33. Favoring Dan into an attack.

34. Bruce's recovering stance.

35. Panning Dan in to an attack.

36. Continue with Bruce's return.

37. Dan's backing up (M.S.).

38. L.S. Bruce bouncing with occasional feints and play—moving.

39. Dan's in rigid stance, observing Bruce M.S.

40. Bruce bouncing.

41. Favoring Dan's chasing and gets Bruce on left cheek.

42. Continue with Bruce close-up registering hit.

43. M.S. favoring Dan with [over?] Bruce's shoulder.

DAN

"How about that?"

(Immediately Bruce snaps [out his nunchaku] and hits Dan after the talk)

LEE

(Bruce moving position with Dan's arms [over Dan's shoulder])

"How about that!"

Dan tries to take advantage, Bruce slips [the attack] and small position, then smiles and hits toward camera.

[Remainder of notes for this fight sequence are missing.]

FIGHT BETWEEN LEE AND CHI

1. Three men come up the stairs. They stop and find the man "Chi." We zoom in to Tien's close-up. Order: Lee, Chieh Yuan, Tien Jun.

2. A L.S. of Chi lying on the dragon bed.

3. From Tien's close-up we pan with Tien, [who] looks to Chieh. Chieh's close-up; he is looking.

4. A M.S. of Chi as he gets up, pulls the curtain, and looks.

5. Same as 7 can be shot. Close-up of Lee.

6. A M.S. of Chi as he deliberately turns on the red switch.

7. Same as 4 can be shot. A top shot of everyone, including red area of arena.

8. A M.S. of Chi tracking as he walks to the middle of the arena, into the red

zone, no expression. Behind him is the stairway [to the next level]. As he speaks, we zoom in to his eyes.

CHI

"As you gentlemen know, red spells danger. Therefore I advise you people not to step into this warning arena. If you want to go on living, stop here and go back downstairs. Life is precious."

Or:

CHI

"As you know, red spells danger, and I advise people not to step in this warning area. That is, if you want to live, better stop here and go back downstairs."

9. A M.S. of three people's reaction. Chieh and Tien both look back with the exception of Lee [who is looking with] airtight awareness as he pushes everyone to one corner and stops.

....

1. Side low angle of Chi looking toward Lee.

2. Same side low angle of Lee looking toward Chi. As he moves, we track back; Lee enters the red light without flinching, a committed determination [is displayed on his face].

3. Tracking-in angle (same speed) toward Chi as he stands there motionless (the same determination).

4. Same as 7 can be shot. A top shot of the two staring at each other at the firing line (in the red arena).

5. Favored angle, a close-up of Bruce in (subliminal white color plus deep breathing)—the beastly killing determination (look through)—without changing (casual, deadened).

6. Chi, close-up of preparation.

....

11. Favoring Lee in a two-man shot as Lee relaxes, smiles, and puts his hand back; while keeping his smile, initiates a "lightning" right finger-jab feint, follows instantaneously with a low/high hook kick (fluid speed, intense grace and powerful—1-2-3). Chi flew across camera and lands.

....

1. Hold [on] Chi's landing, but immediately gets into his stance.

2. Tien's and Chieh's reaction.

3. P.O.V. Lee and Chi squaring off, Lee in right stance, Chi in right stance. Lee is playfully serious, snapping a hand at Chi; the second one, Chi retaliates with a kick while Lee dances away.

4. M.S. as Lee changes his stance, tracking in to a one-two feints and connects with a right cross ("lightning").

5. Chi staggers back.

6. Favoring Lee as he runs into a spin kick, knocking Lee back—but keeping his cool.

Tien urges Chieh to move on.

TIEN
"You are my brother. I will let you do this first deed of merit. You go ahead. Wish you success."

CHIEH
"Thanks!"
Tien appears complacent.—Chieh exits.

7. Hold L.S. as Chi attempts to block Chieh's way (Chieh is already in motion). Lee intercepts.

8. Chi moves toward lens.

9. Lee's side, hook, spin.

10. Chi's backing up.

11. Lee trying to stop Chieh recklessness, but he goes up—awareness.

12. Favoring Lee in cool movement—time—a beat—Chieh screams and falls and dies.

....

7. Chieh is dead.

8. Chi dashes.

9. Lee's hit toward camera.

10. Chi backs up and moves forward with feint.

11. Favor Bruce; he is thrown. Bruce's "cool" acceptance.

12. Tien's reaction, looks toward stairs—rushes forward.

13. Techniques (Lee's superiority) groin shot.

14. Tien's reaction.

THE FIGHT BETWEEN LEW [KAREEM ABDUL-JABBAR] AND TIEN JUN

1. Tien jumps up to a confident natural stance.

2. Kareem sitting.

3. Tien gets into a stance of confidence.

4. Kareem gets up.

5. Tien is shaken (with panning).

6. Shadow shot.

7. Kareem M.S. as he takes off gown and screams.

SECOND DRAFT

1. Tien Jun breaks in the door. Puts on the martial art posture!

2. A shot of Lew.

3. Reverse shot over Lew's shoulder of Tien Jun's uncertainty.

4. A neutral shot of the two with height contrast shadow on the background.

5. C.U. of Lew's determination.

6. C.U. of Tien Jun's expression of fear.

7. Low-angle close-up of Kareem's determination and confidence as he screams, cut.

8. Shot favoring Kareem as he kicks, James ducks while the heavy bag splits; sand leaks out.

9. M.S. Tien. He is scared. Sand keeps pouring out. He looks at Kareem.

10. Close-up of Kareem to C.U. of eye glasses.

11. Close-up of Tien's frightened eyes, pull back to head close-up as he screams and moves (cut).

12. Low-angle hand-held camera toward Kareem. Kareem's outstretched hand grabs as Tien's hands come up; Kareem pushes.

13. A side shot of Tien's face being grabbed, and as his two hands come up, Kareem pushes Tien out of shot.

14. We see James Tien flying back (from trampoline) into the shot (a spectacular crash). Kareem's legs enter shot. We

zoom into Tien's losing of coolness. As he looks down we pan low to a:

15. Close-up (low angle) Kareem deadpan look with shades [on].

16. L.S. As Tien gets up, Kareem gets into a series of kicks (side, hook, side, straight punch, or spin kick).

17. Cut to Bruce's sequences. As he ends, he gets into a stance and hears heavy thuds and [sees] dust from upstairs.

18. Tien's rolling as Kareem's foot attempts to crash him. He grabs it and after a struggle pushes him off and gets up (show relative size of hand and foot).

....

1. Hold Tien falls, Lew walks in and picks up Tien by the neck.

2. Close-up of Tien struggling from the choke (Lew in shot).

3. Close-up of Lew's deadpan (Tien in shot).

4. Tien makes a desperate kick and Kareem lets go. We zoom in to a pissed-off feeling of Kareem; as he moves, we cut.

5. P.O.V. camera slowly moving forward as Tien backs up and he is scared, calling Dragon [Bruce] to help.

6. Bruce finishes foe . . . screams [are heard] near door.

LEE'S FIGHT WITH KAREEM ABDUL-JABBAR

1. M.S. as Bruce jumps up [the stairs]. Tien is thrown across the screen. Bruce looks/cut.

2. A shot of Tien. He is dead.

3. M.S. of Bruce as he advances; he looks and stops. Camera zooms in to a close-up.

4. Over Bruce's shoulder. A shot of Kareem.

5. Tracking close-up of Bruce after flashback dialogue; as we pull back, he gets into a stance.

6. Kareem steps backward and sits down as we track in to a close-up.

7. Close-up of Bruce as he yells/cut.

8. As Bruce launches a kick, Kareem out-reaches him with a straight kick, knocking [Bruce] down.

9. Hold [on] Bruce falling and he looks.

10. Kareem rocking [in his chair]. Stops and rises.

11. Two-man shot (both facing each other) as Bruce rises, and as he attempts something, Kareem right lead stop [hit], right hook kick. [Bruce] blocks Kareem's right lead [but is knocked] down [by the] hook kick. Bruce rises and drops again.

12. Close-up of Bruce—thought dialogue (thought).

13. Close-up of Kareem as he yells.

14. Top shot favoring Bruce. As Kareem plants his side kick, Bruce trips him.

15. A shot of entangled feet.

16. Shot of Bruce exerting force (see Kareem if possible).

17. Shot of struggling of the entangled feet.

18. Close-up shot of Kareem's ease.

19. Shot of feet as Kareem is winning.

20. Tracking close-up of disgusted Bruce. As we pull back, Bruce rolls away and immediately up while Kareem moves and just sits there.

21. Bruce close-up as he moves forward.

22. P.O.V. track-in shot as Kareem reaches out with his two palms (side angle).

23. Bruce jumps back into a stance.

24. Tracking close-up of Kareem's eyes. As we pull back, we reveal his two out-stretched arms.

25. With Kareem's two outstretched hands in the foreground, a M.S. of Bruce.

LEE

"The best advantage of Mantis is that it can ignore death, has no distracting thoughts and can concentrate in fighting against the attack from outside."

As Bruce relaxes into a natural stance, we zoom in to his close-up of determination.

26. Kareem lowers his two outstretched hands, and he gets up. We zoom in to his close-up.

KAREEM

"Little fellow, you must have given up the hope of living!"

27. Close-up of Bruce.

LEE

"Ah-ah, on the contrary; I do not let the word *death* bother me!"

28. Close-up of Kareem.

KAREEM

"Same here, baby."

29. Close-up of Bruce.

LEE

"Well, what are you waiting for?"

30. Hand-held camera as Kareem kicks toward camera: side, hook, side.

31. Bruce blocks the last kick as he backs up.

32. Favoring Kareem as he right hook/left straight/right hook/right side [kicks? toward Bruce] and gets hit by a stomach punch.

33. Bruce follows [with] another stomach punch. Left cross/right hook, knocking Kareem back. Kareem ducks, but he [Bruce] gets a left hook from Lew, and down Bruce goes. However, he angrily gets up.

34. As Kareem hook kicks, Bruce's left hook kick lands on his planting left foot—right low/high and knocks him down.

35. Bruce walks into shot wanting to punch the outstretched Kareem; he gets thrown out of shot; rises (O.S.—glass cracking), sits up, turns, looks.

36. As Bruce rolls over, Kareem comes across screen left; he pushes Bruce's head on the broken glass. Zoom struggle; zoom back as Bruce raises his two legs and presses into a handstand.

37. Favoring Kareem as the two feet [of Bruce] come down (with a hard tingling sound) on Kareem, striking hard on his ears and knocking him back into his stance, disturbed.

38. Bruce moves back to the center but not without his defiant gesture of licking thumb and inviting gesture.

39. Kareem, from his stance, touches his two ears and moves forward.

40. Favoring Bruce as Kareem comes into distance, and as he comes in with a side [kick], Bruce times his planting of foot and groin-thrusts him, knocking him back.

41. Kareem staggers back and immediately launches forward out of shot.

42. Top shot favoring Bruce as Kareem enters shot, coming in with a hook, and as Bruce attempts to bridge gap, Kareem snaps out his front lead [punch], but Bruce slips it [over his] right shoulder, then ducks the following left cross and bobs up and immediately [delivers a] right hook or swing to [the] ribs of Kareem. Kareem staggers back, and as he comes again with a right hook kick from a left stance, Bruce ducks and scores from underneath [with] a groin shot, and Kareem drops.

43. A reverse shot and Kareem dropping down and rolls over and looks up.

44. A low-angle of a standing Bruce as he licks his thumb and walks back "agiley." [As Bruce walks] away, the camera tracks him (or zoom in to) a close-up with thought dialogue:

LEE
(Bruce smirks)
"The bigger the body of the giant, the more difficult for me to prevent being crushed when he falls every time I knock him down."

45. Low-angle: Over Bruce's shoulders we see Kareem rising and immediately launches a flurry of kicks: (1) right hooks (2) right side (3) left spinning side kick (4) right low-high hooks (5) right side kick and (6) another spinning left side kick.

46. Bruce moving back from last spinning left side [kick]—he pauses to look up.

47. A close-up of Kareem: [he] is a little short of breath.

48. Close-up of Bruce—thought dialogue:

LEE
"Look at him. Give him the fatigue bombing!"
Bruce moves.

49. Top shot over Bruce's shoulder favoring Kareem. As Bruce makes a fake move on him, Kareem immediately snaps front (1) right lead, (2) right hook kick—a one-two combination and a right hook kick as Bruce times his planting [foot] but without actually scoring. Kareem backs up. (Note: Maybe more thought dialogue [here] between Kareem's recognition, then verbally telling him: "This little son of a gun can sure move fast!") More

fight (fighting due to anger) verbally or thought flashback to illustrate theme.

50. Insert of foot on knee.

51. Favor Bruce [as he] knocks Kareem down with two punches and jumps on top of him.

52. Close-up of Bruce as he pushes hand and secures a [arm and neck] lock.

53. Top shot of two men struggling.

54. Close-up of Kareem's struggling.

55. Top shot to level: Kareem flips Bruce over. Wants to elbow Bruce, but Bruce elbows him while Kareem backhands him, knocking Bruce down. Both stand, favoring Kareem.

56. Tracking favoring Bruce. As he attempts to come in, Kareem blocks his left side kick and right punches him, grabs his head, and [delivers] another right cross— Bruce drops [but is] immediately up and reaches for screen.

57. Insert of Bruce fumbling breakage of paper window; turns and looks.

58. [1] Kareem attempts to advance but stops by the light.

59. [2] Track pulls back as Bruce runs toward Kareem and digs a few hooks to his stomach and a final dynamic high hook (kick? punch?); as Kareem staggers by it, he grabs Bruce's arms. Bruce head-butts him (insert stomping Kareem's foot), pushing him back.

60. [3] Continue tracking with pushing away. Reverse-angle favoring Kareem as Bruce (with back facing camera) slips Kareem's right lead over [his] right shoulder [and] weaves out of Kareem's left cross. Bruce comes out with a very dynamic hook [that] snaps Kareem's neck back, and as his head snaps back, his knees buckle and his feet fall out underneath him on the mattress.

61. [4] Reverse-angle of Bruce as Kareem hits the floor, and as Kareem gets halfway up, Bruce throws a heavy right cross on his chin, knocking him back down.

62. [5] Kareem falls on the ground. A blur-sharp-blur of Bruce standing there.

63. [6] Tracking, favoring Kareem as he hurriedly adjusts his nearly fallen glasses, and as he gets up, we pan him getting up and [he] does a step-and-slide side

kick. Bruce backs away, then edges back. Kareem also backs up, then Kareem attempts another kick—Bruce backs up away, then edges back. The third time Kareem side kicks, Bruce jams into a groin shot, knocking him down on shot.

64. [7] Favoring Bruce as he unleashes a powerful right hook, a full snap cross, then a leverage hook, knocking him down.

65. Kareem falls down (breathing heavily). Sticking his hands out while looking up. He is tired.

66. M.S., then . . .

KAREEM (THOUGHT DIALOGUE)

"This tough son of a gun is wearing me out!"

Then he gets up [but] the light [from the window] bothers him again.

[8] Bruce is panting and moves. Bruce, tired, shakes the front and rear hand:

LEE (THOUGHT DIALOGUE)

"I am already very tired. No, no, Hai Tien, he must be much more tired than you. Calm down."

67. [10] Kareem backs toward the stairways. First a pause, then as he moves once more between the stairways, we zoom in to his sensitivity to the light and turns his head [away from it].

68. [11] Bruce looks, turns, and looks back [as] the camera zooms in to the source of light. Then tracking begins. As he slowly backs into the windows, we follow him with track. He nonchalantly pokes holes in all the windows.

69. [12] Reacting more sensitively [to the light], Kareem walks to the bottom of the stairs to avoid the strong beam of light with his arms [shielding eyes].

70. [13] With Kareem as we see Bruce circle across the stairways and come across to the [temporarily blinded] Kareem, who suddenly faces him with back toward camera.

71. [14] A close-up of Kareem's eyes.

72. [15] A "red" color filter (or something). P.O.V. of a surprised Bruce.

73. [16] A shot (maybe from other side of stairway) as Kareem attempts a move and immediately reacts to the light. [He]

turns and [heads] back to the stairway as Bruce pursues and jump-kicks.

74. [17] Kareem attempts to snap a punch, as Bruce slips it over the left shoulder, Bruce whips a powerful right hook to the stomach, then double hook [to] the head as Kareem bumps his head and pitches forward.

75. [18] With Kareem down and instinctively he climbs to the entrance of the stairway.

76. [19] P.O.V. pushes into a blinded Kareem and stops.

77. [20] Close-up of Bruce (with Kareem's fist in foreground).

LEE

"You have done your job, my friend. Please let me pass and go upstairs!"

[This dialogue was shortened to: "Why continue? Just let me pass."]

78. [21] Close-up of hand-shielding [his eyes] Kareem.

KAREEM

"You have forgotten that I, too, am not afraid of death!"

He moves forward swinging a wild right hook.

78. [22] [Although this is cut 79, Bruce has it written as cut 78.] Over Kareem's shoulder shot as Bruce backs up from [Kareem's swing] a one-two and Bruce lands with a powerful right hook, followed up with a leading right-hook kick to the head. Kareem falls; Bruce jumps on him with a neck lock.

79. [23] A shot of Kareem landing on the floor, and as he rolls over on his hands and knees, Bruce jumps into shot with a head lock. [Bruce crossed out the preceding techniques.]

77. [24] A close-up tracking of the two as Bruce says,

BRUCE

"Please! Let me pass!"

78. [25] Kareem shakes his head, and as he gasps for breath, he crawls out of the shot after a few tracking shots.

79. [26] Tracking, we see Kareem back as he swings Bruce up, crashing through the bed. But Bruce still hangs on. Bruce somehow got out and he yells:

BRUCE

"Please! Just say [you will] let me pass!"

80. [27] Close-up of Kareem shaking his head. As we pan to his hand on the broken bed.

81. [28] Kareem trying to arch upward. Bruce is forcing the motion.

BRUCE

"Just say 'yes!'"

Kareem arching [his back], [his] hand stretched. Bruce's expression is also in. Suddenly Kareem collapses. We track him to a close-up.

82. [29] A top shot from the stairs with Kareem's body lying there, Bruce sitting. He turns and looks up the stairs. Tiredly gets up and staggers toward James's [body], then walks downstairs.

NOTES ON POSSIBILITIES ON KAREEM'S FIGHT WITH BRUCE

Keeping distance intermix with thought dialogue.

Kareem: "This man fights like a wildcat!"

BRUCE LEE'S SCENE BREAKDOWNS FOR THE GAME OF DEATH

This excerpt contains the creation of a character, Lee Guo Hao, who later is the hero in Lee's epic martial-philosophy screenplay *Southern Fist/Northern Leg*. Lee Guo Hao, or "Lee Gok Ho" in Cantonese, is the Chinese name—meaning "National Protector"—with which Bruce and Linda Lee christened their son, Brandon.

For an explanation of the abbreviations and numbering used here, see page 250.

1. Aboard Kai Tak airplane (interior—day)
   [a] Kid and girl, with kid wanting to sit in window seat.

   [b] The "professional" announcement of trip, mentioning the stop over in Korea en route.
   [c] The recognition.

2. Plane takes off from Hong Kong (exterior—day)

3. Plane (interior—day)
   [a] Kid's initiation of conversation for contrast with martial art nut's nagging—make him a spectator (mention Lee is taking a tour of Southeast Asia with sister and brother); Yu Ming's

wonder of Lee's quitting [the championship fight].

[b] Flashback intercut with appropriateness.

    [1] wild and primitive (insert with appropriate intercut—my blank look—from now on).

    [2] technical stage (Yu Ming's admiration).

    [3] nonchalant stage (boy's aggravation—reproach).

4. Plane landing in Korea

[a] Announcing the one-hour stopover. Kid insisting or I like to see Korea's airport interior.

[b] Yu Ming's friendly handshake, wanting to talk more on way to next stop.

5. Korea airport interior and phone booth

[a] The usual tourist routine at airport, with kid wanting cold drink.

[b] Paging Lee.

[c] Sharp and cold conversation of Tien.

6. Korea airport entrance with nice car outside

Time one thug opening door, getting in, starting engine, with Lee's casual line of "Nice weather," with two "wooden" thugs on each side—rigid with only eyeballs moving.

7. Brief car ride in Korea.

8. Boss's house (exterior—day)

[a] When one man comes out to greet Lee, Lee walks away and suddenly turns to the two expressionless thugs:

LEE

"Thank you!" (blank expression)

    "Man! That's a big snake!" (the two thugs react normally)

    "That's more like it—don't be so stiff."

[b] Then Lee walks toward camera and blocks lens.

9. Boss's office (interior—day)

[a] First Change: With the block out, the door is opened; Lee walks in.

[b] Everybody is here; the kid is being entertained, Nora is scared, everyone looks. And we zoom in to Tien as he tells the rest of the martial artists that:

TIEN

"This is *the* Lee Guo Hao, 'the Yellow-Faced Tiger' as foreigners refer to him."

    And we cut to Tien's particular interest.

[c] P.O.V. of Tien on Bruce's fancy clothing.

[d] Kid coming over innocently with toys. Lee, after brief look at worried Nora:

LEE

"It's very 'kind' of Uncle——"

    [e] Interrupting introduction/meeting (as a whole line) by saying he would like a cup of tea.

    [f] Reaction of Tien and others, showing Bruce's unpopularity.

10. A hallway and two guest rooms [exterior] or [interior]
Bruce sends kid away to play or get a drink.

11. "Brief" stay at girl's room
[Lee tells Nora] Not to let kid know.

LEE

"Stay inside and don't run around!"

12. Out of girl's room into the other guest room and closes door

13. Boss's office

    [a] Second Change: Lee enters with hip fashion clothes.

    [b] From hanging up of phone to tapping of fingers on table. Boss's deadly warning that luckily Lee did not spend too much time with girl and boy; otherwise they will have to be eliminated for knowing too much.

    [c] The introduction of people (handshake introduction).

    [1] Huang Chia Da—$2,000 and mother's operation

    [2] American—he is practical

    [3] Hsie Yuan (Chieh Yuan)—$700; he is strong and loves to show his strength, simpleminded)—Chieh Yuan's reaction.

    [4] Lee Kun—he costs cheap because he is an alcoholic and a cheap petty thief

    [5] Tien—so far cost me the most because he is efficient and is the current Asian champ

TIEN

"By the way, I do not like retired and undefeated champions."

    As Lee starts to walk away, Tien won't let go.

TIEN

"On top of that, for a retired champion, you sure have a bad memory. I've just spoken to you at the airport not too long ago. How can you have forgotten my voice?"

    (Pause for P.O.V.)

LEE

"You know something, you sound tougher than you look."

    (Release handshake)

[d] Boss offers money and coolly gets turned down, but Lee has to do it anyway because boss further warns him of the relationship of the boy and girl's lives and his goal.

[e] Briefly mentions mission but will go into details tonight in the projection room.

(Cut directly to)

14. Projection room (same room as above—[i.e., meeting room])—possibly Nora will be added
The exterior—the electronics must be taken care of.

[a] From a blurred image of the Temple of the Leopard, and the introduction of each man's skill and each attacker's duty—with Lee and Tien to watch over the whole [operation], particularly "Together to fight the Tower of the Unknown."

[b] Mention the only survivor (Huang) of many previous attackers, but unfortunately Huang is committed at local nuthouse and is no use because he cannot tell much, aside from the comment: "Unbelievable agility and power!"

[c] Lee's built up Huang's kicking ability.

[d] Boss mentions tomorrow's meeting at 11:00 A.M. and asks everyone to rest.

[e] Bruce asks permission to use car to visit Huang.

BOSS

"Of course you can use my car, but I can tell you it's a waste of time."

LEE

"Thank you for letting *just* me go."

BOSS

"Ha! Ha! That is why I like you. You know you have to come back!"

14. Boss's house (exterior—morning)
Tien is with chauffeur, shoptalking, and suddenly Bruce comes out.

11. With Tien's complaint of car to Boss—(exterior)
[a] Tien bitching to chauffeur.
[b] About clothes.

TIEN

"I sure don't like the way you dress as a martial artist."

LEE

"How does a martial artist normally dress?"
(Tien's hesitation)

LEE

(Continuing)

"It is not how he dresses—that's his own personal taste, anyway—but what really counts is what is behind those clothes of the martial artist, isn't it? By the way, have you looked at how you dress lately?"
(Tien's look)

12. Sanatorium hallway and padded cell.

13. Boss's office (with Tien beside him)
    [a] [Nothing written.]

TIEN

"You have a bad habit of being late."

LEE

(Purposely ignoring Tien)

"You want your job done, don't you?"
    [b] Boss assures Lee that boy and girl are fine and know nothing about the project.

LEE

"You have no choice anyway. You need me, and by the way, don't you or anyone in this house lay even one finger on either one of them!"
    (Tien laughs)

BOSS

"I can assure you that my guards personally will take good care of them. And I might even be generous enough to let you see them anytime you want—but don't even try or think that you can leave this house. My generosity, you see, has a limit."
    [c] Establish purpose of meeting, set date of attack.
    [d] Ask them to take tomorrow morning easy and conserve your energy for today.

15. Training garden
    [a] Everybody training with Bruce. Nora and the kid, and the payment.
    [b] About Mantis—pull girl away and back with tears in her eyes.
    [c] About money.

LEE

"I want you to remember me."

BOY

"Why? I see you every day."
    (Nora is sobbing)

Add Tien's bossing everybody—especially Chieh Yuan.

Start to walk toward camera. Camera zooms in on boy and girl as they look.

[d Bruce then walks and hides Lee Kun.

[e] Tien's instigating with Chieh Yuan to fight Bruce; Bruce turns tide.

15-a. Shows night before [scene 15—in Nora's room]

[a] Everyone's expression as Bruce walks out to have some air.

[b] American seeing Bruce is eating, sitting near to American; mentions game of death.

[c] Add water turn off, water dripping.

16. Boss's house (exterior)
The small bus (like *King and I* music).

[a] Everyone equipped out with music—stop—everyone waits.

[b] "Good morning, fellas."

17. Bus to temple.

18. Preparations to break in.

19. The big fight.

20. The arrest.

21. The airplane.

REFERENCES

Broer, Marion R., Ph.D. 1960. *Efficiency of Human Movement*. Philadelphia: W. B. Saunders.

"Bruce Lee: The Ted Thomas Interview." 1994. Boise, ID: Little-Wolff Creative Group.

Campbell, Joseph, with Bill Moyers. 1991. *The Power of Myth*. New York: Doubleday, Anchor Books.

Carriere, Jean-Claude. 1994. *Violence and Compassion*. New York: Doubleday.

Dyson, Geoffrey H. G. 1964. *The Mechanics of Athletics*, 3rd ed. London: University of London Press.

Ellinger, Herbert. 1996. *Buddhism*. Fort Walton Beach, FL: Trinity Press International.

Grigg, Ray. 1994. *The Tao of Zen*. Boston: Charles E. Tuttle.

Heidenstam, Oscar. 1963. *Modern Weight Training*. London: Nicholas Kaye.

Kopell, Harvey P., M.D., and Nancy C. Kester, M.D. 1969. *Help for Your Aching Back!* New York: Grosset and Dunlap.

Lee, Bruce. Handwritten notes titled "Buddhism's Eightfold Path," from *Commentaries on the Martial Way*, vol. 7. Bruce Lee papers.

Lee, Bruce. Handwritten essay titled "Living: The Oneness of Things." Bruce Lee papers.

Lee, Bruce. Handwritten notes titled "Newton's Three Laws of Motion," from *Commentaries on the Martial Way*, vol. 7. Bruce Lee papers.

Lee, Bruce. Handwritten notes titled "Zen," from *Commentaries on the Martial Way*, vol. 1. Bruce Lee papers.

Lee, Bruce. Handwritten paper titled "Economical Expressing—a Way of Liberation." Bruce Lee papers.

Lee, Bruce. Early 1960s. Letter to Eva Tso.

Lee, Bruce. 1961. Handwritten essay titled "The Tao of Gung Fu." Bruce Lee papers.

Lee, Bruce. 1963. Essay titled "Descartes," from Lee's philosophy notebook, dated January 13, 1963. University of Washington. Bruce Lee papers.

Lee, Bruce. Circa 1970. Handwritten notes for *The Silent Flute*. Bruce Lee papers.

Lee, Bruce. 1971. Essay titled "Jeet Kune Do—Toward Personal Liberation." Bruce Lee papers.

Lee, Bruce. Circa 1971. Handwritten essay titled "The Ultimate Source of Jeet Kune Do." Bruce Lee papers.

Lee, Bruce. Circa 1971. Paper titled "Additional Notes on Jeet Kune Do."

Lee, Bruce. Circa 1973. Handwritten essay titled "In My Own Process." Bruce Lee papers.

Lee, Bruce. Circa 1973. Handwritten note titled "What Is an Actor?" Bruce Lee papers.

Lee, Bruce. 1975. *The Tao of Jeet Kune Do*. Santa Clarita, CA: Ohara Publications.

Little, John. 1996. *The Warrior Within*. Lincolnwood, IL: NTC/Contemporary Publishing Group, Inc.

Little, John, ed. 1997. *Jeet Kune Do: Bruce Lee's Commentaries on the Martial Way*. Boston: Charles E. Tuttle.

Little, John, ed. 2000. *Striking Thoughts*. Boston: Charles E. Tuttle.

"The Lost Interview," with Pierre Berton. 1971. Boise, ID: Little-Wolff Creative Group.

Nietzsche, Friedrich Wilhelm. 1954. *The Antichrist*, ed. and trans. Walter Kaufmann. New York: Penguin.

Novak, Philip. 1995. *The World's Wisdom*. San Francisco: Harper Collins.

Rahula, Walpola. 1959. *What the Buddha Taught*. New York: Grove Press.

Turgend, James. February 1974. "Stirling Silliphant's World of Oscars, Emmies, and Gung Fu," in *Fighting Stars*.

TV and Movie Screen. 1966. "Our Marriage Brought Us a Miracle of Love," in *TV and Movie Screen*.

Watts, Alan. 1957. *The Way of Zen*. New York: Pantheon.

Watts, Alan. 1996. "The Middle Way" in *Buddhism: The Religion of No-Religion*, ed. Mark Watts. Boston: Charles E. Tuttle, p. 20.

Watts, Alan. 1996. "The Wisdom of the Mountains," in *Buddhism: The Religion of No-Religion*. Boston: Charles E. Tuttle, p. 80.

INDEX

ABOUT THE SUBJECT

Bruce Lee (1940–1973) is considered the greatest martial artist of the twentieth century. A true Renaissance man, Lee was a talented artist, poet, philosopher, writer, and actor, apart from being a formidable fighter. His insights into philosophy, physical fitness, self-defense, and moviemaking have been enjoyed and lauded by millions of people around the world for almost three decades. He is the founder of jeet kune do, the first martial art to be predicated on total freedom for the individual practitioner. A learned man, Lee attended the University of Washington where he majored in philosophy. His personal library contains more than 2,500 books on topics ranging from Eastern yoga to Western psychoanalysis. His philosophy and example continue to inspire athletes and artists from around the world.

ABOUT THE AUTHOR

John Little is considered the preeminent Bruce Lee scholar in the world by the Bruce Lee estate. Selected by Linda Lee Cadwell, Little is the only person who has ever been allowed complete and unrestricted access to Bruce Lee's writings, library, scripts, choreography notes, family and professional photographs, essays, college notes, recordings, and manuscripts. In addition, Little has conducted exhaustive research with many of Lee's former students, friends, colleagues, family, and associates.

He is the leading philosopher on Bruce Lee and the author of *The Warrior Within: The Philosophies of Bruce Lee* (Contemporary Books), the first formal presentation of Bruce Lee's philosophy. Little is also the editor of *Bruce Lee: Words from a Master* (Contemporary Books), and the highly regarded twelve-volume Bruce Lee Library Series (Charles E. Tuttle Publishing Company), which he has assembled from Lee's surviving papers with the full sanction of the Bruce Lee estate. In 1998, Little produced, directed, and wrote the score for the Warner Home Video documentary *Bruce Lee: In His Own Words*, which won the prestigious Toronto and Montreal World-Wide Short Film Festival awards for best documentary. Little's shooting script for this film resides in the Margaret Herrick Library in Beverly Hills, California, a branch of the Academy of Motion Picture Arts and Sciences.

Since 1994 Little has lectured internationally on Lee's significance and philosophy; he has been writing about Lee since 1976. He is a graduate of McMaster University's philosophy program and is the director of the Bruce Lee Educational Foundation.